Growing Up

while

Going Down

the

RABBIT HOLE

FRANCES SMITH

PAGE PUBLISHING, INC.
Conneaut Lake, PA

First originally published by Page Publishing 2020

ISBN 978-1-6624-1227-1 (pbk)
ISBN 978-1-6624-1228-8 (digital)

Printed in the United States of America

To all who read this history shared and benefit from doing so.

PREFACE

I wrote this book on a dare. By that I mean I dared to take on an effort so herculean I could not fathom how I might actually accomplish it. Sometimes even reading a book, especially one that is lengthy, is a mental challenge. Now, vexed by the relentless idea of writing something as complex as a book about my early years, with a sense of dread I realized that while I have toiled through several extreme challenges as an adult, writing a book was a type of involved undertaking wherein I was an untried novice. Many a day I questioned whether or not I could do justice to a matter of such import.

Not only would a book be monumental in scope compared to any writing I had ever done; it would require a depth of understanding of my past that I hoped I possessed. I questioned my abilities and feared the effort would either drive me mad or result in decided failure after suffering considerable torment trying to succeed at such enormity. After years of suffering from indecision and the unrelenting burden of an intuitive knowledge that this mission was my cosmic assignment, I gave in, gave it to God, and began to write.

I slogged along through my doubts and fears because of my belief that I had no choice. Rather than diminishing, the sense of purpose I had harbored in my heart for years had only grown in intensity. Like Jonah in the Bible, I resisted, my excuse being I lacked the ability such a project would require. The story was immense in many ways, and how I might reduce it to a manageable length and format were tasks my mind wrestled with a long while before I took up the gauntlet. As I struggled to write, laboring over each line and spending countless hours rewriting, the inevitable began to occur in barely discernable instances. A welcome newcomer moved into my neighborhood of fearfulness. Like a shy child peeping from around a

5

corner, confidence began to show itself. The uncertainty of whether or not I could well relate my own story had held me hostage for too long; I was earning my way free from those shackles.

One vital aspect I realized early in this effort was that I had to think about only one memory at a time, to dedicate all my ability in a focused plan, necessarily keeping other memories at bay until I had related to my satisfaction the small story on which I worked. The better I managed to do so, the more effortlessly the natural flow of the story presented. Mentally and physically I had to break down this big story of twenty years into stories little enough they were manageable. The process reminds me of the quilting craft. Many times the quilting squares are the initial focus. Once all the small, individual pieces have been styled, they are fastened together to make a large covering. I learned to write about small stories and then went back and wove them together as the bigger, ongoing narrative.

I also wrote my story to silence those whose prodding had gone from pleasant compliments to what felt like arm-twisting. For a long while these suggestions felt flattering. That my life's story appeared interesting enough and that those voices expressed a belief in my ability to author a text appealed to my vanity. But over time I had grown weary of what had begun to feel nearly like oppressive nagging. None of them had ever written a book. They had no idea what they were actually talking about. They would not be the one wanting to pull their hair out at times, tasting the gall of exasperation or confusion, being unable to sleep because the mind could not be still, or experiencing a myriad of other manifestations of the creative process of a novice writer. These supporters appeared not even to care about any suffering that I might endure, so insistent on the end result were they.

At the risk of sounding trite, the foremost reason I wrote this book was to connect with people. My sincere wish, my basic desire is that by becoming acquainted with the young girl I was and young woman I would therefore become, anyone experiencing any or all the kinds of adversities I faced (and particularly the negative effects of same) gleans a sense that they are not the first one to suffer so. Neither are they alone. Neither is life hopeless. Neither does discord need to continue to dominate, but that it most certainly will if recovery does not occur. Such a person absolutely needs to understand that desperation is a godsend if one realizes its message, because if uninterrupted, such a path of turmoil, discomfort, and devastation will increase to damage more severely, cripple more hideously, and poison more with accumulation.

The good news is that regardless where in the downward spiral a person finds oneself, she or he can absolutely break the bonds that destroy and learn to live a natural and prosperous life well lit by love and truth. Such is completely possible. I recover a bit day by day. The healing will never be a completed process, and that I consider a wonderful reassurance. Yes, I wrote this book in hopes of helping people. My hope is that anyone might benefit from reading this account, and my belief is there are multitudes as stricken and afflicted as I was.

As the case has been countless times in my nearly seventy years, I had to overcome much fear and doubt, even laziness, disappointments, and some of life's serious disruptions, to actually complete this book once I started. It has been roughly a decade in its gestation. Today I offer it for your edification, reading enjoyment, and a simple opportunity for you to get to know this beautiful child God created and the journey that was her first twenty years.

The reader will surely understand my story continues beyond the point the book ends. My hope is the reader will be dissatisfied that they cannot know more how this saga plays out and whether their sense of impending doom will be correct or not. I will confess there is much, much more that is integral and needs to be told, but concluding this book where I did seemed appropriate as well. As this is my first foray into the world of professional writing, how readers receive this book may influence whether or not I assume a second undertaking and pen a second book.

To this point, involvement in this project has been another journey of tremendous proportions for me, and with all the discomfort associated with it, no doubt an equal growth experience! Most of all, I obeyed what I believe was my Lord's will, and that elates me and provides a unique sense of peace. After all has been said and done, I am thankful. For all the effort this book represents, I am improved because of it, and that is my true life's work.

PRESCHOOL YEARS

The many places my family and I called home during my child-hood years are the linchpins that organize and frame my early memories, each residence generally associated with a particular year of school through junior high school. During the period of time I was a preschooler until I was ready to enter high school, my family lived in sixteen different dwellings, primarily around our hometown in southwestern Kansas, but reaching into Colorado and Oklahoma at times. Without fail we named those places, opting to remember folks associated with the location or designating simple words that indicated something about the characteristics of our rental. These names remain beacons in my memory that clearly demarcate days long past. These days and the many experiences they included remain clear and are unquestionably important parts of my growing up yet also constitute a kind of perilous descent.

As a child of preschool age, I remember two places we called home. The first was Trailerville. If the mobile home village had a formal name, it is lost to the ages. I do remember it being a park that had more than a few trailer spaces, was busy, and literally close-knit. The dirt passageway through the park was severely washboarded, which must have been hell on cars as they crawled along while being violently agitated. To us youngsters, the mess was just a fun time.

Trailerville was located at the southernmost end of my home-town Ulysses, a rural southwestern Kansas farm community that sat on huge natural gas fields integral to its economy. Trailerville was imminent when we passed Russell Binney's small grocery store. Doing so was somehow exciting, like exiting Canaan and reentering the wilderness. With our family of six and the size of trailer homes in those days, life was truly close-quartered.

Snapshot memories decorate that section of my mind. Pocket doors, blond-colored wood paneling, a round window not unlike a porthole of a maritime vessel, the narrow corridor that divided the berth in which I slept from the built-in bureau are but a few of the images of our trailer home that my mind captured and has stored for over half a century. Life seemed a lot less complex in those days, and our humble abode was simple but nothing I ever thought merited an apology. Listening to the radio with the rest of my family, watching my mother sprinkle clean laundry, then roll up the garments and stuff them into a plastic zippered bag, and finally enjoying the smell of those clothes as she ironed them were ongoing routine pleasures.

Life was filled with many sorts of interesting, entertaining, remarkable occasions, one being when my newborn sister Stacy joined us at home. I was rapt watching my mother lay her on a towel on our small dining area table and bathe her. Stacy's shriveling umbilical cord concerned me because it was ugly and looked like it must hurt. In fact, I thought it must be an injury. Why else would that baby have something so painful looking there on her belly that Mom had to take care of?

As if it were only yesterday, I remember my father's utter frustration late one afternoon when he was home alone with us five kids. Stacy was walking, but not old enough for potty training. It was warm weather, and she was clad in nothing save her diaper. With the frequency and certainty toddlers demonstrate, Dad saw she had messed her diaper. Choosing to try to ignore the sag, odor, and priority this turn of events involved, my dad waited as long as he could to try to address the smelly situation, hoping my mother would return from wherever she had gone.

In 1956, diapers were cloth held on by baby pins, at times reinforced with plastic pants. There were no easy-stick tabs positioned just right depending on whether the diaper was made for a little boy or little girl. There were no wipes, flushable or otherwise; neither was there easy, genteel disposal of toddlers' raunchy messes.

At some point Dad admitted defeat and gave in to the task at hand. Grimacing and muttering under his breath, he did get the diaper off, then wiped and cleaned the baby's bottom, and flushed away the poop. The rank, soiled diaper he left, aftermath with which Mom had to contend. Now it was time to get a diaper back on Stacy before the situation got nasty again. With an unforgiving audience of critics, Dad folded the clean diaper several times, trying to get all the points and corners to where they could be pinned without sticking the baby, whose arms and legs were moving impatiently. Several times this man whose talents lay in shifting gears on pieces of heavy equipment and gross manipulation tried to get that diaper safely secured. Each time, however, as soon as Stacy got up and began to move about, the diaper just as quickly eased down around her ankles.

Finally, Dad resorted to something with which he was a bit more adept. He gave up on the diaper pin and simply tied the diaper on his baby girl. Dad felt pleased, proud of his resourcefulness. Little Stacy quickly arose and busied again herself with her newfound mastery of walking. Not immediately but nevertheless, the elusive diaper seemed to jump off her hips and ease its way from the top of her legs to the top of her feet. We kids looked at Dad for a cue on how to react to this latest development. The look on his face was a mixture of exasperation and resignation.

He immediately corralled his toddler, freed her from the constraints of a diapering gone awry, and that was that. Stacy reveled in her natural state, and Dad was satisfied having found a solution of sorts despite its inherent risks. My eyes opened really wide in disbelief knowing this was highly unordinary and would be equally unacceptable to my mother. With Dad, life was never dull.

Before I started kindergarten, we left Trailerville behind but not the trailer. We moved less than a mile northwest to Pearl Carter's. Even though Pearl's last name was Carter, we were not related. She was a white-haired, rather round woman who seemed friendly enough. Zoning must have been relaxed because at Pearl's, there were three or four trailers parked on the northeast quarter of that residential block. The remaining homes were attractive, well-kept, stick-built homes, among which the trailers must have looked markedly out of place. Around our trailer stood a fence six feet high, not attractive picketing, but the heavy wire sort made to contain livestock on a farm.

Somewhere we kids had acquired an old, broken-down mattress covered in striped ticking and had managed to hoist it halfway over the fence. We now had a saddle on our horse and were ready to ride. My older siblings, Bruce and Gayla, and I were determined to have fun on our mount. With their help and coaxing, I found myself six feet off the ground, trying to stay in the imaginary saddle that straddled our metal horse/fence. The fence was strong enough to lend some support to the unsightly mattress but was not meant to bear a load. It was beginning to totter unsteadily under the stress of being morphed from fencing to equine.

My muscles soon wearied, and I needed to dismount but found myself in a precarious situation. The horse was bending to and fro, trying to buck me off. Staying in the saddle was becoming very difficult. On the ground beneath the mattress, we kids had used our old metal toy table as a platform from which to mount our steed. I called for my brother and sister's help. No answer. I pleaded and whimpered for my pardners to get me down. They told me to get down myself. I screamed and cried for them to help me. Instead they ran behind the rear of the trailer, out of sight.

Realizing the difficulty was mine to resolve, I tried to hold onto the saddle to dismount. Alas, old, flat mattresses hanging taut across a wire fence leave little to grab hold of, and I fell to the ground, hitting my left arm on the metal table leg on the way down. There was not a single blade of grass at Pearl Carter's, only dusty Kansas dirt from which I picked up my wannabe cowgirl self and went inside bellowing to my mother. Eventually my siblings showed themselves, uncontrite and unrepentant.

After two or three days of unsubsiding pain, my mother took me to the doctor to see about my arm.

Where do children acquire some of the notions they possess? We arrived at Dr. Brewer's small office four blocks east of our trailer. Despite being in serious pain, I refused to get out of the car. When my mother commanded me to get out, I simply could not, resolute from fear. Her glare made me cringe. I wailed that I didn't want a shot. My mother insisted I wasn't going to get a shot, but I was positive she was merely lying to me to get me to yield. Always tall and stout, I proved to be the ultimate handful as my mother wound up having to forcibly extricate me from the front seat of the car and drag me, screaming, into the medical office for examination. I had broken my left humerus, a small concern compared to the shot issue.

By the time I entered kindergarten in the fall of 1956, we had moved our trailer to Nettie Lane's. A quarter mile or so south and one block west of Pearl Carter's, we remained within a three-block radius of where we had been living. Moving trailers back then (we never called them mobile homes) must have been an easy job considering the number of times my dad did so.

Nettie and Pop Lane were people I liked. Nettie worked at Duckwall's behind the candy counter, so I knew her from going and having her weigh out a few cents worth of candy as often as I could. She was patient and always talked nicely to us kids. Her husband, Pop, always wore overalls and smiled a lot. Their two grandsons, Bobby and Billy, were close to me in age and had the same names as my parents, which seemed amazing to me. The Lanes were nice people, and my life while at their most basic rental property wasn't unenjoyable at all.

At school one of the things I was required to know was my address. Each student had to stand, face the class, and recite their name and address to their fellow kindergarteners. Caring about doing well in school from early on, I asked my mother more than once what our address was, but to no avail. I don't remember if I was given some explanation about having no street address; I only know we had none. Because I was often sent into the post office to the window to ask for "Robert Carter's mail, General Delivery," I do remember that was as close as we got to any kind of address at that time. At any rate, I was mortified because I couldn't get my assignment prepared. Not about to be lacking in front of my classmates, I managed a solution. When time came for my recitation, I said I lived at 402 North Parkway Street. I can only presume I had heard that street mentioned somewhere along the line, and it wound up serving a youngster's needs nicely. Necessity is the mother of invention, and I gave no more thought to my made-up address.

One day at school during recess, a classmate named G. D. Reed and I collided head-on at considerable velocity. Our foreheads absorbed the force of the impact, and we were both knocked a bit silly. Not uncommon then, my parents had no telephone, so calling my mother to come get me from school was not an option. My teacher was concerned enough that she decided to drive me home. My head hurt so badly I was nauseous as Ms. Swayze escorted me to her car, a two-door Mercury with a white top and pumpkin-colored body. We left Sullivan School, drove east two blocks to the highway, and turned north. Nettie Lane's was south! We drove for several minutes and came to Parkway Street. All too soon Ms. Swayze pulled the car to the curb, put the transmission in park, and turned off the engine. The gig was up. I was busted.

Nauseous from the head injury and about to vomit, reeling from my throbbing head, humiliated from being caught in a lie, and frightened about how I was actually going to get home, I burst into tears and confessed my shameful plight. I told my teacher I did not live here, that in fact my house was a long way away over by Sullivan's elevator. Rather than being angry with me, my teacher was curious and concerned. I told her there was no address where I lived. She asked if I knew how to get to my house from where we were. Thank goodness Ulysses was a small town.

One thing I learned from the head-banging incident and a few other futile attempts at lying, it was a choice for which I lacked the required savvy or luck to be convincing or successful. Thankfully, my head injury was inconsequential, my pride being the part of me seriously jeopardized.

To this day I don't know why I was the young student with no address. I do know I often suffered much anxiety created by ordeals like the school assignment. That situation exemplified how our lifestyle, growing family, and lack of communication would tax our family time after time.

While at Nettie Lane's, I played a lot with a girl who lived across the alley, Marty Monroe. Her given name was Martha, and she was a year older than I and very much a tomboy. Being older, Marty was usually in the lead, and I had no problem following. The Monroe family lived in a house provided as part of Earl Monroe's employment with the railroad. The house seemed so big and capacious and had a huge yard as well. I surmised with a house and yard that size, the Monroes must really have a lot of money.

In addition to Marty and her parents, the Monroe family consisted of an older brother, Mike, who was about the same age as my brother Bruce. With dark hair, dark eyes, a beautiful smile, and friendly manner, Mike was really cute. Gayla had a big crush on him, and she got teased in no small way about that. Additionally, Mike had type I diabetes, and with the insulin and hypodermics, I was fascinated. With my fear of needles and shots, the idea of him having to give himself injections every day was obsessive.

There was a younger girl in the Monroe family too, and like the situation with my younger sister Stacy, being younger than we other kids automatically excluded them from our activities.

Mrs. Monroe was a friendly woman named Shirley who was a relaxed sort. I remember seeing her more than once walking around their house with only a bra on her upper half, smoking a cigarette with hair dye processing on her head. Upon first seeing Marty's mom clad like that, I was ready to bolt, but gauging my response from hers, I could see it was no big deal, so I treated it that way. Being able to be that relaxed was a nice feeling.

One day Marty and I were across the street to the south of Monroe's, playing on land with several piles of skids and pallets. On that equipment storage site, there were also several large tanks, ones much bigger than the propane tanks that typically sit beside farmhouses in rural settings. On these tanks were Mobil Oil's logos, the red winged horse. Of course, we had no business being there, but the place was too nearby and alluring. The man who supervised the lot, old man Fogelman, had run us kids off before, but we never heeded his boundaries.

Fogelman was nowhere around that afternoon as Marty and I went toward the inviting stacks of skids piled six to eight feet high. To us young girls, they were mountains we needed to climb, escapes we had to make, an exciting world that was too captivating to resist.

We were having great fun climbing and jumping off them—until I landed too hard. Not actually having had skydiving lessons, and absent the understanding of rolling to prevent injury when I landed, the last time I jumped out of my make-believe airplane, I landed with a thud. I slammed my left arm to the stony ground and fractured it a second time in as many years.

This time it was the forearm I hit, and there was no doubt it was broken.

I clenched my right hand around my left wrist and ran home screaming at the top of my lungs, "I broke my arm! I broke my arm!" Despite my ungodly fear of shots, the pain was such that that day, there was no fight from me about going to Dr. Brewer's office for treatment.

First Grade

During my first-grade year, we moved again, two block east and as many north and nestled our trailer between houses occupied by folks with whom we seemed to have little in common. Toleration and peaceful coexistence were not our mindset. Unfortunately in our reality, *different* meant "more than" or "less than" instead of simply "different." Although there were no other trailers around, at this location, the houses were smaller than those that surrounded Pearl Carter's and much plainer. Yards included some grass but also plenty of dirt and weeds. As the lot we lived on did have some grass, there was a sense we were moving up in the world. This place we called Margie Hagerman's.

We actually lived directly across the street from Margie Hagerman and her four kids, who were friends and classmates of ours. Margie's husband had been killed in a car crash a couple of years earlier. Our families had long known one another. We kids got along well, and going across the street with my mother to Hagerman's was enjoyable. Margie was a kind and friendly woman who looked out of ice-blue eyes and whose normal facial expression was a smile. Not only that, she had an air conditioner in her house that always kept it nice and cool. She was an employee in the office at the carbon black plant several miles outside town. As my mother never worked outside the home save one short period years later, I was curious about mothers who did so. That Margie knew how to type, wore fancy clothes to her job, and made money for her family left a lasting impression on me.

Margie's facial hair grew into a bit of a mustache toward the corners of her mouth. My eye for detail riveted on that feature, and though Margie's little 'stache was not heavy or coarse or off-putting, my fascination with the unusual caused me to wonder intensely why Margie had a mustache while other women did not. Well, most women anyway.

At the city library there worked a woman who had not only a mustache but also a beard! Though Margie was a brunette, her mustache was soft looking, like peach fuzz, and she never had to shave it. The woman at the library had black hair, with whiskers like a man, and I could tell she shaved her face and her neck. Her neck was very fleshy and hung down underneath her chin, and the black whisker stubble was as clear as the nose on her face. Her arms and legs were also very hairy, and her body was not only big but rotund as well.

Compounding the effect of this woman's appearance was the completely opposite appearance of her library coworker. The coworker was a petite, middle-aged woman who had graying blond hair, was not overweight, and was feminine looking like most other women.

Even so, both library ladies were very similar in a couple of ways. Neither was friendly, and both eyed us kids with disdain whenever we entered the library. I oscillated between fascination, fear, and suspicion whenever I encountered these women. To begin with the library was quite a different sort of place. Its bookish smell and enforced stillness, its sterile environment that seemed almost akin to the town hospital, were never welcoming. Coupled with the unfriendly troll and crone who stood guard there, the library was never a place in which I felt comfortable so did not frequent.

At Margie Hagerman's, the neighbors on our side of the street weren't nearly as nice as our friends across the street. Next door to us to the north was August Kissner. He was a cantankerous old man in his sixties and had no use for youngsters or their antics. He lived alone in his house, a white stucco that was generic-looking except for a simple front porch that ran the width of his modest dwelling.

We had not lived there long before things between August and the Carters were on the fast track downhill. Old man Kissner never hesitated to express his dislike toward us kids by yelling, cursing, and otherwise exhibiting his contempt for us. He would have been better off adopting a different approach because he was old and outnumbered. We were relentless at harassing him. We would knock on his front door and then hightail it to a hiding spot, toss pebbles at his windows, throw rocks onto his roof, anything we thought of to antagonize, upset, and frustrate the acerbic old man. Things escalated till our dog, Rin Tin Tin, turned up dead one day. Our parents were positive August Kissner had poisoned him. We waged cold war with August, conducting frequent sorties behind his Iron Curtain for as long as we lived beside him.

The Devil's Hole was a big depression in the ground on the other side of August Kissner's house. As an adult, I learned it had been created when someone had excavated to put in a foundation on which to build, but nothing had ever been erected there. Weeds, trees, trash, and debris were thick in the hole. It was a foreboding, mysterious, intriguing place made more so by its proximity to the evil August Kissner. That hole provided the Carter kids and the Hagerman kids many hours of adventure and suspense. Like cats playing in cardboard boxes or with empty paper bags, we kids entertained ourselves superbly in that play area. A playground built by professionals could have been no more appealing to us than was this gathering spot.

Our tenure at Margie Hagerman's was a busy time filled with mischief. When not consumed with August Kissner, we clashed with the neighbors on the other side of our trailer, the Scroggins. Even their name sounded offensive. People we looked down on we called cruds. Scroggins were definitely cruds. They had an outhouse, their house had no paint on it, and their lot was overgrown with trees and vegetation. Mrs. Scroggins looked really old and wore clothes that looked like something out of the *Grapes of Wrath*. I remember three children: a nearly grown boy named Arthur, an older girl named Iva (a really weird-sounding name), and a little girl, Eileen. Everything about the Scroggins seemed to offend us, so it was only natural to declare open season on them.

One late afternoon, my mother's younger sister Betta was babysitting us five Carter kids. With two of her own preschool toddlers, she had her hands full. Also present was another aunt, Mom and Betta's younger sister Karen, who was more like a cousin than aunt to me. Across the street to the south of Hagerman's was a lot

19

owned by the Scroggins. It had several tall trees that provided a lot of shade; thick, beautiful grass; and irises that were in full bloom. The irises proved as tempting to us as Bathsheba was to David.

Dusk had arrived when Karen proposed a really daring idea. She wanted to sneak across the street, her minions accompanying her, and pick some of those pretty flowers. I remember being especially scared, not wanting to be an accomplice, but unable to say no. So under the cover of near darkness, several of us sneaked. Following Karen's lead, we commenced picking the stately flowers. Not much sooner than we had begun, a tall shadowy figure sprang up from the grass several yards to our left. It was Arthur Scroggins, and he was yelling at the top of his lungs. Busted again.

A few minutes later outside our trailer, Aunt Betta stood posturing with the police. She appeared to be angry with us kids, but knowing her, under her breath, I imagine she wanted to laugh. She called Arthur Scroggins a pervert for lying in the grass, spying on us, and the whole Scroggins bunch a nest of weirdoes. I was in mortal fear of what my parents would do when they returned home to the row we had created. As it turned out I recall no punishment being meted out by my parents. Who knows what they really thought. No doubt the Scroggins and August Kissner were ready to throw a block party when we moved on.

Most memorable about the time we spent living at Margie Hagerman's was something far more sinister than our trouble with neighbors and something I kept to myself a very long time.

My father had a younger brother of about eighteen years who was mildly retarded. The rules of that family prohibited anyone from formally acknowledging his slowness, and since it didn't exist, appropriate attitudes and behavior were taboo for discussion. The family's unspoken yet effectively communicated policy was denial with no possibility of exception. How else does one explain leaving a young man with raging sex hormones, without normal decision-making skills and judgment, in charge of vulnerable children?

One evening, that uncle, Bud, was our babysitter. Darkness had fallen, and we kids were inside. At some point I fell asleep on the couch in the living room area. I don't know how long I had been asleep, but I began to awaken because I was being disturbed. As a half-asleep six-year-old, I couldn't make sense of what my uncle was doing pressed so close up against me. I felt his breath on my head and face and heard strange sounds coming up from his throat. His arms were around me, and his hands cupped my bottom, pressing our loins together. Highly aroused, he was near climax. I was not really frightened. Mostly I was confused, wondering what my uncle Bud was doing. I did not protest or ever let him know I had awakened. Somehow I knew that he was doing something bad. Since he was doing it to me, I was a participant of sorts, so I felt guilt and shame. I also knew it was something I had better not tell anyone.

Bud died a few years later when I was ten years old, but not before he fondled my budding breasts as a soon-to-be ten-year-old. In later years I would also learn I was not the only child he molested.

As my first-grade year in school ended, so did our time at Margie Hagerman's and trailer living too.

SECOND AND THIRD GRADES

O ur next move was clear across town, a mere block from infamous Parkway Street! We moved out of the trailer and into a house my grandmother and step-grandfather owned. The house was constructed primarily of cinder blocks. It was large, with several bedrooms, an upstairs with two areas that had been partitioned off and plywood nailed onto the topside of the rafters. They were close enough to being rooms we called them that and played in them whenever the temperature was not too hot. The house sat on Lotus Avenue and Main Street on a good-sized corner lot. There were several mature trees that provided shade, equally as many shrubs, and even some grass. Most of all, there was so much space inside and out, the house seemed as big as a castle. There was a detached garage with a small apartment on one end, in which my parents once lived when Bruce was a toddler and Gayla an infant.

My grandparents had been living in the house but were moving several miles from town to begin farming on land they had leased. I later learned my parents tried to buy that house but were ultimately unable to secure financing. This place we simply called Grandma's. I was elated to live in that house. There was a lot of space in which to live comfortably: to breathe deeply and easily, play, enjoy privacy, and successfully stay out of our mother's hair.

To the north of our house, two more houses sat on the block. These were the homes of the Kibbee and Cooper families. They were large families too, and we kids all attended the same school, played together at home, and got along well. Even our parents were friends and socialized together. All was copasetic. Life was great, for a while anyway.

In the first few years of my life, Dad worked at the carbon black plant a few miles east of Ulysses. This was a blue-collar work with job security, benefits, and a simple routine of shift work at a production facility. Dad was a personality with which all that didn't much agree. He had wanderlust, and the sense of confinement spawned by too much routine did not fulfill him.

For a while Dad also worked for a local road-building contractor named Barney Rogers. I recollect those days, recall what Mr. Rogers looked like, and still remember a couple of Dad's coworkers. Dad was a heavy equipment operator and had steady work with Rogers too. Still Dad was listless and in need of higher wages for his large family.

By the time we moved to Grandma's house, Dad was working as a dozer operator on pipeline construction jobs. He would continue in this line of work till he retired. He felt real passion about being a cat skinner, earned a good wage (but without any benefits beyond that), and got to travel to wherever the jobs were. Unfortunately, this was also a turning point in our family life since Dad was no longer at home a lot of the time. My mother had five youngsters to care for day in and day out, a household to manage, and all that comes along with those responsibilities. One of the most heartbreaking, insufferable memories of that timeframe occurred around this time and had to do with Dad's absence.

I was a Brownie scout. It was February and time for our troop's father-daughter banquet. I was so proud being a Brownie. Uniforms have always been appealing to me, and getting to wear the first one of my life that year gave me a very strong sense of pride. Perhaps that pride was a two-edged sword though. Experiencing it was a very uplifting feeling, yet when I lost face at that banquet that year, the pain was awful.

As in Ms. Swayze's car a couple of years earlier, I wound up reliving the mortifying sense of helplessness, confusion, shame, and inferiority I had suffered at what should have been an occasion of delight. Feelings antithetical to what childhood should be about crashed down on me like the world had fallen off its axis.

Perhaps the adults in my sphere perceived this situation as no big deal, but the fact was a young child was tormented acutely by a situation that could have been easily avoided.

At any rate I was the only girl in our troop of twenty or so Brownies to show up at the banquet with no father. In kindergarten my responsibility was to know my address and recite it. Now, in Brownies, there were also responsibilities, and in this instance, those responsibilities were to attend the function, bring my father, and when my turn came, stand and introduce my father and myself to the others present.

Again I was in dire straits, unable to do what I was supposed to do. I was frightened, embarrassed, in tears, and feeling so very less than the other girls. Every other Brownie had succeeded that evening where I failed. Instead of my father, accompanying me were my utter embarrassment and humiliation and the relentless sense that there was something completely amiss about me. Knowing the nature of the function and with four or five uncles in town, why a stand-in father was not secured is unfathomable. Nevertheless, I showed up at my Brownie banquet fatherless.

Thankfully, my troop leader's sensitivity and her husband, who was also the brother of my aunt Karen's husband, rescued me. Sally Smith told her husband, Henry, of my plight, and he agreed to be my father for the evening even though he had his own daughter to accompany. Through the graciousness of sensitive folk, I was saved from complete humiliation, although inside, a pernicious toll had again been exacted.

It never occurred to me to be angry with my parents over the latest painful situation. This time and so many others, I was simply overcome with intense emotions, confusion, and lack of counsel. Subsequently some of the conclusions I eventually drew, on a level far deeper than words can extend, exacerbated the unhealthy scenario. As this troubled child, I did my best to deal with life's vexations. I guess the key part of that statement was that I was, after all, only a child.

After moving into my grandmother's house, there was a time when his pipeline job must have been near Ulysses, because Dad was able to be home after work in the evening. I don't know why, but at some point, there in my grandmother's house, one of Dad's pipeline coworkers began living with us. His name was Paul. He had been there long enough that I felt comfortable around this man and enjoyed the way he engaged us kids. One day at work, he suffered a broken leg and wound up with a large cast that went from his toes up past his right knee.

My parents' bedroom was off the living room to the north. Heading east off the living room was a long, dark hallway. On either side of the hallway were rooms, seven in all. Bedrooms, bathroom / laundry room, and at the far end dining room on one side and kitchen on the other all connected via the hallway. Paul's bedroom abutted the living room on its east side.

My younger brother Lonnie, two years my junior, was my best friend and wonderful pal. We were pretty much inseparable, a welcome relief to the impatience and combativeness of my two older siblings. Our younger sister Stacy had been born two years after Lonnie. She was a sickly, asthmatic baby and had to be hospitalized a lot because of her illness. Coupled with the fact that she was several years younger than the rest of us, Stacy pretty much grew up without the benefit of a sibling who was also a friend.

One evening as my parents were in the living room watching television, a very different scene unfolded on the other side of the wall not more than a few feet from them. Lain up with his broken leg, Paul was a friendly middle-aged guy with a wide smile who joked with us kids and paid us some attention. Lonnie and I had taken our easel-style chalkboard into his room and were taking turns writing on it while conversing with Paul, who was perched on his single-sized bed with his injured appendage.

I was sitting on the side of Paul's bed between turns at the chalkboard when he placed his hand on my right knee, beneath my dress. Involuntarily my head turned back toward Lonnie and the chalkboard. As with my uncle Bud, it was as if my voice had been stolen. Paul quit speaking as he moved his hand from my knee to my thigh, especially rubbing the inside of my thigh. I kept my eyes and head straight ahead. I believe my neck would have broken had I tried to turn it, as if not seeing what was happening would nullify it. Paul simply continued to move his hand up my leg, and I remained mute. Also from the experience at the hands of my uncle Bud Carter, I remembered the sounds sexual excitement creates and

25

how those sounds are stifled when the sexual contact is taboo, illegal, and because the child's father is sitting *not more than a few feet away*!

As with my uncle, I also felt overwhelming confusion. I knew what Paul was doing was wrong, so why was he doing it? And why was I just sitting there? Worst of all, why did it feel kind of pleasurable since it was wrong? I wondered if other children were like me. The only explanation I could come up with to answer this sickening knot of thoughts and feelings within me was that I was just a very, very bad person.

Soon the monster's hand eased my legs open far enough that he could get his fingers inside my panties. He easily parted my labia lips and stroked the moist area he had trespassed and was now violating. He massaged my clitoris some before reaching backward and finding the opening to my vagina. He didn't penetrate me with his finger, probably realizing hurting me would increase the odds of his discovery. Finally he withdrew his wet digit from my clothing and was finished.

As it were, Lonnie realized the nature of what was happening just a few feet from him. Although I uttered not a word about what had happened, in days that followed, Lonnie alternately pleaded and insisted that I tell our mother what Paul had done. Why a little boy of kindergarten age would have sexual savvy of that degree did not enter my seven-year-old mind. I don't remember how much time passed before I summoned courage to recount what had befallen me. Finally one evening as she was washing dishes, Lonnie by my side, I walked down the dark hallway to the kitchen and Mom. It was a conversation no child should have to have.

Standing behind my mother perhaps four or five feet, I announced that I wished Paul wouldn't have come back to our house after he broke his leg. Immediately my mother ceased washing dishes and turned around to face me. Her eyes narrowed, and she asked me why. Her voice seemed to express as much suspicion as concern. My chest was so tight, my fear was so gut-wrenching I wished the floor would open up and swallow me. I have no doubt I couldn't have gotten through that confession were it not for the strength and courage my little brother's love and presence provided.

Telling my mother what happened was as traumatic as the molestation itself. When I finished with the revelation, my mother said not a word to my brother or me. She hollered at my dad, "Bob, get in here!" in a tone I shall never forget. Dad came into the kitchen, and Mom then said to Lonnie and me, "You kids get out of here." It was a lifetime of terror before my father exited the kitchen. I fully expected him to beat me, possibly kill me, or even worse, not love me any longer because I was such a bad girl. Waiting for whatever was going to happen to me next was beyond horrifying. I felt utter terror.

Dad went to Paul's room, entered, and closed the door behind him. We kids could not hear what was said, but after a few minutes, Dad came back out. Like Mom, he never said a word to Lonnie or me. I had grown old from the stress of it all. I had no idea where I stood, if Dad still loved me, what I was to do or not to do. To this day I don't know if Paul admitted to his crime or not. At that moment, inside myself I fractured, but this breaking was not of bone. It was I, Frances Ann, separating from who I really was.

I remained broken for decades. I had landed in a hell that would require scores of angels helping me navigate a horrendous web, seeing me back to and through that time when I was violated by a pervert, then dispatched by a coup de grace executed by my parents and their bungling, so that I might pick up the pieces of that shattered child I had been, retrieve my genuine self, and begin integrating the two.

My cache of tools for this great work included the healing power of love, hard work, much determination, and education. Overcoming the ghastly, crippling evil dealt me would be akin to slowly, steadily, laboriously straightening a bent, twisted, and gnarled tree that was actually intended to be tall, straight, and strong and reaching gloriously homeward toward heaven. That work eventually and necessarily became a life's work.

As my life unfurled, this catastrophe would manifest itself countless times and in countless ways. The toll of this train wreck grew greater every day I grew older, and life became more complex, and the stakes grew higher.

Dad had given Paul time to gather his belongings and get out. When he emerged from his room, Paul carried his suitcase with one hand, nevertheless maneuvering his crutches with that hand and the other. He shuffled down the hallway, into the kitchen, and out the back door, got into his car, and left. Then, as if nothing had ever happened, my parents' deafening silence screamed that I was never to speak of this disgrace again.

I didn't realize then, but this watershed moment decimated me. I had no champion. The standards imposed upon us children were severe. Except for my older brother Bruce, and Stacy, the baby, we kids were expected to toe the line. When we didn't, Dad meted out strong, swift physical punishment. Now, here was an adult who broke sacred rules and ignored basic moral imperatives, but Dad didn't even raise his voice to the awful man, let alone whip the bastard like he did us kids. What was fair about that? Unless perhaps what Paul had done wasn't really so bad. Unless what I had experienced and all elements relative to such trauma were not that important.

Men are willing to fight for people, land, ideas, and other things that are valuable and important to them. Dad himself had fought in World War II. However, that day when I was a violated seven-year-old, there was no fight on my behalf. The price I would wind up paying was harrowing. Indeed, my molester was removed from our home, but that was the only price he had to pay. My wounds were not attended to. I was given no explanation, comfort, or reassurance. I was simply left alone, to deal with what had happened to me, to try to make sense of it and somehow live with it, whichever way I could. Above all, my parents communicated to me perfectly, without ever speaking a word, that they were the ones in need of protection. I was never to make them uncomfortable by mentioning this ugliness again.

My soul and spirit were critically wounded. I was in shock and needed life-saving attention to facilitate healing and ensure the best outcome. I never received even simple first aid. I was far too young to understand family dysfunction and how it ran rampant among us. Don't think, don't ask, don't feel were our religious tenets. Already a nervous and very anxious child, I was henceforth depressed. I tried for dozens of years, in untold ways, to redeem myself in my father's eyes. Decades later during recovery, I wrote my father a letter requesting he discuss this event with me. Dad never acknowledged my request. He went to his grave unwilling or unable to summon the courage to grant my need.

The devastation Paul's behavior visited on me, compounded by my parents' mishandling the situation, was understandably profound. Outwardly I continued to march, putting one foot in front of the other and going about the business of life. Inwardly I had been rendered unrecognizable. The innate guidebook our Creator instills in us was in shreds. All parts of my being that weren't flesh and blood were scrambled. Insecurity and self-loathing were demons that had been provided an opening, and they immediately moved in. They would live there too long and wreak untold havoc on me. Absent vindication and education, for many years the light instilled in me by God himself was precariously dimmed.

Life that autumn was to prove brutal in another way as well. About the same time as life at home was turned on end, in the tiny town of Holcomb, Kansas, forty miles from Ulysses, the Clutter family met their fate at the hands of ex-convicts Hickok and Smith. I remember watching the newscasts, hearing grown-ups talk about the murders, seeing my mother begin locking the doors, and taking other precautions people never worried about hitherto then. Even the grown-ups were frightened and cautious. I was terrified. More than fifty years later, any discussion of that slaughter still causes blood to run cold.

The heinous circumstances of that crime destroyed much of America's remaining innocence, just like Paul Brooks's molestation of me as a child in second grade altered my life forever.

First Move to Colorado

I n the summer of 1960, I had just finished third grade. That season my family embarked on what was to be a three-month adventure, enjoyable or not, depending on one's position within the family. My parents had attempted to purchase my grandmother's house on Main Street, where we had lived for two years, but their attempts were unsuccessful. With past practice a reasonable predictor of future behavior, we were overdue for a move, a situation soon remedied by our relocating to Colorado.

Today Florence, Colorado, is the home to two state prison facilities and widely recognized as the home of the federal Supermax prison that houses some of the most notorious criminals in America. Its economy is now largely based on the penal business, but in 1960, that distinction lay decades in the future.

As a young girl I loved Florence, Colorado. Two hundred forty miles northwest of Ulysses, Florence was a town with old buildings constructed with red brick characteristic of that area and distinctly different looking from those in Ulysses. The rows of houses in Florence mostly displayed grassy lawns and trees, fed partly by two storm drainage ditches that ran through the town and their diminutive offshoots that traversed the residential plats in this attractive little burg.

These ditches were temptresses, nothing less. They beckoned to be investigated and used as play areas. Florence seemed kind of like a grown adult in its maturity, whereas Ulysses was younger, pimplier, if you will. Florence was scenic, beautiful, and inviting. Ulysses was dusty, hot, and windy. I was excited and happy about moving to Colorado.

The beauty and inviting atmosphere of Florence were power-ful draws, but one factor existed that surpassed all others: family. My Uncle Jerry and Aunt Jene Elliott lived there with their three kids, two of whom were cousins close enough to my age to be rele-vant. They had moved to Florence from Ulysses a few years earlier. Jerry, Mom's handsome younger brother, never seemed to mind all us Carter kids being around. Aunt Jene was easy-going and treated us kids fondly. She had black hair with natural curl in it, kept a lot of candy and cookies and sweet rolls and doughnuts in her kitchen, and was always glad to let us have a generous amount of these fancy sweets. That I felt so welcome and comfortable at their house endeared them greatly. Going to Colorado to visit the Elliotts was always a wonderful dream come true, and now we were preparing to move there ourselves.

My cousins Jerry Jene and Sheree were two and four years younger than I, respectively. Though younger than I, they were great playmates and friends. At two years old, their baby sister, Terry, was often disagreeable and was given to throwing temper tantrums that frightened me. She would frequently hold her breath and turn an alarming purple. We kids were reassured by the grown-ups that she would pass out before she would die from not breathing, but that thought failed to reassure me. Avoidance was the strategy I employed toward Terry.

Since we always traveled the same route to Florence and went as often as possible, I knew the way at a young age. Visits made there and to Pueblo were memorable. My mother had quite a bit of family in that part of Colorado, and when traveling, we called on several older relatives whose homes and hospitality were inviting and whose caring scrutiny felt welcome. Such visits were important as I gained a valuable sense of who we were and from whom we had descended. Going to Colorado was always enriching as well as fun.

What prompted my parents to venture away from Ulysses was no doubt financial motivation, hoping for steady employment for Dad at a good wage. As soon as school was over in the spring of my third-grade year, we moved out of Grandma Valta's house and Ulysses and relocated to colorful Colorado.

I don't recall the actual move, but the house we found to rent is etched in my mind forever. Bigger than anyplace I had ever lived, it was an old two-story with light-green plaster on the outside. It sat atop a hill with no neighbors nearby. Because of its elevated location and size, it did seem like a castle, so naturally that was what we named it.

Unlike most of Florence, our castle had no grass, no lawn, nothing green except the color of the stucco. This house was even larger than Grandma Valta's, so despite its landscape of rocks and dirt, it still seemed we had made a big step upward. We were at the foothills of the *Rocky* Mountains, after all, and there seemed to be as many rocks on the ground as there were stars in the sky. Those rocks provided hours and hours of free, if not safe, entertainment for my brothers and me that summer. There were more rocks to be lofted than we could ever hope to, not that that kept us from trying.

One day upstairs in the castle, in the bedroom Gayla and I shared, Lonnie and I were busily absorbed entertaining ourselves when in wandered Bruce. I wish I could recollect otherwise, but whenever Bruce came around, trouble was never very far behind. Before long, Bruce opened the door that accessed a step-out porch off the bedroom. Out on the small balcony he quickly discovered a good-sized wasp nest. Not content with simply observing the insects while respecting their space, Bruce proceeded to knock down the nest. In an instant he was gone, and Lonnie and I were left in a room rapidly filling with wasps seeking to destroy those who would destroy them and theirs.

As he sprinted toward the castle's interior, Lonnie screamed at me, "Run, Fran, run!" Scores of incensed dive-bombers filled the air in the bedroom. I was petrified and made the worst possible choice, though not an unfamiliar one. Instead of running as Lonnie instructed, I froze in terror, then crumpled onto a nearby chair, drew up my knees to my body, wrapped my arms around my knees, and with utter futility, buried my face between my arms. I sat there screaming as the angry, displaced enemy reenacted Pearl Harbor on a miniature scale. I don't remember who was responsible for my eventual rescue. I only remember the painful wasp stings I suffered and the loathing I felt toward Bruce.

That summer Lonnie and I spent wonderful days of exploration and adventure. We fueled our bodies during these delights with a dietary mainstay we truly enjoyed: mustard sandwiches. An occasional slice of American cheese fancied up our self-made rations, but most of the time, the plies of white bread united with plain yellow mustard were eats we thoroughly enjoyed. As often as not, we spent the daytime hours playing with our cousins, and in colorful Colorado, life seemed wonderful.

Later in life I would learn that summer wasn't nearly as glorious for my mother as it was for us kids. I didn't realize our mustard sandwiches also signified the lack of much bologna or other meat. I also learned my mother necessarily spent a lot of time doing laundry for the seven of us in the bathtub at that house, obviously without a washing machine of her own and apparently without funds to go to a laundromat. I can only imagine how such demanding labor and financial-fueled stress worked on my mother's nerves.

I have little recollection of life without the realization of the importance and necessity of money, or how little of it we possessed. As long as I can remember, my sharp young mind picked up all different kinds of cues from my mother about money, everything related to it (which was everything), and our lack of it.

The hope for work and financial steadying was apparently short-lived, and before school began in September that year, we were back in Ulysses.

Fourth Grade

In conjunction with our return to Kansas, my dad got a job that temporarily moved us into the ranks of Marty Monroe's family. This job wasn't with the railroad, but it did come with a house as part of the deal. We moved to the very northwest corner of Ulysses, out to the fairgrounds. Dad had been hired as caretaker of that complex, and "the fairgrounds" was the next place we called home.

A pleasant old house at the edge of the grounds was home during my fourth-grade school year. The house was good-sized, with three bedrooms and a large country kitchen. Very plain without being run-down, the house had a lived-in, friendly feel to it. In front of the house facing south, there was a large grassy yard and several very tall well-positioned shade trees. From the kitchen door facing east, there was also a gravel driveway area with space for several cars. Fifty feet or so northeast from the kitchen door sat a mostly finished structure we kids dubbed the garage. All this sat on a couple of acres that comprised the residential portion of the fairgrounds. I really appreciated the abundance of space we had inside the house and out. We now resided not in town but at its very edge, within easy walking distance of friends and family, but a nice distance apart from others.

The garage was not a garage at all, built in no way to house any type of vehicle. It measured perhaps forty-by-thirty, the roof and windows had been finished, and to the exterior walls tarpaper had been affixed. Inside, insulation had been installed, and toward the northern end, about a third of the walls and floor had been finished in plywood. Simply put, my brothers and I had an exceptionally large comfortable area to call our own.

As for the remaining area, exposed floor joists served as the spine of this wood skeleton. For Lonnie and me, this framework became our tight ropes, balance beams, cliff edges, or rope bridges spanning volcanoes or any other exciting, mysterious, scary, and pseudodangerous setting. If we toppled from our vantage point the joists provided, there was as much fun to be had crawling on the ground beneath them, digging, burrowing, burying treasures in secret hiding holes. We were limited only by our lack of imagination.

Much like the Devil's Hole at Hagerman's, our adventures in that building occupied many hours of time and provided much entertainment for my brother and me. Bruce hatched and raised pheasant and pigeon eggs beneath light bulbs in washtubs on the floored portion of the garage. Outside were a couple of ragtag coops that were home to a dozen or so pigeons he had managed to acquire. My older brother had a real gift for being able to grow things from seed, be it animal or plant life. We lived around his animal husbandry setups with healthy interest while knowing to observe their off-limits status, which was not difficult since being too close to Bruce very long was never a good idea anyway.

As well as our enviable play area in the garage, Lonnie and I had a lot of room to roam outside too. The fairgrounds were a large area for a couple of kids, as we would later find out in a very different respect.

Other distractions and responsibilities at our new place came with the names Daisy, Lily, and the triplets. These clan members were goats that were a part of our expanding menagerie. Daisy was a brown goat with yellow eyes that looked as evil as she behaved. As often as not, she reared up on her hind legs in aggression toward me. I was terrified of that goat. Lonnie always told me to kick her or bust her in the face and she would stop bullying me. Although I did try, I never found the courage to stand my ground with that beast.

Lily was an all-white goat with long horns and a sweet disposition. In the spring, she presented us with pure-white triplets, which were really adorable and fun. We learned how to milk the goats, and Mom made fine-tasting gravy with the milk. The goats roamed and foraged freely in the yard and the nearby fairgrounds, and their bleating and the tinkle, tinkle of the bells around their necks I recall with fondness.

During our tenure there, my father flexed his entrepreneurial muscles. He had wrangled an old farm truck somewhere and had removed the sideboards. Somehow he secured access to other pieces of equipment integral to wheat harvest and the hay business: a swather, rake, baler, and even an old combine. Trips to the hay fields with Dad were great times. Riding on the combine with him during wheat harvest, itching from chafe thick in the air, eating wheat out of the grain bin of the combine, watching the grain fall from the upper end of the machine's auger into the beds of the waiting trucks to be transported to the elevators were exquisite treats. All this also allowed me closeness to my dad if in proximity only. One takes what they can get.

At times Dad's hay hauling operation required additional hands. One such worker was a young man whom everyone called Zero, a label that denoted his mental, social, and educational lack. Such insensitivity did not register to me then. I was nine years old and was unable to discern most of the outrageous facts present in my own life. Zero himself never expressed displeasure at his belittling moniker. To this day I have no idea what his name actually was. Through adult eyes I shudder at the callous and demeaning attitude the men around me exhibited toward that young man, but back then, even if I had had the mind to question my father's behavior, I would not have done so. At this age I already possessed the clear understanding to never dispute the behavior, authority, motives, and character of those about whom I cared the most, feared the most, looked up to the most, needed the most.

Curiosity, disagreement, questioning, such behaviors were a foolish gamble in my young life, and I learned early on how it feels to roll snake eyes at a crapshoot. Dad's size, willingness to lay hands on us, and years of practice effectively kept us kids at bay when our father felt unsure, uncomfortable, or otherwise unable. If the subject at hand were the workforce, politics, current events, or other impersonal subjects, one was safe in engaging Dad. On the other hand, to try to communicate about feelings or anything else with which he was not comfortable meant my father would snuff out any attempt to compromise his internal buttresses, no matter how harsh he had to behave in order to be effective. And so by time I heard a young adult being called a Zero, I was adept at avoiding the physical or emotional rebuff I would suffer, had it even occurred to me to make my father uncomfortable by questioning that insulting label.

Questions directed to my mom could be equally risky. While the consequences of overstepping my boundaries with her did not meet with physical discouragement, they involved forms of rebuke that made the blood in my veins feel ice-cold. The wrong inquiry of my mother would produce irritation and unnerving looks coupled with a silence that would make me want to become invisible, even if I didn't understand what wrong I had done.

Conveying disapproval, discomfort, and disgust without ever uttering a word was a technique my mother employed until it was a part of who she was rather than a choice. This tenor created such a precarious zone, venturing there was simply a no-brainer. More than once I asked what I thought was an innocuous question only to be shot through by the projectiles launched from her eyes. Soon I learned I couldn't trust my own judgment not to offend, so I had to find other sources to tap when my curiosity, interest, confusion, and other ordinary instances in growing up needed response. Like the Iron Curtain, these walls existed much too long and prevented the development of closeness, trust, and a sense of safety and ease.

This pathological family dynamic prohibited normal growth of relationship and destroyed countless fledgling interactions. Intentionally or not, my parents cultivated this mandate of silence with the false notion it would protect them. Unfortunately, their need to protect themselves many times prevailed beyond the idea of first protecting their children's well-being. Had they not been fraught with internal injuries from their own childhoods, I imagine things could have been a lot different within our family. Wounded beings simply cannot do as good a job at anything as they could if they were whole. Ultimately, the truth of this standard was that it simply perpetuated pain and pain's offspring.

Although I realized early on that questions for either of my parents were a gamble of sizable risk, situations sometimes forced taking the leap. Keeping my mouth shut was equivalent to silencing my brain, so my job became figuring out which questions would be benign and which would register as strikes against me. Trying to do so was confusing, and I committed serious fouls at times.

While probably five years old, I was still pretty much a novice at this skill of chance taking, and one day I erred badly. In the kitchen area of our trailer home, I offended my mother when I asked her how babies got out of their mothers' bellies. The look she shot me was one of narrow-eyed suspicion and displeasure. With furrowed brow and frost-coated words, she told me I was too little to understand. Immediately I knew I had gone out of bounds. I knew my mother was more than a little unhappy with me, but I couldn't understand exactly why. I was too young to yet know this question would violate her comfort zone, but her eyes turning to slits in her head was something my mind immediately filed away for future reference.

My question would not be dismissed, so I gave answering it my best shot. The nearest I could figure was that the belly button must open up so the doctors could get babies out that way. Thank goodness it never occurred to me to ask my mother how the babies got into their mothers' bellies!

After the childbirth question, I was left feeling insecure, guilty, and anxious, but no less curious. I didn't understand the nature of my violation, nor did I know for sure how to avoid repeating it. I did conclude that seeking answers elsewhere was probably a pretty good idea. I could not help but continually wonder why I thought about things that were unacceptable to my mother, whose attention I needed, whose affection I was starved for, and whose approval I wanted.

Life is neither easy nor often pretty for those on the lower rungs of the social ladder. Keeping our heads above water was our daily, unrelenting objective, which stymied a more genteel refinement and lofty consciousness. These were qualities for folks whose lifestyles and mindsets were foreign to ours. My molester, Paul, was not the only boarder my folks took in while raising a family. During the years we lived in our homes on wheels, Mom's brother Bob would often bunk on our sofa, a family friend named Junior Humphries also stayed with us a while, and during the time we lived at the fairgrounds, we had a fourth boarder.

Johnnie Humphries was one of fifteen children in a family renown if not well regarded in Ulysses. Margaret and Orrin Humphries were good friends of my mother. They always had a smile for us kids and were welcoming and liked to hear how we were doing. My aunt Betta was married to the oldest Humphries offspring.

As a preschooler, I well recall walking across the street kitty-cornered from my grandparents' house to the lawn of the courthouse. I sat there with my aunt Betta and her two toddler daughters and listened while she hollered up to the third floor, where the jail and her husband, Bill Humphries, were housed. As my aunt and her husband did their best to visit and share some time with one another, we kids had fun playing on the courthouse lawn, enjoying time spent together as cousins often do.

I later figured out differently, but as a kid, I thought Margaret Humphries might be part Gypsy. At times my mother would tell us of Gypsies coming through Ulysses while she was a child and how afraid of them she was because my grandparents had warned her that the Gypsies would steal children away from their families and subsequently raise those children as Gypsies. In pictures I had seen that Gypsies had pierced ears, and Margaret Humphries was the only woman I knew with pierced ears, so I concluded Margaret must have been a Gypsy or escaped from the Gypsies or something like that. Why else would she have pierced ears when no one else did? Nevertheless, her pierced ears fascinated me. To make us kids gasp in awe and amazement, Margaret would sometimes take out her earrings and show us the holes in her lobes. That was as mysterious and exciting as anything kids today have for titillation!

Apparently, Orrin's toes fascinated me as much as Margaret's ears did because I mortified my parents one day with a request I made of him. I was perhaps three, even four years old and quite remember the incident. By this age I was practicing some obsessive-compulsive behavior that soothed some of my stressful anxieties but also left me with guilt because I did not ever see anyone else engaging in some of the rituals I enacted to make the world around me feel more orderly and inviting. So why did I have this need? I knew I was different, and different was not a good thing to be. All this, coupled with a sense of compulsion and not enough social reservation, did me in.

Things that didn't seem to bother other people, I often found very troubling. Unfortunately, Orrin Humphries's appearance was a bit grungy, which apparently did work on my mind because while enjoying time together as families one evening, I made a request that left everyone in deafening silence. Although it had been worrying me all too long, to everyone else my request came out of nowhere. As pretty as I was innocent, I walked across the living room of the Humphries's home toward Orrin. I stopped just in front of where he sat. With his self-rolled cigarette dangling from his bottom lip, his salt-and-pepper hair grown a little too far over his ears and down his neck to look neat, his banjo at rest on his crossed legs between songs, I waited till he looked at me. Looking directly into his pretty blue eyes, I stated my business. Eager to get the job done so I could quit thinking about it, I simply asked this old man if I could clean between his toes!

It is probably safe to assume that those present did whatever necessary to make sure they had heard me correctly, since what they thought they heard me ask surely wasn't what I *had* asked. My mother's heart no doubt missed several beats. I am sure she was speechless for a time. However, the horror of this unusual child of hers making such a revolting request catapulted her the distance to me. She grabbed my forearm and yanked me toward her, digging her nails into my flesh to express her anger and disgust. Dad's face contorted in disbelief, and his head shook back and forth, no doubt involuntarily. Not only did Orrin's toes not get cleaned, with my parents I racked up another strike about how different and disconcerting I could be.

Now, at the fairgrounds five years or so later, I didn't realize it, but Johnnie Humphries was a bit slow mentally, like Dad's brother Bud. Johnnie was one of the middle children in that family and was about eighteen or nineteen when he stayed a while with us. He was very soft-spoken, had a handsome face and pleasant manner. Being around him was not difficult—with one exception. Living amongst us, I witnessed another aspect that made association with the Humphries not only unorthodox but indeed somewhat heretical: they were Catholics.

My parents never, ever took us kids to Sunday school or church. My grandmother Bea parented us in that regard, and as a member of the Church of God, the lens through which she viewed Catholics was not one of approval. Suffice it to say, Catholics were looked down on. They were the cruds of the Christian world, and now Dad had one living with us. When we sat down to supper of an evening, Johnnie Humphries had to bow his head and pray silently and then make the sign of the cross on his chest with his hands. On Fridays, Mom had to cook him fish sticks to eat. Never did my family bow our heads and pray before we ate, and we never had to worry about when to eat fish or not. By this time of my life, what I knew about Catholics told me that this situation in our home was way too close to a belief with which I was to have nothing to do. Apparently, Johnnie didn't have to live with us very long because I managed to withstand the exposure to his religion without any lasting ill effects.

The downside of living at the fairgrounds was that Dad had the responsibility of cleaning up after the county fair and carnival that always accompanied it. Dad's responsibility trickled down, and the fact was Bruce, Lonnie, and I were the peons that comprised his workforce. Of course Dad was glad to have the abundant child labor we kids represented. Who could blame him? It was summertime and very hot as we sat out with our broom and rake handles that had nails protruding from their ends and functioned as spears. The amount of paper and trash left lying on the ground after several days of community festivities was enormous. Working in the August heat and daily Kansas wind was awful. The job was a lot to try to wrap my nine-year-old mind around, and it seemed like it took forever to accomplish. We kids received no monies for our efforts, so motivation was hard to muster. With noncompliance not an option, I managed to persevere. I have never looked at soda cups, sno-cone cups, cotton candy holders, corn dog sticks, popcorn containers, napkins, straws, or people the same since that ordeal.

Toward the end of our tenure at the fairgrounds, my aunt Karen took me aside one day. She was gentle and sensitive in her approach, but the subject matter upset me nevertheless. Karen was eighteen then and always kind, caring, and affectionate. As a child she taught me how to bowl, played board games with me, bought me trinkets and gifts, and never considered giving time and attention to me a burden. She cared about who I was and how I was doing, and being with her always felt good, except this particular day.

At the fairgrounds house one afternoon, Karen took me aside and said she wanted to talk to me. She explained to me that I was a big, tall girl, and my body was beginning to change, that I was developing breasts, and I needed to start wearing a bra.

Immediately I became really upset. Again I felt like I was breaking some rule. No other girl in my fourth-grade class wore a bra yet. Even my sister Gayla, two years older than I, had no hint of budding breasts. This situation wasn't fair, and it somehow compounded the feeling I held that something about me was askew, even bad. Not even my body would cooperate with trying to be good.

Not even Karen suggested normal development was something to celebrate. Even if she had, because of the toxic emotions that plagued my psyche, I would have discounted such a suggestion immediately. Additionally, why Karen instead of my mother was talking to me about my developing breasts is poignant. Like so many other times, what my mother was thinking is a question to which I will never have the answer.

I can only surmise Dad had had enough of his agricultural business venture and tending the fairgrounds and cleaning up after the community, because between the time the county fair ended in August and the school year began in September, we moved from the fairgrounds. Packing and unpacking were tasks at which my mother must have been an expert. The day we left the fairgrounds my mother cleaned that house, swept and mopped the worn linoleum throughout as if we were moving in, not out. Dad always said there was no excuse for being dirty, that soap and water didn't cost very much. To her credit, Mom ascribed to that same philosophy.

FIFTH GRADE

A ll too soon life at the fairgrounds was bygone. From there we moved a few miles east of Ulysses to a place that was originally a schoolhouse and sat on perhaps two acres of land. This place we called Bullock's, after Roy Bullock, who owned it. A county road bordered the south side of Bullock's, and surrounding the place on the other three sides were fields of crops. The house, its semicircular driveway, Bruce's pigeon coops and livestock enclosures were nicely nestled in this niche. It was a pleasant enough setup, and although Bullock's house was small but nice enough inside, my distinct memories are of the outside.

Along with the goats we already had, Dad brought home a Shetland pony one day. From my days on our mattress equine at Pearl Carter's, horseback riding was an idea that made me ache with longing. Now courtesy of Dad and the pony, we had a horse of sorts! At first I had great hopes of being able to ride every day. Unfortunately, that pony had other ideas, and rightly so. He was not the noble, intelligent, dignified steed like I watched on *Fury* or *My Friend Flicka*, popular television series about horses. Although Dad said he bought the pony for all of us kids, Dad had to have had first-grader, maybe 50-pound Stacy in mind when he bought that pony, not fifth-grader, 110-pound Frances!

That pony would have become swaybacked carrying me far, but for a sweet while, I was in denial about that fact. Gayla would never have considered riding that pony and getting sweaty and dirty being outside. At fourteen years, Bruce was far beyond pony years, and Lonnie was a nice-sized eight-year-old, big enough to feed and water the pony but too tall and heavy to beautifully ride, like Miss Bonnie Blue Butler did in the pony scene in *Gone with the Wind*.

That pony was not only too small for us to ride but was cantankerous and ornery with no tolerance for us kids. He would kick at us with his hind legs whenever we were near. He was uncooperative when we tried to catch him and routinely bit us. All he amounted to was another mouth to feed, and an unlikable one as well. Between the pony kicking at and biting us and the damned goat rearing up on me like she did and some geese my mother had flogging us mercilessly, harmony with the animals existed mostly with our dachshund Dutchess.

On the first day of school, we five were outside waiting for the bus. Stacy, not quite six years old yet, had a small tricycle that was nearby. Bruce had the idea to race to see who could go fastest on the six-year-old's trike. As with the Shetland, we were much too large, but our older brother could be very persuasive, and Lonnie and I accepted his challenge.

I placed my right foot on the metal plate between the trike's back wheels, stooped over, and grasped the handlebars and began pushing hard with my left foot, going as fast as I could around our racetrack. Oops! I hit a rut in the driveway. The trike lurched violently and toppled forward. Inertia splayed me onto the ground. I picked myself up, dusted off my dress the best I could, righted the trike, and began again, undeterred and needing to recover precious time.

With confidence matched only by urgency, I bore down and was moving at a nice trike clip, when a second rut really did me in. Sticking my arms out in front of me to brace my fall proved catastrophic. The energy compounded by my weight snapped my right forearm in three places.

I didn't board the school bus that morning. Rushed to the hospital's emergency room, I got a healthy dose of ether after which the doctor set and casted my arm. The first week of school that year I spent in Bob Wilson Memorial Hospital rather than Leona Trueblood's fifth-grade classroom.

Breaking my arm in three places the first day of school that year was a portent of an extremely challenging year to come. The fall of

1961 through the spring of 1962 would be as tumultuous on the outside as were the internal changes my body was undergoing.

Having to spend several days in the hospital was as stressful as would be expected for a ten-year-old who had an irrational fear of shots and all things medical. Undoubtedly it was no less stressful to my parents as there was no health insurance, and living close to the financial edge was simply our way of life. I missed the first week of school and left the hospital with my right arm sporting a heavy cast that extended from close to my armpit to the knuckles midway on my fingers.

This situation also meant as a right-handed person, I now had to write with my left hand. Doing so was an enormous struggle. At the end of the first marking period, when I received grade C on my report card in penmanship, I was furious with my teacher. Normally my handwriting was neat and graded highly. How to assign my grade must have been a quandary for my teacher, but that consideration never entered my ten-year-old head and, if it would have, would have been no consolation anyway. All I did realize was that I had little use for Mrs. Trueblood after she gave me that C.

My injury was serious, and I had to wear that cast a long while. The day I was to have it removed I felt jubilant. Finally this prosthesis would be history. I couldn't get rid of it fast enough. Eventually convinced the oscillating cast saw would cut through the plaster of the cast without cutting my arm, I watched closely as the doctor cleaved the well-worn club from one end to the other on the outside of my arm and then again on the inside till it was rendered two halves. Next he took bandage scissors and cut the elastic bandage that constituted the innermost part of the albatross. Finally he lifted the top half of the cast off my arm. Joy!

Actually the joy was short-lived. What my eyes and nose beheld was not what I expected. The arm was shriveled and looked pathetic. My arms were rather hairy to begin with, but at least the hair was very light-colored and not too noticeable. At this point, even though light in color, the hair was very long and lay in curls the length of my forearm. There was so much hair it looked nearly like the hair on my head. Had I had dark hair, I am sure it would have resembled that of a chimpanzee. There was simply much too much hair on that arm!

The skin on the arm was yellowed and the top layer dead and in dire need of an extreme exfoliation. That arm looked more dead than alive.

As if the hair and skin weren't enough, the crowning insult was the odor. After nearly four months inside a cast, the whole mess smelled dead too. Copious amounts of dirt, sweat, and germs infested that cast and the skin of that arm and hand. My eyes began to well up with tears that soon began rolling down my cheeks.

As if my senses had not already been inordinately offended, the next thing I knew, the damned arm scared me half to death. Still shocked by the prune of an arm I beheld and the rotten stench it exuded, the thing suddenly expressed a will of its own. It began to levitate. Startled and pushed over the edge, I began to wail. I was afraid if I tried to move my arm, it would break again, and here it was, suspended in midair at shoulder level.

Time did stand still a bit. I was frozen in shock and fear. Finally I heard a voice, faint as if it were far away. It reassured me that everything was all right. Skeptically I allowed the doctor to touch my arm, interrupt its levitation, and bring it back down to earth. He wrapped it in elastic bandage again and explained there was nothing wrong except the arm had borne so much extra weight for so long it had grown accustomed to that weight. The physical law about there being an equal and opposite reaction to every action was exemplified by my arm that day. But my not knowing anything about physics at that time turned the levitating arm into one of the most frightening moments of my life!

Throughout those months as my mother took me to Dr. Dodson's office for checkups on my broken appendage, I consoled myself with the idea that when we did depart the doctor's office, Mom might let me go get a cherry limeade at the drugstore two doors down. One such day I was to suffer a watershed moment in my life brought on by my pursuit of one such liquid refreshment. Even though every person encounters these turning points, by their nature they are significant, and the pain or elation they provoke pocks our hearts and imprints our minds forever.

After my checkup while still in the examination room, I asked my mother if I could go to Minor's Drugstore to get a cherry limeade. Immediately the doctor interrupted my mother's response and set upon me. He looked directly at me and curtly stated that at 110 pounds, I was overweight for my age, and I needed to lose weight. I was startled by his quickness and intensity. There was no compassion for the youngster I was, no gentleness in his voice, no detectable concern for my feelings or my health, only his accompanying frowns of judgment, impatience, irritation, and disgust while he ambushed me with his demeanor and impaled me with his ruling.

From that moment on till decades later, when that man would take his own life with a firearm, I despised him. His judgment about my weight and appearance was only the first of countless such incidences that would abort any fledgling self-esteem I might begin to muster about my maturing body, any idea of self-acceptance I might entertain, any belief that I was pretty, attractive, and a desirable female. Indeed, coupled with the significant family dysfunction that meant I received negligible attention and affection in everyday life, absolutely no healing after being molested more than once, why, being overweight and its stigma was just another huge nail being driven into my emotional coffin. I was tattooed with, depression moving toward despair. My physician's smugness furthered the battering I had begun to suffer years earlier by my sister Gayla, with her unchecked taunts that I was a fat pig. In his office that day, Dr. Dodson simply made it official.

I knew well how to simply keep going by placing one foot in front of the other, and I did so again that day. I walked out of the clinic that afternoon after having been marked for life. Outwardly I reacted rather stoically, but inwardly I had suffered another important assault on my being. I don't remember my mother saying anything to the doctor about his gruffness with me or to me in the privacy of our automobile. As we rode home, my fragile sense of self seemed withered and tried to evacuate my body through an invisible hole in the car's floorboard. By that time, enjoying a cherry limeade was the farthest thing from my mind.

As if life were not heavy enough already, late that fall my younger brother Lonnie and I developed grossly chapped lips that afflicted us an inordinate amount of time. Naturally the constant dryness and subsequent licking in vain attempts to moisturize them was an ugly cycle. Our lips and the skin around them were scabbed, cracked, burning, and bleeding. I remember Lonnie and I even pulling our lips simultaneously in the direction of both corners of our mouths to try to get some relief from the awful sense of tightness the chapping caused. That only made matters worse, but it does illustrate our desperate discomfort. It seemed we could think of nothing *but* the chapped lips; hell could be no more miserable. This malady was very painful, extremely uncomfortable, and just as unsightly. I was embarrassed to go to school with my mouth looking awful.

The split and scabbed-up lips did eventually heal and left no scars around my mouth. Interesting is the fact that a simple case of chapped lips became an extreme case and the idea we children were not given the simple treatment of Chapstick. I am puzzled whenever I think about this ordeal as to what our parents were thinking. Money was always scarce, and all us kids knew it was a critical, ongoing issue, but common sense says a tube of Chapstick, even one that we could have divided between us, would have been financially manageable. Whatever the explanation, nothing will ever change the fact that my brother and I suffered immensely during the weeks our lips were so mangled and awful looking.

To this day and without fail, I have a plethora of Chapstick and many other brands of lip balm tucked into and secured in every part of my world. I may suffer a lot from different maladies during this lifetime, but untreated chapped lips will never again be one of them.

The graying of the sky that comes as fall approaches winter was like my inner light, except at ten years old I was not in the autumn of my life: I was in my springtime and should have exuded the newness and freshness, the promise and uplift that come with that season. Due to incidences of neglect, deprivation, and injury, my light was waning. Instead of young I was already aged.

As with the ordinary combustion engine, our Creator embeds a spark of divinity in each of us. Since the Creator cannot err, every spark is perfect. This spark combines with fuels like love, nurturing, protection, and caring guidance to make light, and it is the energy from the light that propels us, just as mechanical energy created inside an engine drives a car. Part of the difference in human beings, then, springs from the fuel used when causing the spark to combust and produce energy. I was not getting enough quality fuel to be who I would otherwise have been. Absent a regular supply of the fuels that God intended, in some essential ways, I was growing as much down as up.

Grandmother Bea was short and plump and always trying to take off pounds. In her home was a contraption she called a stoffer. Whether that was the manufacturer's name or the name of their product, I am unsure, but I clearly remember the term and what the weight loss machine looked like. It was close in color to the pink associated with the Mary Kay line of cosmetics, was close to six feet long, and sectioned into three parts. The machine sat perhaps a foot and a half off the floor and resembled a three-piece flashy pink cot. No doubt that contraption had cost my grandmother a pretty penny, as do most products that promise weight loss.

Grandmother would sit down on the middle section of her machine before totally reclining along all three sections. Next she would take a sandbag that was a couple feet long and a foot or so across and lay it across her midsection lengthwise. Having gotten nicely situated, she would press the button to turn on the machine, at which time it would begin gyrating. Held in place by the sandbag, Grandma would lie there and relax while the machine caused her body to roll back and forth while shaking and shimmying, her roundness held firmly in place by substantial undergarments and a bag of sand. Completing the picture was the satisfied grin she unfailingly wore, no doubt the outward expression of the idea that fat and inches were melting away thanks to this novel gadget.

I doubt my beloved grandmother really ever lost a pound or an inch due to that machine, but I have no doubt she got her money's worth by being able to get off her feet, relax, and close her eyes for a spell and enjoy the rhythmic hum of her pink helpmate.

Another item in her cache of weight loss strategies was to go to TOPS meetings. The acronym meant Take Off Pounds Sensibly, and the philosophy was just that. Members attended weekly meetings in members' homes. As participants arrived, the first order of business was the weigh-in. Some members could not wait to get on the scales; others held back as long as they could. Clearly individual attitudes matched the degree of sensibility the person had exhibited the prior week.

After everyone had arrived, weigh-ins were finished and recorded, and the clock indicated it was time to convene, the members seated themselves in the living room of Mrs. Sam Wiebe to share testimony, recipes, encouragement, and garner resolve to sensibly take off pounds in the week to come. When all business was concluded, so was the meeting, at which time the attendees gathered at one side of the room near the kitchen to enjoy refreshments. The diet soda Tab was brand-new then, so at that time, diet foods and drink and lite versions of things to eat were marketing ploys of the future. Nevertheless, I am sure the ladies employed the use of their low-calorie recipes and remained sensible.

In this group of TOPS, members were a dozen or so women, all around the age of my grandmother or older. With one exception—*me*! My grandmother strongly urged me to come with her to TOPS. She stressed that learning the tenets of this organization and applying them might help me lose weight, and the benefits I would see would surely be worth the effort. Numerous examples from my life to that point illustrate that saying no was not one of my strengths. I did not want to go to TOPS but did not have the wherewithal to tell my grandmother no.

Never have I had even one recollection of feeling normal when it came to my weight. Long before I was old enough to begin school, by the time my brain was mature enough to retain conscious memories, that singularly painful, powerful word (*weight*) and the denigrations it spawned, had ravaged my mind and left an indelible identity hardwired into my brain.

In the immediate past, Dr. Dodson had chided me about my weight with his words, tone, and facial expression, reinforcing great fear and feeding the very emotions within me that made me want to seek comfort in food. Now my grandmother had said essentially the same thing as the physician had, albeit in a different manner. Her actions were full of love and caring and without cruelty or words meant to be hurtful. Unfortunately, none of that worked to make my presence at the TOPS meetings with a houseful of postmenopausal, gray-haired women at various levels of obesity and soon-to-be senior citizens any less humiliating.

The months I attended TOPS with my grandmother, and her peers turned out to be no more than another roundup at which I received another branding to be carried with me through life. At times the best intentions fall short and have mixed result.

My fifth-grade year started out roughly and only got worse. That time span was accompanied by many profound changes in my world. Life's stressors grew in number, complexity, and significance. Managing not to drown in waters already much troubled, became more difficult each day. A painful and challenging childhood was about to become much more so.

My fifth-grade teacher was a short, plump, heavy-breasted woman whose eyes all but disappeared when she smiled or laughed. I remember her as one of two teachers in my K-12 years that liked me and took a bit of a personal interest in me. Unfortunately at the time, I didn't perceive her actions as such. In fact, Mrs. Trueblood and I must have clashed rather regularly because my mother was at the school several times to meet with her regarding my attitude and behavior.

One day that fall, Mrs. Trueblood took me aside, and the discussion that followed would become a part of that shadowy, dark place inside myself where I tried to lock away experiences that were difficult to understand and react to appropriately, were confusing if not traumatizing. Such experiences were housed in the cellblock along with guilt, shame, and fear.

How clearly I recall the building of my elementary school, a well-built, fine old structure where my own mother had attended school in the 1930s. My fifth-grade classroom was on the west side of the second floor of the school. It was located between Mr. Sparks's sixth-grade classroom and the middle stairwell. Mrs. Harp's fifth-grade classroom was opposite the stairwell, and opposite our class-room door was the Health Room.

Why the Health Room was so named none of us students knew. With the feel and appearance of a first-aid station, the Health Room was never used for anything relating to health issues during the five years I was a student at Joyce School. This area looked like the place a school nurse would have occupied had there been one. There were never any lights turned on in the Health Room, so it was dark compared to the rest of the school, with a cold look and feel to it. The upper half of its hallway wall consisted of nontransparent glass. Inside against the north wall was a couch where an ill student could have lain. Against the opposite wall sat an adult's desk and a couple of chairs. One afternoon when my teacher instructed me to follow her to that room, I knew it could be for nothing good.

I sat down as Mrs. Trueblood bade me and waited nervously for her to begin. Being alone with her felt odd and uncomfortable. Finally, she began by telling me we were both females, that she had a daughter who was in high school and with whom she had had a talk like this at one time. She remarked how I was a tall girl whose body was becoming that of a young lady and that meant it was developing inside and out-side, and those changes meant I would soon experience other changes.

The talk was reminiscent of the chat my aunt Karen had had with me the year before about wearing a bra except this occasion was much more uncomfortable. This woman was not my family; she did not love me. In fact, I was appalled and furious because this liberty she was taking with me was making me feel extremely uncomfortable and upset. My stomach was queasy as the outrage I felt toward my teacher was strong. I detested her for what she was saying. Why me? Why not any other girl? I needed control in my life, and what I was hearing was that my body was morphing into something over which I had absolutely no control. This feeling was horrible, I did not know how to handle it, and I had nowhere to turn for solace.

There were several parts of my life as a child from which my mother completely divorced herself. Going to church fell into that category. Even as a child, I resented my mother's absence, participation, and lack of guidance but was powerless to chink away at the armor with which she separated and tried to protect herself from situations with which she had negative associations, one of which was church.

In fact, neither my father nor mother would fulfill that part of their parental responsibility, seeing to their children's spiritual life, growth, or development. While my mother would absolutely not take us to Sunday school and church, she did ensure we were always dressed and ready to go when the honk of our grandmother's car horn signaled our ride had arrived. Aside from attending our Christmas programs, weddings, or funerals, neither my mother nor my dad set foot inside our church. Consequently, I never worshipped with my mother or father, sang hymns or prayed with them, felt the contentment of sitting beside them in a pew, nor wept in joy or anguish as one often does in God's house. My developing body, clearly obvious to the world around me and the latest source of distress I was experiencing, was just another important part of life about which I could not turn to my mother for guidance or support. I felt so alone and confused.

I knew about menstruation. While a third grader, I had snooped in Gayla's dresser drawer and found literature on that subject and had read all about it. Such things, relevant in ways, were taboo to inquire about otherwise. Innocent curiosity and natural questions I formulated, I had long ago learned to associate with a sense of wantonness and luridness and most likely proof that I was a very lascivious, immoral girl. I knew better than to ask my mother about such nasty things.

So why had my teacher isolated me from the other students, taken me into this dark, secluded room, and began this conversation with me about my body? I felt as I had with my molesters, my uncle Bud and Dad's friend Paul, as if something evil was happening yet again, and being the bad person I was, somehow I had asked for it.

Mrs. Trueblood maintained a reassuring smile on her face that infuriated me even more. She talked differently than she did across the hall in the classroom, which also felt weird and suspicious.

Ultimately, I disregarded everything she said—the changes taking place in my body, preparing for becoming a young woman physically, and all that was hygienically related to that. I felt dirtied again, different from everyone else with yet another secret to protect.

In the springtime of that school year, all of us girls in fifth through eighth grades would officially be educated about puberty and its inclusions. From Joyce School, we fifth and sixth graders were bussed the ten blocks or so to Sullivan School that housed grades K-8. As we students entered the gym/cafeteria, our mothers were already seated. As instructed, each girl sat down in the seat beside her mother, an eighth-grade teacher named Mrs. Bogue greeted the group and introduced the film that was about to be shown. Never had my mother spoken one word to me about puberty, menstrual periods, or becoming a young lady physically. It was just like going to church and praying. Those were things I did not do with or in front of my mother, and if I had been forced to, I would have been extremely uncomfortable. That part of my life didn't include her or my father. They had never included themselves in it.

Now this new part of life that completely unnerved me was suddenly being addressed openly, as if I should be comfortable with it and with my mother sitting here beside me while I was put through such an ordeal. There was not that kind of closeness between my mother and me to withstand the pressure such unseemly, private, revolting subjects delivered. Actually, I am sure she was just as uncomfortable as I was, and unsurprisingly, after the tortuous tea was over, my mother and I continued our silence toward one another.

Not having the kind of relationship with my mother that permitted openness, honesty, and safety, I was embarrassed and completely ill at ease, as if I were breaking really important rules. I wanted to run away. I didn't want my mother knowing I knew about this stuff. Busted again! I couldn't understand why some of the mothers I knew were even smiling. This scene went beyond distressing for me to agonizing. My life would never be the same again, but that didn't mean I wasn't going to resist the change.

When the horrible film was over and the lights were turned on, I felt sick to my stomach. And then the teacher who was hosting thanked us for coming and directed us to the tables where the cookies, butter mints, and punch sat. I saw everyone there as rule breakers. Even the school had gone to hell! Five months later I would have my first period.

I attended grade school in the same building my mother had. Joyce School was a lovely, well-constructed two-story solid-brick building that felt safe. Generally, I liked being at school and did well with minimal effort. I enjoyed the predictable routine, clearly defined expectation, rules (even when I broke them), and the consequences I might expect. It all made pretty good sense. I felt at home with people who were educated, inspired by their demeanor and knowledge. I liked being one of the first to be selected in the classroom contests and playground games. I needed the recognition I got for my performance there. Most of the time at school I felt good about myself.

Moving from house to house was a way of life. As a child I never questioned why we moved so often even though leaving a few of the places was not easy for me. Moving a family of seven twice within a few months couldn't have been any easier for my mother, but that was exactly what we did. We packed up, left country life behind, and moved back into town.

After beginning my fifth-grade year living at Bullock's before Christmas, we occupied a house that came to be called the Mexican Shack. The name was not an expression of contempt toward brown-skinned folks. Rather it was our expression of the social and economic level at which we found ourselves manifested by the appearance of the house and lot. More than the house itself, the corner lot on which it sat had a definite run-down, needy look about it, a condition we associated with that of most Hispanics, a good number of which lived in my hometown. We were back to living in a small, rather run-down-looking house with absolutely no grass, only Kansas dirt giving the outside its bleak complexion. No flower, not even a weed in bloom decorated that thumbnail of earth we occupied that winter and spring.

The savage goat Daisy, the ornery, biting pony, the gentle goat Miss Lily and her three kids were relegated to the annals of Carter history, and we moved to the east side of Ulysses onto Court Street. While we could no longer have the bigger animals, there was enough space between the house and the alley my brother Bruce could bring along his beloved pigeons. They were housed in two coops that rested a few feet from a fifty-gallon gasoline barrel Dad had co-opted somewhere.

This new acquisition of Dad's was about four feet high, four or five feet long, and probably about four feet in diameter. Years after I was bucked off our mattress horse at Pearl Carter's and the ordeal with the disappointing pony, I had found another steed. I spent many hours mounted on that metal horse with the mechanically operated gas pump mane and face and, in my mind, traveled many miles and lived through exciting adventures, well occupied by my own imagination.

There were two grade schools in Ulysses. Whether by stroke of luck or divine attention, in all our moving we stayed within the boundaries of the same elementary school. I have since realized not having to change schools was important and provided a much-needed sense of stability and belonging.

This year in my childhood was the most difficult one yet and would yield more than one pivotal moment in its wash. However, one of the best, most exciting, happy times in my entire life I enjoyed that winter as well.

My parents managed to buy a small electric piano, and around the middle of my fifth-grade year, my grandmother Bea began paying Mrs. Mona Collins, a lady from our church, to give Gayla and me piano lessons. Happiness. Pure joy. Utter excitement. Ecstasy. At the piano I felt like I was receiving life-giving blood and oxygen from the keys. I wanted to be there always. I needed to be there. I was alive and happy when I was on the bench practicing my piano lessons. Doing so washed away all cares as long as my fingers were on the white and black keys. No one could have ever done anything that would have meant as much to me and provided me such a meaningful opportunity to express who I was and experience happiness and joy doing so.

My grandmother Bea also provided me with a second important opportunity at this same time, the worth of which was invaluable and the memory and learning I took from it edifying from that time forward. She asked me if I wanted a job so I could earn money for myself and help out her and my grandpa. She offered me the job of cleaning their laundry every day after school and once on weekends.

In that offer, she also included doing housework for her. I did not have to be asked twice. I jumped at the chance.

Even by this time some of my family in town were soliciting me to help them around their homes. I was already well acquainted with chores like cleaning ovens, sweeping and mopping floors, dusting, vacuuming, and the like. I always did good work and responded to guidance and correction about my work, so my help was sought fairly often. I have since realized since I was big and strong and in ways quite mature for my age, those characteristics worked in my favor, attracting these opportunities for some income.

Once a week I would vacuum and dust my grandparents' house, empty garbage, wash windows if needed, scour sinks and the commode, and any other tasks my grandmother assigned me. Her standards were high, but that did not bother me because mine were too. Grandmother and I made a good team, and she taught me a lot about this part of life.

The job I assumed of cleaning the laundromat I enjoyed immensely. I felt important because I was involved in their business. I was earning money regularly, and having funds with which to buy things for myself felt absolutely wonderful.

After school each day I would walk east one block to Main Street and cross to the one hundred block of Central Avenue. My grandparents' home and laundry sat at 117 East Central. The laundry and house were attached via a small office area that basically housed a desk and rolling chair, a really old cash register from which we made change for the customers, and a couple of shelves that held odds and ends. The ceiling in this space was probably no higher than six and a half feet; the room measured maybe seven feet across and perhaps ten feet deep. On the outside wall was a window perhaps three feet across and two feet high. Up against that wall sat the desk and chair facing west, and this was my grandfather's throne. My memories of him sitting at his desk, hat on and cocked slightly to the left, elbows resting on the desk and cigarette in hand, as often as not, packaging coins into paper rolls, or simply gazing out the window thinking of whatever was on his mind warm me and remind me of how much such scenes in my childhood helped provide a much needed sense of safety and stability.

My grandparents at work in and around their home and business was like going to church on Sunday and seeing folks I had known since birth, sitting in the same places in the pews where they sat week after week. Such pleasant scenarios support a child's sense of security by conveying order, echoing a sense that all is in its place and well. A child possesses no greater need and can be given no greater a gift than what my grandparents bestowed on me with their presence and ordinary, daily routine.

After arriving at my job site, I would first gather up all garbage strewn about by customers and deposit it in its rightful place. After emptying the three large garbage cans out back, I proceeded with my wipe down. Tables used to fold clothes, chairs, rolling carts used to transport laundry, windowsills, doorknobs, machines that vended change, laundry products, and soda pop were all things I washed and wiped off daily. Anywhere else I might see dust, spills, or crud, I was responsible for making look clean and neat. Next I would sweep the concrete floor; that was no small job both in size and navigation. Working in and around customers sometimes made me nervous, but I also liked being around the bustle that was energizing. Weekly I was responsible for washing the big windows that comprised the majority of the front of the building. The entry door had a set of muntined panes I was responsible to keep free of fingerprints or anything else detracting from the sparkle of clean glass. Depending on weather and debris, part of my job was to sweep the entrance to the facility, which was a concrete slab running from the building to the sidewalk. That was not a favored part of the job because the concrete was worn and chipped, fractured and leaning in places. Getting it clean with my broom was simply not easy and required more time than I liked to devote to it.

Next on my daily chore list was to wipe down all twenty washers. By this time, the old machines with the rollers were obsolete, and in their place sat automatics with the coin box affixed to the tops. These machines got surprisingly dirty in twenty-four hours, and my job was to clean them. I would make me a bucket of soap and water and with a good-sized rag would begin my rounds. I washed the inside of each machine first, then the top, and last I would wipe down the front and sides of the machines. By time I finished, the machines looked nice and fresh, like broad white soldiers standing there at attention and ready for close inspection.

After filling my bucket with fresh water, I next proceeded to the dryers. There were eight of them, four against the west wall and four against the south wall. Grandpa did not make me deal with the lint traps on the undersides of the dryers. Instead all I had to do was wipe down the fronts, doors, and handles and make sure the drum was clean and ready for use.

Unfailingly, I put off the worst task of my entire regimen till last. When I could no longer avoid it, I would force myself to proceed to the public toilet. Scouring the sink, cleaning the mirror, emptying the garbage can, and sweeping the floor were not really that bad most of the time, but again, putting off the most offensive part of the job till last, I would then have to confront the commode. That part of my job should have included a sliding scale for pay: the filthier it was should have brought more money to my hand, but I had no idea about the fine points of salary negotiations when I was ten years old!

Human beings are nothing less than astonishing in how inconsiderate and gross some choose to be. So many customers must have had an aversion to flushing a commode because more often than not, they left it for the next guy to do. How such big messes can be wrought during a function that can generally be successfully contained I don't understand to this day. At any rate, the nastiness I often found in that bathroom and had to deal with nearly made me gag.

I learned early on, however, my grandmother would cut me no slack just because the place was gross and nearly made me sick. One day I ventured into a particularly disgusting insult in the bathroom. The commode bowl, tank, and seat were smeared with feces. Had the mess been a result of someone experiencing a gastric explosion through their rectum, it would have been horrendous but without the insult of intent.

This mess was not the result of someone who had digestive issues and didn't clean up after themselves. This was someone awful who was a degenerate. Not only were all parts of the commode covered with waste, the pervert responsible for this filth had also smeared it all over the walls. That I didn't quit my job on the spot indicates my value of money. I wanted to cry, but the situation was so beyond anything I had ever seen I was stunned beyond tears.

Eventually I composed myself enough I began to slog through the nightmare, and after a harrowing glimpse of how lowdown some people can be, I found myself finished with the toilet and ready to do my final and favorite part of my job.

Refilling the pop machine was heavenly. I would get the key from Grandpa's office and open the door face of the big machine. There were at least ten rows of pop bottles lying on their side on shelves with just enough angle when the bottle a customer chose was pulled forward and dispensed, the whole row would move downward till the hole created by the bottle the customer was now enjoying was filled.

My job was to inventory how much of each type of pop was needed to fill each shelf, then go to the storeroom at the opposite end of the building and get the bottles I needed, transport them to the front where the pop machine was located, and restock the machine. Grandpa took care of emptying the money bins and reloading the change compartments in the machine. He was the brains of this operation, and I was the brawn.

After I was finished with the pop machine, I was also finished with my work for the day. The best part came next. My grandparents had told me I could help myself to a pop each day after my work was done. The laundry was neat and clean by then. I always felt good about my work, and once a week I got paid as well. Life at work was sweet!

When I returned to work the day after the nasty toilet ordeal, my grandmother's expression was not pleasant. In true no-nonsense, all-business fashion, her mouth was a bold-print straight line across her face with the corners dipping downward just a bit. Dead serious, my grandmother's eyes burrowed into me, and I felt an overwhelming sense of dread.

"Fran, you did not do a good job on that bathroom yesterday. I want you to go out there and do it again, and do it right this time. A job worth doing is worth doing well," she continued.

I looked down at the floor and felt sick. I did not enjoy displeasing my grandmother, and even more to the point, I now had to deal with that awful mess a second time.

I managed to summon all the fortitude I had, quell my body's need to gag and vomit, and once again began cleaning literal shit, desperately hoping I could manage to get it to my grandmother's satisfaction before the awful, filthy mural of excrement truly did overwhelm me. One of the most disgusting, nauseating tasks I have ever had to deal with in my lifetime I somehow saw through, and the lesson I learned at the hands of my grandmother has served me excellently through every year I have been on this earth. Fortunately, the toilet malefactor never again tagged the walls and commode in the laundromat's bathroom with his organic graffiti during the time I worked for my grandparents, so I was spared a repeat of that awful mess.

I felt happy when at my grandparents working or hanging out. At home the atmosphere was choking, and discord flourished.

As often as not, after we kids were in bed, the fireworks between my parents would begin. Within the Mexican Shack, my older sister Gayla and I slept in bunk beds in a room adjoining the living room, where our parents' destructive bouts occurred. Like clockwork, the hissing, accusations, physical contact, and emotional scalding interrupted our sleep. In our bunk beds, one of us would whisper to the other, "Are you awake?" *Of course we were awake!*

As empathetic, sensitive, and extremely emotional as I was by nature, toward my parents I remember feeling neither sorrow nor patience for their pain and difficulties. I felt fascinated in an odd sort of way, and true to the either-or type of logic exhibited so often by the adults in my world, they and their strife disgusted me. I had had ten years' experience in severe family dysfunction by then. I had become desensitized to the sufferings of those closest to me, especially when that suffering was likely to make mine worse.

Effects on children from such injurious ordeals in life like this period of disharmony cannot be overstated. My guts were tied in knots all the time from the negativity and the uncertainty of the looming outcome of the diseased marriage. Even worse, I simultaneously loathed and laughed at my parents and in particular my mother. Even though my father's hand was heavy when he delivered punishment to us kids, Dad's heart was actually soft toward us, and as children, we somehow viewed him as a victim of sorts when it came to his relationship with our mother.

Neither of my parents finished high school. My father was the eldest of nine children, born in 1925 to an alcoholic father and young mother who farmed for a living. At age fifteen or so, there was a row between his father and my dad, and the old man kicked Dad out of the home. That course of events abruptly ended Dad's school days. Eventually he was taken in by his father's bachelor brother in southern California and from there was drafted into the army and served in the European theater during World War II. After the war and his discharge from the army, Dad set out from Texas en route to California. He traveled through Ulysses to visit his mother, and during that visit, he met my mother. Dad was never to see California again.

Dad was a very intelligent person, a voracious reader, a hard-working man with a gypsy-like need to wander, a person full of dreams about small businesses he wanted to establish, things he was going to do or make for us kids. Dreaming came easy for my dad, but realizing them simply did not happen. After several hurtful disappointments, I learned not to count on things Dad talked about doing for us or with us. As far as I knew, he was a faithful husband, the best father he knew how to be, and a dependable provider. As long as I can remember, Dad handed over his paycheck to my mother. She would endorse his name to cash his paycheck and obtain the family's funds. When working away from home on pipeline construction jobs, Dad mailed his paycheck home for Mom to cash and manage.

Though he experienced many difficulties throughout his walk on earth and never managed to acquire much materially, life and its capriciousness and indifference never embittered Dad. Always fond of a few French and German expressions he learned during the war, I often heard either "C'est la vie" or "C'est la guerre." And he meant it. He laughed often enough, often to himself with a knowing smile on his face. He ranted and raved sometimes as well, but that was not his nature, and it rarely overshadowed his being able to see the lighter side of things.

Dad had the most piercing blue eyes and the way he sometimes looked at us kids with those peepers thrilled me. His eyes spoke what his mouth was unable to utter. The love and pride he felt for us were conveyed easily in his eyes. To see himself in us, to observe his link with immortality was his ultimate need, and it had been fulfilled.

In all things there is a plus and a minus, an upside and a downside. My relationship with my dad was no different. As should be the case with any little girl, my dad was my prince. As my prince, I longed to be as much like him as I could. Tragically telling, I never recall trying to emulate my mother. Dad was big, strong, proud, seemingly unafraid of the world, commanding, and quite selfless in most ways. His work ethic was impeccable. He was a self-starter and, as a worker, set high standards for himself and achieved them.

As I grew older, I wanted to be smart like he was, to be able to talk with him about politics and places he had gone and experiences he had had. I wanted to connect with him. I wanted him to be proud of me, because I regarded him so highly. I wanted to be big and tall and physically strong like he was. In high school, I learned German to help create a bond between Dad and me. As Dad had done in the 1940s, I joined the army and served our country, earning an honorable discharge after serving eight years during the 1970s. Whenever Dad was at home, I hung around him outdoors, foregoing time spent indoors on more traditional feminine interests. I helped him tinker with cars, do hard physical labor, despite my mother's disapproval and concern for my female body. I needed Dad to pay more attention to me, to display more affection and approval, and I tried all I could think of to earn it.

I never was able to attain what I sought so long. Only much later would I learn there was no way I ever could have. It was not mine to *have* to earn; it was his to give me, freely, naturally, abundantly, and unconditionally. Sadly as a child and as a young woman, I had no realization of this. Instead I learned to live with the awful belief that if I violated certain limits, Dad would stop loving me. As a kid I saw this kind of savagery time and again within Dad's side of the family.

Turning on one another easily and viciously was practically codified in his blood ranks. Most terrifying was that I couldn't tell where these awful, lethal limits were. Although it was no real comfort, all I could figure was my best chance in avoiding the limits and being cast out was to be the best girl possible. Surely that would ensure not only avoiding crossing the limits but earning me the attention, love, and affection I desperately needed. This unmet need and nearly primal fear took its toll on me growing up and quite some time thereafter. It exhausted me in many ways and would show itself in behavior and choices through the years that caused great pain and suffering, setbacks, and indescribable misery.

The inner world was the realm Dad never had the fortitude to explore, to understand and accept as integral and valid and just as much a part of who we are as the outer world is. When the time did eventually come that I pressed him to have that discussion with me, he simply refused, unable to care what might happen to me in doing so. He never mustered the courage to look past the veneer into the world that cannot be seen with eyes but comprises who each of us is, as much as does our physical body.

My mother was the third of eight children, the eldest deceased as an infant. Born in 1927, Mom was the oldest daughter in a family also headed by an alcoholic father. My grandfather was thirty-three years old when he married my grandmother, who was sixteen and pregnant when they wed. Grandpa was a binge drinker, and when he imbibed, it would last days, weeks, even months. Consequently, Grandma had to function as head of the household and earn the living on a continual basis. In turn, this meant my mother had to function as an adult in terms of household chores and also tending to her younger siblings. Mom believed her mother's viewpoint was that Mom was a babysitter for the younger children before she was a daughter. Believing so poisoned my mother's relationship with my grandmother, the effects of which endured the rest of their lives.

During my mother's ninth-grade year in school, she, a female cousin, and several other girls skipped school one day. For this they were all expelled from high school. With the exception of my grandparents, all the other parents intervened on their daughters' behalves, and their teens were subsequently allowed to return to school. My grandparents' failure to advocate for their daughter ensured my mother's school days were over. No doubt this was a vital turning point in her life both from an academic perspective and no less from a self-esteem point of view.

At the Mexican Shack on Court Street, it was the early 1961. Kennedy was president. Civil rights had not been legislated yet, the women's lib movement was ten years or so in the future, the first moon landing was eight years in the future, and gas was less than a dollar a gallon. My mother's life was a part of those times, and although many women's lives were rich and rewarding, my mother's world was quite a difficult place to live. Mom's lot in life had been cast. Never enough money, too many children, and the crippling weight of unmet needs overwhelmingly burdened and disfigured her. Hopelessness, helplessness, cynicism, and resentment grew in her heart's garden. They were weeds that choked gratitude, curiosity, confidence, abundance, and security till such edifiers withered on the vine. The scourge that dominated her inner self increased the scope and pace to which my mother yielded her true self and traveled the path that led to a negative existence rather than a full and productive life.

Early in her life, my mother concluded she was homely, without talent or individual specialness, intellectually mediocre at best, without much worth or value. She considered herself good for little but the least. Throughout her life she never matured emotionally much beyond the difficulty and suffering of her childhood and teen years. That stunting compounded her inability to shape her attitudes as well as her physical world. Mom never realized she possessed power and strength and, believing otherwise, forfeited those assets. Hence conditions in her life never improved much, and predictably she became withdrawn, acerbic, and increasingly unpleasant. Her unresolved pain and anger took ugly tolls on her, Dad, and us kids; her insecurities and false beliefs wreaked havoc on her body and spirit. Joy for her did come at times from us children, especially when we were infants and preschoolers. As we grew, however, our needs and demands became more complex, and Mom was largely baffled at how to meet them. Unfortunately, what she turned to increasingly, what brought her the most relief and escape during her lifetime, was simply cigarette smoking and withdrawing inside herself. Unfortunately, what gave her some relief only served as one perpetuator of our family's discord and unhappiness.

My mother had a consciousness of lack, which usually meant she believed she had so little of anything there was none with which to share or give, whether it was material things or wealth accumulated in knowledge and experiences. Socially she was extremely uncomfortable and judgmental and found disdain with most people to the point she had little to do with anyone besides her husband, children, a few relatives and even fewer friends. She was never comfortable with anyone who was upright enough to dream, and if such persons exhibited the tenacity and ability to make dreams a reality, they were spurned accordingly. Mom's way of protecting her own sense of inadequacy was simply to find fault with those of such who did not share her malaise.

One of Dad's brothers met a young woman in Arkansas while he was in the military. He married her, and my aunt Joy lived the rest of her life in southwestern Kansas. Joy was a friendly woman whom I enjoyed being around growing up. She always had a glass of sweetened iced tea in hand, cigarette in the other, and spoke with an accent acquired in her native Arkansas. Understandably, she also exhibited influence of the Southern culture in which she had been raised. Mom never cared much for my aunt Joy and her ways and was not happy to see either her or my uncle Pete when they would drop by. One of Joy's greatest offenses was that she belonged to a sorority of sort. The sisterhood was not a collegiate connection, rather a social enterprise. My mother never forgave Joy for trying to be snooty and hobnobbing with others of the same ilk by belonging to that sorority.

Beside some characters in literary classics, my mother was the most excellent example of a tragic figure I have ever known and testimony to the brutality our society effects on females from birth to death. My mother also epitomized the power of one's self-image to manifest outwardly. Whether hale and hearty or rife with frailty, first comes thought followed by realization. Without arrest, the obliteration of her true self succumbed to her awful opinion of who she was.

In early photos I have of my mother, I see eyes full of light and life. I see a child and young girl and teenager and young woman beautiful, playful, alluring, attractive. In artifacts of family history, I glimpse some of my mother's soul at points during her lifetime. Through poetry she composed; art she painted; garments, hats, scarves, and linens she knitted, crocheted, and sewed, Mom's abundant talents and potential were envious and evident. Her musical talent was one I marvel at and covet to this day. Having taught herself to play the piano, organ, and accordion, she possessed the special gift of being able to hear a piece of music and sit down and render it with little effort. Mom was unique, special, innately artistic, and had been apportioned a generous number of God's greatest gifts. That she had become convinced otherwise at the hands of life's mobsters warrants reiteration. Debasing herself and all that comprised her was a genuine tragedy.

What her personal desires, hopes, and aspirations were I do not know. My best guess was that she lived with a need and desire to feel valued and affirmed that haunted her till the day she died. Events, choices, circumstances, unrecognized and unmet needs she suffered over the course of her childhood and young womanhood set a course for my mother that was never changed. An adulthood fraught with immense responsibility and hardship, a dysfunctional marital relationship, and needs continuing to not be met further wore down her spirit and reshaped her inwardly and outwardly till she looked nothing like God's magnificent creation she was truly intended to be.

My dear mother's emotional malignancies eventually developed into a full-blown fear of living that sentenced her to a small cell of a world and the waste of most of her potential and talents. More and more she withdrew from people and life. Her comfort zone and tolerance for people became smaller and smaller as the years passed, and by old age, she was barely recognizable.

Looking at life through this lens of subjugation served to imprison Mom's soul and spirit in what must have been an agonizing dungeon. All this is particularly heartbreaking because my mother had a wealth of talents and traits that could have been developed to serve her famously. By choosing to believe day by day what was not true about her, my mother cultivated an outlook that yielded accordingly. Looking back over such things as photos, combing my memories from my earliest years forward, conversing with many, including my mother, about days and events gone by, I have come to understand none of this calamity happened hastily. It was an insidious disease of the heart that slowly acquired momentum over the years and snowballed as it continued to consume the special soul our Maker had sent to inhabit a body and travel through life on this earth.

Why parents do or don't do some things while rearing their children is fodder for educated guesses and speculation and, ultimately, a reminder of human imperfection. No parent, regardless how pure their intentions, is exempt from at least some poor choices.

At the Mexican Shack, spring had arrived, and the relief the newness and rebirth provided was life giving. The evenings were mild, and we kids were outside a lot of the time. Bruce was fourteen, Gayla was twelve, I was ten, Lonnie was eight, and Stacy would have been six years old. One evening our parents called all of us into the living room. We sat more or less in a circle. Bruce was to my right, and Stacy was to his right. To my left was Gayla, and to her left was Lonnie. Dad and Mom sat between Lonnie and Stacy.

Nothing could have prepared us for what they were about to ask of us. They explained that since their marriage was not working out, they were considering getting a divorce. Regardless, they had agreed to do whatever *we kids* wanted them to do! If we voted for them to stay together, they would. If we voted for them to divorce, why, that was what they would do.

Without gasping in surprise or indignation, resisting or questioning, we kids simply sat there and decided how we would vote. Gayla and Lonnie went first and were adamant that the folks remain married. I voted next. Not realizing why at the time, I voted in favor of divorce, the lure of peaceful, quiet nights and the desire for the knots in my guts to relax driving my logic. Bruce refused to vote either way, stating he didn't care what they did. At six years old, Stacy had the swing vote. Stacy voted in favor of them staying married. The marriage was saved. My one dissenting vote left me feeling painfully conspicuous. It haunted me many years, and during that time,

I believed it to be a strike against me that would probably never be forgiven.

At some point during that winter of domestic unrest and their nightly engagement, my father grabbed my mother's left arm with his and booted her in the rear end, breaking her tailbone. Coupled with intense resistance with which I viewed my developing body, my sense of being fat, the long-standing effects of being molested that would never be recognized or dealt with, as well as six others in the family who all had just as many and just as serious albeit different issues, the domestic turmoil was awful and revved up my anxiety, nervousness, and depression. I chewed my fingernails to the quick, chewed on my lips and the inside of my cheeks, and filled the hole in my soul with food that brought comfort. The manifestations in my siblings were no prettier, and implications for all of us were foreboding.

These acute adversities that presented themselves during that year coupled with the long-festering malaise ever present in my life. Together, this sort of emotional diverticulitis flared in proportion to the amount of stress I experienced, and as it were, stress was as present as rain in monsoon season.

The rate and pace these challenges rained down in my life during that year oppressed and depressed me. I was in a serious struggle to cope with major challenges, and the grip I held on my stability was becoming tenuous. With stressors growing in number, frequency, and intensity, the bombardment was indeed wearing me down.

Like the story of the lad at the dike, I was trying all I knew to plug holes and keep the torrent that would drown me contained behind the dam. Sadly, the holes were appearing one after another and my supply of fingers, toes, even my nose with which to plug them was being exhausted at an alarming rate.

My means with which to hold back the flood wasn't the only thing that was depleted. I was exhausted, drained of strength, all but consumed. Without relief of some sort, the torment in my life was gaining the advantage, and how much longer I would be able to stave off its advance was a question fraught with dread.

While struggling along during my tenth year of life, an opportunity presented itself through which I bought some time in the contest life was having for my health and sanity. Because my burdens were never alleviated through proper handling, they continued to accumulate. Fortunately, that spring I experienced a kind of respite and relief that allowed the crumbling dike inside me to fail and the torrents of emotion to flood out of me. The moment didn't heal all that was sick inside me, but it did lance the carbuncle in my soul and clean the wound so I could continue to function. It also changed my life as a child of God.

This turn of events occurred at church one day in the spring of 1962. Later in life I would learn each denomination has its own set of rules governing Christian rituals, like communion and baptism. Another such part of a church service that varies within the Protestant body of believers is the altar call.

Baptists, for instance, offer an altar call at the end of each Sunday service, but within the Church of God, doing so was more sporadic. That Sunday our minister conducted the service and at its conclusion segued into the altar call, prompting, urging, pleading, even exhorting and warning congregants to come to the altar and find peace with God if they were already saved but living a life less than what they knew they should be. The pastor stressed if any member had never confessed their sins to God and accepted him as their Savior, then with utmost haste they should walk down the aisle, fall on their knees, and get saved. He lovingly stated if the Lord was calling, if he was talking to your heart and you knew you were a wretched sinner otherwise headed for hell, then you needed to heed his voice and come and repent and be saved.

Standing there beside my grandmother, the preacher's words pierced me as surely as if they were arrows released by an expert archer. They found their mark, and my heart winced. Inside my chest began to feel heavy and very full, as though it was about to explode.

Anguish, injuries, tension, frustration, anger, guilt, shame, the ingredients that simmered endlessly in the cauldron of my soul, began filling my throat, and I was about to vomit. Rather than coming up my throat, the toxic sludge began to spill out of my eyes, and tears began coming in waves. With my right hand, I reached for my grandmother's palm and clasped it. She returned the gesture and turned her head toward me. Fortunately, we were near the left end of the pew, and as I tugged at her, she followed as I shuffled to get out of the pew. By this time I was desperately trying to stifle the sobs shoving to get out of my chest. Our arms entwined by this point, Grandma walked the twenty feet or so to the altar with me, and as she got to her knees, I fell to mine.

The sobs broke free then, and I was wracked with them nearly to the point of not being able to catch my breath. A decade worth of putrefaction found its way to the surface and, having escaped its bindings, stampeded through my being. I knelt prostrate before God and man with my grandmother holding me as I wept and convulsed until the garbage that had been stored inside me compromised my bulwarks and overran all my entrenched defenses.

With the congregation standing and quietly singing "Just As I Am" and "Softly and Tenderly," several folks made their way to the altar to claim Jesus as their savior or get straight with God and rededicate their lives to him if their Christian walk had slipped and needed a course correction.

After the hymns being sung had been repeated several times, the swell within me had produced its biggest and most intense waves, and my body's writhing and nauseating emotion began to decrease. All the energy freed in that breakdown was on its way to the bosom of the Lord.

As I became calm enough to listen and respond, the pastor explained that we are all sinners who have fallen short of the glory of God, but he sent his son Jesus to shed his precious blood in payment of our sins, and if we believe in him as the son of God and accept him as our savior, our slates are wiped clean, our spirits sealed against further contamination, and our souls saved from eternal damnation. The pastor asked if I believed this, and I said yes. He then said a prayer with my grandmother and me, asking Jesus to come into my heart and save my soul.

After praying with my grandmother and me, the preacher also huddled with each person who had come forward and ministered to them. After he had done that, he explained to those of us remaining at the altar we could return to our seats or stay at the altar if we felt the need to remain there.

Except for my grandmother and me, everyone stood and walked back to their seats. I was simply unable to stand, unable to stop the silent tears from flowing from my eyes and running like a river down my cheeks. So I stayed at the altar, still prostrate before God and my church family. Grandma remained with me, still on her knees with one arm around my shoulders, praying to God on my behalf. Meanwhile the pastor was concluding the Sunday morning service in the usual fashion, and after the closing prayer, the members of the congregation began exiting the church. It was after everyone else had left and only the preacher, my grandmother, and I remained that I was finally composed enough to stand and prepare to leave the church. She and I thanked Reverend Taves for his prayers and guidance. With Grandma leading, we made our way to the pew where our belongings remained and departed the church for home.

My eyes were horribly red, already swollen and puffy and hurting from the sunlight. They would require ice packs the rest of the day to preclude them from swelling nearly shut and soothe the misery with which they pulsated. I felt as though an incredible load had been lifted from me even though I felt extremely embarrassed at having been in such a state in front of the entire church. I lay on my grandmother's sofa for the better part of the day that remained, not yet far from a crumpled heap. My grandmother stayed closed to me that day and conveyed her pride that I had given my heart to the Lord. That she and I shared that very personal, important event in my life only strengthened the strong bond that existed between us.

That my parents were not there didn't matter to me then. In fact, had they been there, the Holy Spirit and all the garbage inside me simply would have had to wait. I could never have exposed myself like that with my parents present. They had voluntarily excluded themselves from that significant part of my life and all it entailed. As was often the case, they had no idea what I had gone through that day, what I had struggled with and why, and what I had gained.

Looking back through older eyes, I have often wondered if no one present that day ever thought that it was unusual or concerning for a ten-year-old to be completely distraught as I was, whether my collapse was from a life that was full of sin, a spiritual sense that appeared mature beyond my years, or from other factors that would render a child as broken up as I was.

Somewhere in that same timeframe, my mother took a job as a fry cook at Blalock's Café. I can only surmise she did so with financial problems as the driving force. Our financial situation was never stable. Never can I remember not being aware of money and the utter lack of it. At times Mom would have to borrow money from her parents. I was aware of the situation, and the embarrassment I felt was excruciating. My comprehension of our situation propelled my insecurity to levels that were increasingly taxing. I believed we were poor, and I hated it. So Mom went to work. Although her job lasted only a short while, the repercussions went on much longer.

The mystery, whisperings, judgments, violated taboos, sin, and raw betrayal constitute the final volatile, life-changing element living with us that winter. How do children learn of such goings-on? Where has the savvy originated? Who leads the conversation? How deafening is the silence? How cold do the stares and glares become? What happens to the wounded hearts?

My mother was said to have a boyfriend. The nausea I experienced was violent and unrelenting, the rage frightening, the sorrow for my dad indescribable. My world was quaking; what stability did exist was teetering. Our future was pretty much up for grabs. Decades later I have long since realized marriage and its strength or failure comes from both involved. However, in my ten-year-old mind, my affection-starved heart automatically turned toward that either-or way of thinking I saw modeled each day, and it was either Mom's fault or Dad's. Therefore, Mom was the guilty party.

But providence had provided an out. The Carter kids, commandeered to be a marital congress, had ruled, and Bob and Billie would continue as man and wife.

Unfortunately, this mandate also sealed the fate of something as important to me as anything and anyone in my life. My piano lessons ended, and my soul was again broken apart and returned to the wilderness to eke out an existence. My loss and disappointment were unspeakable because in order to mend my parents' marriage, we moved west again, back to Florence, Colorado.

Sixth Grade

We Carters closed the door on the Court Street debacle when we boxed up our worldly goods for transport to our next location. As Mom swept and mopped the floors of the Mexican Shack and Dad returned the keys to the owner, much in our lives had changed. We had changed just as much.

At this point, Dad began working away from home more frequently and for extended periods of time, no doubt a money-driven change of tactics. After such powerful problems became undeniable in my parents' marriage, equally strong efforts at healing their relationship were required. I don't know if the decision was joint or my dad's alone, but after school was out in May, we departed Ulysses and, as we had done three summers earlier, again moved to Florence, Colorado. Two hundred fifty miles would separate my mother from her alleged transgressions, and we would have moral support from Mom's brother and his family, Uncle Jerry and Aunt Jene and their four children, the Elliotts, whom I dearly loved and always enjoyed visiting.

Located a few miles off US Highway 50 near Canon City and the Royal Gorge, I did like visiting Florence and my relatives who lived there but no longer wanted to relocate there. During the three years' time since our first move to Florence, my attitude toward leaving Ulysses had changed very much. I felt emphatic about not wanting to leave my piano lessons, my friends, and the sense of safety, stability, and acceptance I enjoyed at Joyce School in Ulysses. At that time, being able to understand and express my feelings in those kinds of words was a long way away. Even if I had been able to do so, it would have made no difference in my parents' decision to leave Ulysses. The knot in my chest, the roiling in my gut, and my awful-looking fingernails shouted this message; alas, to no avail.

Gayla's attitude toward moving was completely opposite of mine as she was elated to be getting away from Ulysses and the pejorative judgments and effects of some harsh treatment she endured at the hands of two of her teachers, an experience diametrical to mine. Two years older than I, her perceptions were possibly keener than mine, and assuredly, her personality was exceedingly different. Like I, she bore inner scars left by pain and hurt, except that the culprit responsible for inflicting her wounds was a very different type of aggressor than I had known through the years. Completely unaware of her suffering, I did feel its outgrowth: her harsh words and tone, her impatience and surliness, her lack of fondness toward me, her intense aversion to any hint of a close relationship with me.

Not until many years later when we were both in our fifties would I learn from her of this suffering and her strong jealousy of me. Gayla, jealous of me! That thought had never, ever crossed my mind. Still, that explanation did make sense out of many hitherto inexplicable verbal floggings she had unleashed upon me during our childhood.

Stacy, the fifth-born, had come into the world in October 1955 a sickly infant. Asthma and its life-threatening complications resulted in Stacy spending a lot of time in the hospital as an infant and preschooler. Her stays there often lasted weeks at a time, and even when at home, she required a lot of close attention and trips to the doctor. In turn, this meant our mother was often preoccupied with the sickly baby on a regular basis. When hospitalization was necessary and our mother was left to stand vigil day and night among the nuns and other hospital workers, we remaining kids felt the reverberating ripples.

As with any family enduring critical illness within its ranks, asthma took a significant toll on each of us and as a unit. When Stacy was hospitalized, our mother was largely indisposed with her until the crises subsided and the baby could be discharged. Family assisted with the care and oversight of the rest of us. Eight years old or so, Bruce stayed a lot of that time with our grandmother Valta and her family on the other side of town. Help also came in the form of another one of the Humphries boys.

Our parents opened our crowded trailer home in which we lived while Stacy was an infant and entrusted our care to Junior Humphries. Whether or not Junior was his given name I don't know. Of the fifteen Humphries children, Junior was one of the first half dozen. As with most of Margaret and Orrin's progeny, Junior was handsome, tall with dark curly hair, and a friendly, beautiful smile. Probably around twenty years old, he had seriously injured his foot at work and had to have some or all his toes on one foot removed. He was in the process of recovering from his setback yet still had to see to his livelihood, so helping with kids earned his board and keep with the folks.

Junior's foot was heavily bandaged; he hobbled around with the help of crutches and managed to stay upbeat and useful. I don't recall him being anything but kind and patient toward us kids. Junior was an adult present with us little ones who did see to our safety and basic needs. But despite good intentions and honest effort, Junior was not a woman and lacked female prowess in the finer points of how to direct children and their efforts, monitor their outfitting, grooming routines, and the like.

Apparently during this struggle with Stacy's health, there were times when less critical details were not always given the attention they would have otherwise received. More than once Gayla presented herself at school in her third and fourth grade years with hair uncombed, wearing flip-flops on her feet instead of acceptable footwear, and sporting clothes that were less than neat and pristine. A gaunt Appalachian waif she was not, but an Ipana toothpaste or Breck shampoo poster girl she also was not. Until this time, school had been a pleasant destination for my older sister, but understandably, our family's tenuous hold on stability slipped significantly with Stacy's illness and its demands. One of the consequences of that time of struggle was Gayla's realization of how judgmental, mean-spirited, even cruel people can be. Her tender young heart would be hurt and never return to the innocence she enjoyed before her Kampf.

To Gayla's teacher in third grade, instead of seeing a child who was displaying evidence of difficulty by virtue of her appearance and uncharacteristic demeanor, Mrs. Enid Hickok detected the scent of vulnerability and, with the upper hand she held, time and again embarrassed and humiliated my sister for things beyond a third grader's control. The teacher pointed out the deficiencies in my sister's attire, some lack of punctuality, and used ridicule to belittle a young girl into shame and anger. Gayla's performance at schooled nosedived, her healthy attitude toward attendance and participation evaporated, and she gained an entirely new awareness of a set of standards by which one's value and worth can be determined. Gayla also became very angry at our parents' inability to do a better job at protecting her from such belittlement. From that time forward, a large part of my older sister yearned for the security an impressive wardrobe and all its accouterments might help to offer, friends who were of the popular set, and the privileges and advantages that often came to ones so regarded, social settings that would never again relegate her to the ranks of the underprivileged from where she sprang.

To this day the mention of Mrs. Hickok brings an ice-cold tone to Gayla's voice and a reiteration of what a vile witch she was with no business around young children. With a sense of matter-of-fact resignation, my sister states simply, "I hated that woman ever since she was so mean to me."

Therefore, after her seventh-grade year ended and we left Ulysses, settling in Florence was a dream come true for Gayla. Always of average size and never overweight, with a pretty face, pleasing smile, nicely done hair, and a figure pleasing to boys her age, Gayla immediately began receiving a lot of welcome attention. Cute girls befriended her, popular boys paid attention to her; her social calendar was all she could hope for. Life had done a real about-face for Gayla, and to her notion, it was about by God time.

In Florence on Third Street, we moved into a house that suited me just fine. It had three bedrooms, a living room and kitchen that were not cramped, and outside, both front and back yards were sizable and had a lot of grass. In the front yard were a couple of mature trees. The backyard was fenced on three sides, and the fencing on the south side was constructed of cinder blocks, which was interesting since I had never seen a fence made from that material before. There was plenty of room to play, and Lonnie, our cousin Jerry Jene, and

I wandered for blocks in all directions exploring the neighborhood that was filled with lots of trees and felt very inviting. There was a mature feel to this town that was not the case in Ulysses. Many old brick buildings and houses dotted the town that lent to its charm and character.

Next door beyond the cinder block fence was the home of a girl between Gayla and me in age. Her name was Mary Helen Vinto. Like I, she was a large-built girl and tall for her age. Unlike I, she was the only child in her family. She had brown skin and very black, wavy, short hair. My world was broadening. Mary Helen was Italian. I had never been around an Italian before. All I really knew to associate with Italians was Chef Boyardee products, spaghetti, pizza, Christopher Columbus, movies about Romans, and that most were Catholics since the head of the Catholic church was in Rome.

Now we were living beside Italians, and I was cautious yet curious and drawn to them because Mary Helen was smart, friendly, and well mannered, very much like her mother. Her mother's name was Mrs. Angie Vinto. That summer I spent a lot of time with my new friend in her home. Gayla and I even rode with Angie and Mary Helen in their beautiful Chevy Impala to Pueblo more than once. Being invited and included was indicative of their warmth and made me feel really good about myself.

More outstanding than anything else about these neighbors was inside the Vinto's modest, neat, and clean home sat an extralarge and beautiful organ that took up a good deal of their living room floor space. Even better, Mary Helen played that organ like it was a part of her. She worked all the pedals, buttons, and switches effortlessly, as if they were mere extensions of her fingers and toes. Her musical talent was exceptional and, coupled with a lot of training and practice, were like a paintbrush in Michelangelo's hand. The music Mary Helen played was pure sweetness to my ears. Being able to be around this girl and her huge, gorgeous, impressive instrument with which she melded effortlessly, taking in the melodies and accompaniments she shared with the entire block when she turned on her organ and began to play, exhilarated me. This new friend was one of the most musically gifted people I have ever had the pleasure to know. With my love and longing for the piano, being in the presence of someone nearly my own age who was so accomplished and fortunate simply mesmerized me. It also depressed me since leaving Ulysses had also meant the end of my piano lessons.

I celebrated my eleventh birthday in July 1962 at the Third Street house. I remember nothing of that birthday although it is another point on the timeline that became closely associated with three other life-changing events that lay just a few months down the road.

I do remember during that summer my aunt Vicki, Mom's baby sister who was six years my senior, came to Florence and stayed with us a few weeks. Her best friend, Dorothy Bridwell, with whom we were very well acquainted, accompanied my aunt. I was very pleased and excited about their visit.

With Vicki's hair dyed black as ink and Dorothy's a striking red and their extreme bouffant hairstyles standing at attention via copious amounts of firm-hold hair spray, these young women were intimidatingly beautiful and haute couture to me. They wore generous amounts of makeup as well, and Vicki resembled Liz Taylor in the movie *Cleopatra* that was in production at that time. Neither Vicki nor Dorothy suffered from being overweight, and the fancy clothes with which they adorned their youthful figures completed their packaging. To me they were amazing, even mysterious and exotic.

Simultaneously, or so it seemed, a couple of young men appeared almost out of nowhere! Next I recall the four of them getting into a car in which to go on the first of several dates. My eyes were huge with wonder and awe, my mouth silenced by my nearness to a time in life that was as unfathomable to me as the Grand Canyon is wide. The idea of me, Frances, somehow, someday, morphing into a dazzling creature like my aunt was simply beyond my grasp.

All too soon summer vacation was at an end, and it was time to begin school. The Florence High School and immediately behind it the Florence Junior High School were only a couple of blocks from our house on Third Street. In Kansas, elementary school included Grades K-6. In Colorado, sixth grade was the first grade of junior high school. Another difference was unlike Kansas, Colorado categorized within each grade level. Within the sixth-grade level, there were classes 6(A), 6(B) and 6(C). Students were assigned to the sixth-grade class that corresponded with their abilities.

This assignment process proved to be a real punch in the gut for me. I was used to being successful at school. I made high marks, and if I chose to put forth the effort, I could earn very high marks. Thus far in school I had enjoyed my subjects and classmates a lot and did well. One way my mastery and social acceptance were reinforced was that I was always one of the first ones to be selected when the time came to team up. Whether on the playground to play dodge ball, softball, jump rope, or other competitions, my fellow classmates unfailingly wanted me on their side. Inside, whether it was an arithmetic competition at the blackboard trying to solve problems accurately and fastest, reading aloud, or a classroom spelling bee, I was one of the first ones selected by team captains and rightfully so. At school I was used to feeling accomplished and respected and valued. Not only did I enjoy that status very much, I also needed it equally as much to somewhat offset the awful ways in which I felt insecure, powerless, and inadequate.

Now in Colorado at this new school on the first day of class, my world was rocked. I was assigned to 6(B). What the hell! Almost immediately I took a dislike to my teacher, and it seemed the feelings were reciprocal. He was a medium-sized middle-aged man in his forties with closely cropped dark hair. His haircut was short on top and the sides. An imaginary line resting atop his ear extended around the backside of his head to the other ear below which the hair had been shorn practically to his scalp. Mr. Mason wore wire-rimmed glasses through which stared two small beady eyes. He didn't smile much, had skin that shone with oil as often as not, and his voice was a bit high pitched with a pinched sound, as if he needed to relax his throat.

As if all those features were not enough homeliness to have been meted out to any one individual, from the middle of Mason's face protruded a hideous nose. The snout was average size except for its tip. That glob of purplish flesh bulged with veins big and bright enough they stood out even against the purple. It was impossible *not* to stare at this bulbous insult. Coupled with hair too short, an irritating voice, ratlike eyes, flesh that needed continual dabbing to control the offensive oil, and a W. C. Fields-like schnozzola, this first male teacher I had was hideously offensive to my eleven-year-old sensibilities.

I knew nary a soul in my class, no one was unfriendly nor particularly friendly either. The cute boys and popular girls were clearly not eyeing me as a potential candidate for the in-crowd. I wished only to be back in Ulysses. As miserable as I was, I had no way of knowing it was going to get far worse.

As was often the case during my childhood, much of what my parents did and how they went about their (our) lives seemed impulsive and shortsighted. Still affected by the previous winter's domestic upheavals, we kids were also bearing the brunt of being uprooted from our hometown and anything there that anchored us in life and unceremoniously transplanted. Nevertheless, after maybe three months at Third Street, it was time to pack up and relocate into yet another house.

Resistance being futile, about the time school began, we moved into a house not even a mile to the north of Third Street. I left behind the one friend I had made in Florence and continued to march. Apparently in those days signing a lease was not a prerequisite to occupying a dwelling or we would have had to stay put for longer than two to three months at a time. Even with a family the size of ours, moving must not have involved so much effort or logistics, which might have discouraged my parents. As with Dad's wanderlust, the ongoing quest for the best rental property seemed a compulsion of my mother's. The house we moved into was a quaint two-story Victorian just a couple of doors west of Highway 115 that ran through Florence and on into Canon City a few miles north. We were now situated only three or four blocks from where our uncle and aunt and their family lived on Lobach Street. At least there was that plus to this move.

We kids' bedrooms were upstairs, and the hardwood staircase that made a ninety-degree turn halfway up fascinated me with its beauty, sturdiness, and class. That house also had an unfinished basement consistent with homes built circa the early twentieth century, which afforded a lot of storage area. The basement was rather dark and had a dank smell to it, also like many basements in older houses, but didn't feel scary or foreboding.

Very shortly after our move to this house, my folks brought home a beautiful new dark-green bicycle one day. As my parents unloaded it from our car, I saw that like the Shetland pony a year earlier, the bike was far too small for us older kids. It was meant for Stacy. But why? Stacy's birthday wasn't until the latter part of October, and this was mid-September. Of course, it wasn't Christmas, and since those were the two times a year most kids got presents, I couldn't fathom what merited this lavishness.

I had never had a new bicycle. A bicycle is to a child what a car is to a teenager. It is independence, status, a sign one is getting grown up compared to earlier days, a powerful longing satisfied. I am sure I ached with envy but also wrinkled my forehead in curiosity as my parents brought the sparkling set of wheels into the living room. Once there, they finally informed us of the news associated to the bicycle's purchase. Stacy, who had just entered second grade, was going to have to go back to first grade and repeat that year of her schooling. The bicycle was meant to cushion the blow about this unwelcome development in her life. I felt really sorry for my little sister. Success in school was one of my mainstays, and the thought of being made to repeat a grade was one of the worst things I could imagine. I was also thankful I didn't have those kinds of troubles even if the bastards had stuck me in 6(B) instead of 6(A) at school.

Suddenly I recalled that Bruce had had to repeat third grade, and in fact, he too had received a brand-new beautiful green bike a few years earlier. I couldn't, however, remember if he got his new bike for the same reason Stacy got hers. A few years earlier, probably at Christmastime, Gayla and I were given some used bikes our parents had gotten from my aunt Karen and some distant cousins and had refurbished. As dearly as I would have cherished a new bicycle, I wasn't even going to entertain the notion of one after associating it with being used as a consolation prize.

September turned into October, and the uncomfortable days at my new school grew a bit more tolerable thanks to a scheme in which I participated. There was a gas station immediately across the highway to the north of the junior high school. There was one pump, and the tiny building that housed the cash register also contained an inordinately large supply of candy. Never having worked for me before, I nevertheless made another vain attempt at being slick.

Along with other students from whom I undoubtedly acquired the idea, I quit giving my lunch money to the repulsive Mr. Mason. Instead I kept it in my pocket and went to the gas station at lunchtime. I was living large. I bought candy and a bottle of pop instead of cafeteria fare. Life had taken on a little glow, and I felt good about the sweets I was eating and even somewhat smug for being able to put one over on my mother.

One day a couple of weeks into this new routine, I went to exit the gas station, bounty in hand, when who do I nearly bump into but my mother! The frown on her face was so dark and vengeful I figured she would visit the worst punishment upon me that she could think of. Even if I had been able to utter a sound, words would have been useless, so I didn't even try. As several other times in my life, I was again literally frozen with fear.

Mom's face was contorted in an expression of rage. The look of contempt with which her eyes gouged mine traveled on to my heart. Her eyes were mere slits in her head, her mouth choked into a tight purse. She looked like a person possessed, in need of an exorcism. I felt as though she was gloating at my fear, humiliation, and complete distress. I had broken one of the cardinal rules that comprised our family creed of don't ask, don't make the parents uncomfortable, and *don't cause trouble*. As terrifying as the situation was to me, it proved to be just as strange.

My mother hissed at me to get back to school. Mortified, I did as I was told. For the rest of the school day I was beside myself with fear and barely able to function. At the bell, I took as long as I could in walking home, the fear in my gut aging me with each stride that propelled me closer to my doom. Even if Mom didn't beat me till I couldn't walk, again she had seen what a bad person I was, so how would she ever like me or love me? The inordinate degree of fear I experienced from being caught in my deceit was sadly typical of too many moments of terror I lived through as a youngster.

I finally arrived home, unable to avoid my fate any longer. As was the case so many times, the guilty verdict rendered at the gas station earlier in the day had come with the most severe punishment—silence.

I never heard another word about the incident. There was no discussion on the whys and wherefores of my thinking or my motivation. There was no guideline laid out by which I could atone for my violation and do whatever was needed to restore harmony with my mother. My questions, fears, contrition, or plea for absolution were never allowed voice. There was absolutely no way to tell where I stood with my mother and how I should proceed. I felt as though I were in a potentially lethal test where each step could mean life or death, and I had no map, no compass, no one, or nothing to help me navigate this vacuum. As Harvey Keitel's character stated in the movie *Shadrack*, "Death ain't nothing. It's life that's fearsome."

Not suffering a serious whipping was actually no consolation. Had that punishment been established and executed, there would have been a sense of closure and perhaps a tacit indication to move forward. The silence and lack of address constituted an open-ended torture that never reached an official conclusion. My disease, fear of rejection and discomfort, multiplied exponentially that day. The only positive aspect of that day's grinding events was that I did not have to face Dad. Dad had gone elsewhere to work.

Dad was very wary of labor unions, but because most of Colorado's heavy equipment operators were union members, he went ahead and joined the union whose local chapter was located in Pueblo, Colorado. My uncle Jerry belonged to the same union and by and large enjoyed steady work, a rate of pay sufficient to support his family of six, and other benefits associated with collective bargaining. At the job on which Dad was working, there was contention between management and the union that eventually led to a work stoppage, and the union's junior members, one of whom was my dad, wound up without a job.

Subsequent to that wrench in the folks' plans, Dad went back to Ulysses with us remaining behind in Florence. In Ulysses, Dad began working for a man he hired on with many times over the years, Troy Cheek. The office for Cheek Construction was across the alley and half a block south of my grandparents' laundromat.

As if life weren't abstruse enough for me already, fate was soon to heap a rapid-fire trifecta of grave difficulties upon my country, my family, and me.

In October 1962, Bruce was a sophomore in high school. Sports and a young lady named Sandy filled his mind and hours. He and his friend Bob Petersen were both good-looking and experiencing torrents of male hormones with their accompanying effects. By and large Bruce seemed to have few complaints.

Gayla had found her escape from Ulysses and its constraints to be very satisfying. She was cute, proportionate, and pleasing to boys' eyes. She had become friends with a classmate named Karen, and to Gayla's delight, she was becoming a part of the eighth-grade in-crowd with hopes of probably becoming popular. Life for Gayla was decidedly different and more pleasant than it had been in Kansas; folks did not know us, our family troubles, or financial difficulties, and she benefitted in all ways from our change of location.

I was miserable but plodding along. My life with its accompanying pain was nothing new. I had no idea how to change my lot except to lose weight. Closing in on five feet, nine inches tall and puberty changing many things about my body, I still identified with the words Gayla had spit at me so many times through the years: I was basically a big, fat pig. Hence, a body that wasn't fat seemed to be the magic bullet I sought. That was not going to happen, though, because food was one of the few ways through which I was comforted, and giving up that feeling was no more possible than not breathing would have been.

By this time I had been wearing a bra for a year and a half. No more accepting of it than I was the day I first wriggled into it, I detested that torturous garment and having to wear it. To make matters more difficult, Gayla, twenty-five months older than me, was only now beginning to need a bra, a fact that made me feel even more perverse and one that seemed to make her disdain for me even greater.

I was clearly going through the growth spurt associated with puberty. The hair growing under my arms and between my legs disgusted me, but I was powerless to stop it. Despite my obviously changing body and the associated implications, I ignored the fact of what would undoubtedly happen soon. Nor did I ready myself in attitude and with supplies I would need at the onset of my first menstrual period. My position about my changing body was one of rejection and resentment toward it, and the powerlessness I felt in trying to stop it further fueled that emotional fire. I felt no pride or anticipation, just unhappiness. I was fully resisting accepting the facts of life as I understood them, and as was unfortunately the case too often and for whatever reason, my mother was either oblivious to my suffering or unconcerned about my emotional and physical state. For as long as I could remember, my body had been a real problem for me.

From very early on when my sister spewed hateful words in my direction, to being molested the first time when I was a preschooler and now the breasts and the body hair, being me was becoming more and more difficult.

Only several months later in Ulysses when I knocked on the door of my friend Zana did someone spontaneously comment with utmost certainty about how I had changed. When she opened the door and saw me, her eyes bulged and her mouth flew open at the change in my appearance. She had trouble believing how much taller I had grown, how I had a figure, and was so pretty. Her reaction was so spontaneous and genuine I couldn't believe how flattered I felt as her remarks continued. Her attention and sense of awe were a soothing balm to that horrible soreness within me. Not that I knew the word then or would have understood the reasons for it, but my dear friend's reaction to the new me was a vindication of sorts.

That fall in Florence, Lonnie was a fourth grader and had Bruce's friend Bob Petersen's mother as his teacher at the elementary school. He and our cousin Jerry Jene were the same age and were close friends and buddies. Lonnie's life was enhanced through this aspect of our Colorado tenure, and considering some of his soul's secrets, being in Colorado was a respite in more ways than one.

Stacy was back in first grade. Her photos around that time capture the face of a little girl who was there but not always present. Stacy found early on that a make-believe world with make-believe friends and scenarios over which she had control were much more palatable than real life. In more than one snapshot, her eyes reveal a deer-in-the headlight incomprehension and helplessness. Others exude kind of a blank stare. Stacy physically occupied space but went largely unnoticed by us older kids. Whether she found any consolation and enjoyment in her new green bicycle I have no idea.

Enter the dammed communists. The world got very somber that October and terrifying in another way when President Kennedy spoke on television and informed the country of the threat posed by the Russians moving nuclear missiles onto a site in Cuba from which our nation could be attacked from only ninety miles away.

I saw a look in my mother's eyes I had never seen before. I knew well the look of worry, unhappiness, impatience, and suspicion but had never seen fear like this before. She grew more alert as she went about the work of preparing the basement to serve as a fallout shelter as instructed by the government.

Mom began gathering and carrying food and supplies downstairs in case "the bombs went off." Like air raid drills in England during World War II, citizens now began receiving instruction on what to do in the event of a nuclear blast. Later in life I would realize nothing would have saved us from the blast of a nuclear explosion had an attack been directed at NORAD in Colorado Springs, a short distance to the east. Still, in the most agonizing and difficult situations *doing* something endows a person with a sense of hopeful girding instead of helpless surrender. Engaging oneself with a purpose also lessens the likelihood of panic, an inevitable outcome of unrestrained terror.

For fourteen days, tension was thick in the air. We kids remained at home when not at school. Mirroring Mom's demeanor and grim countenance, it was as if someone had died and we were being quiet and respectful, careful not to commit an irrevocable faux pas of any sort. We older kids realized the country could go to war, and such a war would mean bombs being dropped on America and Americans. Our mortality became a real idea rather than a vague notion during those days of the Cuban Missile Crisis.

Finally the crisis was past, war was averted, and outwardly life began returning to normal for America and the Carters in Colorado. That political showdown and what I learned during those two weeks tied a new knot in my gut. That knot was kinked inside my guts along with all the other anxieties, confusion, and trauma that were accumulating as I struggled to survive the emotional tribulation of which my childhood so often consisted.

From that time forward until I was a legal adult, worry about communists, particularly the Russians, pervaded my psyche and affected me profoundly. Knowing these people wanted to take over our country weighed heavily on my heart and mind, yet I knew of nowhere to turn for counsel or guidance on how to combat this mental menace as well as the political and military foe. This newly acquired fear and anxiety simply took up residence with all the rest of my unresolved fetidness I packed around each day.

As were all Americans, my family was trying to deal with the effects of the missile crises on our minds and process what we had endured collectively and as individuals. Still in a state of shock from that ordeal, my family was about to be thrust into another challenge no less grave that would again test our mettle and leave us closer to the brink of disaster than ever before.

By this time it was mid-November. Autumn in Colorado was cool and crisp. Being outdoors was pleasant because the air was brisk, and temperatures were neither hot nor cold. On a Saturday around midday, the telephone rang. Mom answered it to hear my aunt Vicki's voice at the other end. Mom's face suddenly lost all its color, and her voice became a labored whisper. Again I saw fear in her eyes. After a couple more minutes, she hung up the phone and crumpled onto a chair.

After a bit she managed to collect herself somewhat. In a voice unlike I had ever heard before, she hollered for us kids to come to her.

DAD'S INJURY

The Bible says in 1 Corinthians 15:52 that one day in conso-
nance with Jesus's return, those who have accepted Christ as
their Lord and Savior will be changed in the twinkling of an
eye. Restated that means their bodies will be changed instantly. An
instant is all the time required for changes to occur, however apoca-
lyptic or fortuitous they might be. My world changed instantly when
Mom received Vicki's phone call that autumn weekend afternoon.

In their backyard behind my grandparents' laundromat, Dad
had been working on his old blue-and-white International pickup.
He had jacked up the vehicle and secured blocks beneath its frame to
get it high enough off the ground to enable him to lie beneath it and
make needed repairs.

My dad was a tall man with a thick, husky build. He stood six
feet, two inches and at that time weighed probably 240 pounds. With
a large round head, red hair, blue eyes, a barrel chest and extremely
thick, fleshy hands, Dad was handsome and physically formidable.
His body was toned and exuded strength regardless from which perspective it was viewed. In fact, he was exceptionally strong, as we
would soon realize and for which we would be eternally thankful.

While my father lay beneath his pickup trying to make repairs,
it somehow wriggled enough that the supports gave way, and the
truck fell onto him. Dad was pinned between his truck and the
ground, crushed beneath the weight of the steel machine.

How long he lay crushed with his life slipping away no one
knows. Depending on a person's own belief system, explanation of
the remaining facts of this horrific afternoon is open to individual
interpretation.

Troy Cheek, the owner of the construction company for whom Dad was working, had been in his office across the alley and a half block to the south of my grandparents' place. Not only did he depart his office at the perfect time that afternoon, he also chose to drive north up the alley rather than exit his business and drive north on Main Street. Additionally, as he drove north, the rear entrance to the American Legion on his left, he chose to look right and into my grandparents' backyard.

Perhaps it was because he saw Dad's old pickup sitting there, perhaps it was divine intervention, perhaps it was simply chance. But at any rate, Mr. Cheek sensed something was amiss. The truck was sitting in a suspiciously cockeyed way. Then looking with full attention, he realized my dad's feet were protruding from beneath the rear of the work truck. Immediately pulling into the backyard, he tore from his vehicle and ran the few yards to the scene of the accident. Shouting to my dad but hearing no response, Mr. Cheek dashed directly across the alley to Fred Gerritzen's gasoline station.

Shouting at the top of his lungs for help, it was most fortunate there were several men at the station. Together they all ran to where my father lay dying, and with their combined strength and possible supernatural intercession, they lifted up the truck enough that others were able to pull my dad's body from beneath the crushing weight of the International. Bob Wilson Memorial Hospital sat on Main Street four blocks north of where Dad lay. His rescuers loaded my father in the bed of someone's truck and moments later delivered him to the emergency room of the hospital.

My aunt Vicki, who only a few months earlier had been with us in Colorado enjoying fun times, was the only one at home in my grandparents' house that day, so the awful task of phoning my mother with this news fell to her.

As it was Saturday, Mom was fortunate because Uncle Jerry happened not to be working that day. Mom called his house immediately after telling us kids what had happened. The remainder of that day became an awful blur, but somehow we managed to pack a few things and as soon as possible were on the road to Ulysses. Uncle Jerry drove us, and there were never 240 miles that seemed as long to travel as those did that evening. With each of us lost in our own thoughts, not much talking went on inside our car during that dreadful journey.

We arrived in Ulysses well after dark and drove straight to the hospital. Of course, that was before cell phones, so we had received no further news of Dad's condition. As we parked out front of the building where my dad lay inside, his brother Dale, who had been awaiting our arrival, seemed to appear out of nowhere at the car door where Uncle Jerry sat.

Nearly simultaneously we opened all four doors of our brown-and-white 1957 Chevy station wagon and gathered around Dale. He, Mom, and Uncle Jerry were talking in whispered voices, and Dale looked so grim and grief struck he barely resembled the handsome man who was next to Dad in age. Perhaps he was at a loss for words or was overwhelmed at the sight of Dad's children, but whatever the reason, he turned to us kids, stood there with this ghastly look on his face as if he were unable to utter the worst possible words.

I interpreted his silence to mean we had lost our father. "Did Daddy die? Is he dead?" And then all the tears, sobs, and torrents of pent-up fear and anguish discharged like the gush of water when a pregnant female's water sack breaks. Everything inside me that had been suppressed throughout that horrible day flooded to the outside. We kids began to wail.

After what seemed a lifetime, my uncle was finally able to speak and loudly assured us Dad was still alive. In fact, it was a miracle that he was not dead.

"Any other man would have been dead, but Bobby was somehow alive when they pulled him out."

Those horrendous several seconds when I believed my father to be dead were indescribably terrifying. I felt like the bottom had dropped out from under the entire world and I was falling into utter darkness. There were no words to capture the horror and grief I felt. And then, like a soul in a near-death experience, I was zapped from my free fall back into my body. Like the rest of my family standing there, I was again changed. With my father's critical injury and his tenuous prognosis not good, the burden present in my heart and mind had become all but overwhelming.

Accompanied by her brother, Mom had gone ahead of us into the hospital. Once we kids were calmed down enough to control ourselves, our uncle Dale walked with us into the hospital. Hospitals then were not the noisy places they are today who admit visitors freely. In 1962 they were quiet, smelled very strongly of antiseptic, and had rules that prohibited visitors younger than fourteen years. That the nuns excepted this rule indicated the condition of our father. We kids were permitted into his room.

As we entered, Dad lay unconscious and deadly still. Except for an IV line and catheter bag, there were no bells and whistles attached to his body. Dr. Brewer explained to my mother there was not really much medicine could do to help Dad. The doctor furthered that if seventy-two hours passed without Dad developing pneumonia, he would have a decent chance of surviving. Dad would either live or die depending on factors that were largely beyond the medical profession's ability to intervene.

When the hospital staff told us it was time to leave, family members began discussing where all of us kids would stay. Bruce, Lonnie, and Stacy went with other relatives, and Gayla and I went home with our Aunt Tibe, Dad's sister who was the sixth born in that family of nine children.

Aunt Tibe and her husband, Skipper Dahlquist, farmed land out by Big Bow, a whistle stop around ten miles west of Ulysses off state Highway 160. They had four children, the oldest of which was a year or two younger than Stacy. They lived in a three-bedroom trailer house, so with Gayla and me there, that trailer was filled to its gills. That didn't matter though. I felt welcome, wanted, and strengthened by my aunt and uncle and my cousins whom I liked very much.

During the week Gayla and I stayed with Tibe and Skipper, we were even able to think of things other than the crisis our family was going through. My aunt was an excellent cook who prepared lovely meals. She had a loud voice often used to ride herd on her own kids. She laughed a lot, was able to give us needed attention, and make a most difficult time in my life bearable.

Midway through that week, Aunt Tibe told Gayla and me to get into the car, that we were going to Garden (City). She said she was going to take us to J. C. Penney and buy us some clothes. I was elated. Going to Garden some sixty miles away was inherently fun. It meant getting to see all the stores and busyness of that good-sized town, have fun shopping and eating out, and talk and laugh traveling to and from in my aunt's Dodge car that had a push button transmission, which was nothing less than fascinating. Leaving her own children at home with their father, we three proceeded toward Garden and a most special day.

When we got to the J. C. Penney store, Aunt Tibe took us upstairs to the second floor, where the girls and women's clothing was. The smell of the textiles, the old building with its hardwood flooring, the sight of the salesclerks dressed smartly and their businesslike carriage automatically generate a smile on my face to this day. A time certainly long gone now, the difference in business attitudes, practices, and shopping experiences as a customer are losses in America that amount to more substantial lack than mere nostalgia.

I came out of that fancy store that day with the prettiest gold-colored dress in which I felt like a princess. The fabric was an attractive, lively print. There was piping at the neckline and waist of the dress and the sleeves were short, ending about midway of my upper arm. That dress looked very nice on me but not nearly as nice as I felt inside it.

Not only was I the proud owner of a beautiful dress, I also had in my bag a pair of brightly flowered corduroy slacks that zipped up in the back. To go with them, I also was in possession of a long-sleeved navy pullover sweater that was so soft it felt like a cat's fur. I also had a couple of new bras, some new under panties, and some new socks. I felt so loved and attractive in my new clothes, not to mention a notch higher socially since that was the first time I'd ever had clothes from J. C. Penney.

That week in Ulysses was a living nightmare with Dad's outcome uncertain, but this awful ordeal also wound up being equally uplifting. My aunt Tibe showed her love in a myriad of ways that helped me feel better about our future, Dad's recovery, and myself. Gifts like those are never forgotten.

By the end of the week, Dad showed definite signs of improvement, there had been no sign of pneumonia, and it was clear that it would take more than a mere heavy pickup truck falling on Dad and crushing him to end his life. Dad was conscious, had all his mental faculties intact, and was healing well. We were able to breathe almost normally and turn our attention to returning to Colorado and school.

Mom stayed on in Ulysses to be with Dad. Uncle Jerry drove us kids back to Florence to get situated so we would be ready to go to school Monday morning, nine days after our dad was nearly killed.

Hindsight really does lend a vision and clarity to events that can rarely be achieved while in the midst of a fray. Navigating those couple of weeks after my father's brush with death was easy for no one, and how the adults in my life reasoned the plan they did for us kids' lodging while Mom was away I have no inkling. Although I have no doubt regarding their good intentions, a couple of other ideas immediately come to my mind that possibly would have been less apt to test the nerves of children already quite unraveled by the former week and a half of their lives. Unfortunately, I was about to suffer yet another life challenge that proved traumatic to the emotionally frail girl that I was.

My aunt and uncle's house was not large and already full with their four children, so not all of us Carter kids could stay with them. Having resided in Florence only five months or so, I guess friends and options were limited for us. Ultimately Bruce stayed with a friend, Lonnie and Stacy stayed with our uncle and aunt, and Gayla and I were placed with strangers.

Somehow Mom had become acquainted with a woman, although to refer to this lady as a friend probably would have been premature. This woman was gracious enough to open her home, nonetheless, so that was that. Her name escapes me, but I recall she and her husband had two young sons who were more around Stacy's age than Gayla's and mine.

I was completely uncomfortable there despite their kindness. The level of stress I was experiencing was frightful. I was so ill at ease I would not even bathe or use the toilet in their bathroom. I did use the sink to wash my face and brush my teeth, but that was the extent to which I could manage to behave rationally. I don't know how long I could have continued there as distraught as I was, but as it were, fate intervened, and I was overcome.

After the second or third night at the house of the Good Samaritans, I awoke, dressed (without using the toilet), ate the breakfast the lady had fixed, and left for school. I arrived at school with time to spare before the starting bell rang so necessarily went to the girls' bathroom to relieve myself. I was not prepared for what I would find there!

I was fortunate enough to see an empty stall and hurried into it. I immediately pulled down my underwear and simultaneously sat down on the seat of the commode and began to empty my bursting bladder. With relief, I also began to relax and was able to think thoughts beyond how much distress my overly full bladder was causing me.

At some point I glanced down toward my underwear. It was then I saw the crotch of my panties was soiled by blood! I was horrified, mad as hell, and simultaneously defeated. I wanted to run, but to where and to whom? I wanted my mother, but she was 240 miles away. I was in a strange land in a strange predicament with nary one girl coming into that school restroom I could call my friend. My body had been lying in wait, and when I was at my lowest, weakest, most vulnerable point had sniped me perfectly. My heart was racing, and my head was pounding although inside felt like I was dying.

Suddenly the bell sounded for the school day to commence. I knew I couldn't stay in that stall forever. Even though I didn't want to even touch my body, I forced myself to do so and then flushed the stool. Numbly I stumbled out into the hallway, and luckily, I saw my physical education teacher, Mrs. Ahrends. I approached her and told her I was sick and needed my sister. She inquired as to what was wrong, but all I could do was keep repeating that I was sick. Finally she asked my sister's name and what grade she was in. After I gave the teacher the needed information, she told me to wait inside the bathroom and she would bring my sister to me.

That I reached out to Gayla was evidentiary to what dire straits I was in and that I was about to give way under all the stress. What was I thinking, for God's sake?

Several minutes passed and finally the teacher reappeared with Gayla. My sister did not look pleased and crossly demanded to know what I wanted. I said, "Gayla, I started my period," and began to bawl. I was hoping for more from my older sister, but it wasn't to be. Unmoved by my tears, my situation, the humiliation I was suffering, and my being close to the proverbial edge, Gayla nevertheless hissed with cold indignation, "Well, what do you want me to do? I haven't even started my period." Her fury was another gut punch, and I was close to fainting. Unable to withstand even one more iota of life at that point, I was consumed by waves of tears; wracked by sobs of anger, self-pity, and self-loathing; and could absolutely go no further. My reactor had ruptured, and I was having a Chernobyl-scale meltdown.

Even the teacher witnessing this scene appeared taken aback at my sister's lack of empathy and tenderness. She summarily dismissed Gayla to return to her class. Normally no-nonsense and hard-charging, Mrs. Ahrends sensitively began questioning me about how I managed to wind up in this predicament. In little time she had the drama under control. After giving her Aunt Jene's name and telephone number, my gym teacher went to the office and made the call for reinforcements.

Within fifteen or twenty minutes, my aunt entered the restroom accompanied by my teacher. I had been able to regain a bit of my composure, but upon seeing my aunt, tears immediately began streaming down my face again. My dear, softhearted aunt took it all in stride and assured me I was okay and everything would be all right. The helpful teacher told my aunt to take me home and for me not to worry about school, to come back when I was ready. She then departed, and Aunt Jene handed me clean underwear and the supplies with which I now had to contend.

I could not control my body, but by God I could control my reaction to it. My attitude was awful, and I don't know if any words anyone could have spoken to me would have helped me feel differently about puberty and its inconveniences.

I rode with my aunt to her house, and we spent the day together. She talked lovingly and reassuringly to me, trying to help me calm down and get a handle on how to use the belt and sanitary napkins. And to think I thought wearing a bra was distressing! I will always remember Aunt Jene's kindness, patience, and understanding that awful day with a grateful heart.

The only good thing to come out of that experience was that somehow my aunt and uncle found room for me at their house, so until Mom returned, I was with family instead of strangers.

Several decades later I would learn from a mental health professional that my extreme aversion to my body, its development, and the onset of my menstrual cycle was precisely on track because of three conditions that I met: having been sexually molested, physically developing early, and a relationship with my parents that did not include the requisite openness and closeness to heal and foster a healthy attitude toward my body and its normal functions.

Dad suffered his life-threatening injury in mid-November. Not only were the holidays quickly approaching, including the expense that is a part of even a simple Christmas celebration, there was absolutely no income from any source the moment Dad was crushed.

Without any safety net of a unionized environment, the type of work Dad did carried absolutely no package of benefits. There was no such thing as paid vacation or sick time, no retirement plan, no reimbursement for costs associated with his employment, no life insurance, no health-care coverage, nothing but a paycheck. Dad was not eligible for unemployment because there was not a lack of work; he was simply unable to work because of injury that did not occur while on the job. Fortunately when my parents purchased the Chevy station wagon we owned, they also purchased the insurance that covered the car payment for as long as my father was unable to work, so at least our transportation was secure.

Even struggling to live and heal, Dad must have worried intensely about the welfare of his family. I imagine my mother felt like running away, except where was there to go? Thank God for family. By the time Dad was doing well enough for my mother to leave his side and return to Colorado, several decisions had been made. By early December, Mom rejoined us kids and informed us of those decisions.

The farm ground to which my grandmother Valta and her husband Van had moved several years earlier some fifteen miles northeast of Ulysses had a two-bedroom trailer house with a built-on, mostly finished room that was sitting empty on the ground they leased. My grandparents had since moved twenty-five miles or so north of Ulysses, outside a small farm town named Lakin. They lived on ground they leased while farming there too. It was a godsend that that trailer house existed and was not being lived in.

My granddad and Dad's brothers, my uncles Dale, Pete, and John, were going to come to Colorado over Christmas vacation with my granddad's big work truck and move us to the farm, where we would live free of charge while Dad recuperated and became well enough to return to work.

Of course there were mixed, predictable reactions from us kids. Bruce was not glad we were returning to Kansas. He was really enjoying playing sports at Florence High School as well as his new friends and life in Colorado in general. Gayla was as devastated as I was elated. Life in Colorado was more enjoyable than it ever had been in her thirteen years in Kansas. For her, moving to Colorado had been a big gain in all ways, and she hated the idea of moving back to Ulysses. On the other hand, I couldn't wait to pack. I was ready to get back to familiar places, faces, and a scenario where I felt I fit in a whole lot better. Lonnie was more neutral, and as was so often the case, Stacy's voice was as small as she was.

Christmas vacation and the completion of that school semester came as slowly for me as all things do that we anticipate with fervor. Finally, though, time had ticked by, and our menfolk arrived with their strength and vehicles to load our worldly goods. Shortly after Christmas, our caravan traveled down US Highway 50 through the Arkansas River Valley and the familiar small towns that dot that valley, into Kansas, and eighty miles or so farther, arrived at the farm we would call home for a while.

Although leased by my grandparents, the farmland we lived on was owned by a man named Fred Stever, so we simply called that residence the Stever Place and sometimes the farm. Life on the farm was enjoyable for me. My grandparents had lived in that trailer for several years, during which I spent many a lovely day and night there with them. Whenever I was there, I would sleep in my grandmother's bed with her, the motor of the irrigation well my nighttime lullaby, and the aroma of ham, bacon, or sausage and fresh coffee being perked my wake-up call in the mornings. My mind had so many fond memories of that place that moving into it was welcoming and strengthening.

At first Dad was in bed quite a bit, but at thirty-seven years, he was also strong and healed quickly. Week by week he was able to get around more and less painfully. By early spring, he was outside a lot, tinkering at tasks and puttering around the place as he was able. Having Dad at home with us every day and night was a precious aspect of an otherwise awful experience.

In order to feed and clothe us, my mother swallowed the awful dose of pride one must and sought help through the welfare office at the courthouse in town. Having to have help with money, groceries, and clothing must have been one of the most difficult ordeals my parents had to suffer. Despite any of their failings and shortcomings, my parents were from stock that were fiercely independent and proud to be able to take care of themselves and their family. To have fallen to this level was another near-lethal blow to my father's pride, self-esteem, and manhood, no doubt more painful in ways than the accident that rendered him temporarily disabled. I have no doubt it was just as difficult for my mother, but she managed to downshift from always being in barely-making-it mode to survival mode so her feet carried her where she was forced to go.

The commodities Mom brought home from the courthouse had no pretty, appealing labels affixed to the tins. Instead the cans were printed on with government nomenclature. In particular I remember a potted meat product we ate at least two or three times weekly that winter and spring. Mom did her best to prepare it in different ways, but we especially liked it when she would make pizzas of a sort with it by spreading it on hamburger buns and topping it with sliced cheese and toasting it in the oven.

To her dying day my mother spoke of the kind attitude and behavior of the lady that doled out the food and clothing when Mom went to the courthouse. She always said Mrs. Helen Maxwell made a rough time a bit easier by not being patronizing and condescending.

As a married couple that immediately started a family, my parents' lives were no easier than their childhoods. The rate at which their family expanded only increased the demands on them. Every other year for ten years, a new baby came along without much corresponding rise in my father's income or any other increase in security. The need for more money led to my dad increasingly working away from home, which also enabled him not to have to deal with most of the everyday stresses of managing several children and the ever-present curve balls that are a part of life. It also meant my mother pulled double duty, much like that of a military wife whose spouse is often deployed. Such a load would have been enormous for even the strongest and most capable personality.

The years from 1947, when my parents married, till 1962, when we found ourselves living on the farm, had been an incredibly long series of events both trying and edifying, full of laughter and even more tears. That period of time was also full of relocations that symbolized my parents' search for something better over the next hill. That search yielded some worthwhile results but had its downside as well, a sense of stability being the most notable.

Most children have a possession to which they cling and by which they are soothed, reassured, and relaxed. Whether a pacifier, bottle, blanket with silky edging, stuffed toy, or other object, being able to grab hold of something that helps keep the boogeyman at bay is very valuable to youngsters. During my second-grade year, when my life changed at the hands of a molester, I was also fortunate enough to come across such an invaluable treasure. With my mother's permission, soon after school began that year, our neighbors and friends across the street, the Miller family, let me have first pick of a new litter of kittens they had. I chose my kitten and named her Precious, as indeed she was.

Precious was an unsightly, mottled mix of gray and white, but to me she was beautiful. She wasn't even a very friendly cat to most but seemed to understand how much I loved her and realized to whom she belonged. As she grew, I dressed her in doll clothes and pretended she was my baby. At night she slept with me, her soft coat and the warmth of her body coupled with her purring quickly lulling me to a slumber. Not only did I love that cat with all my heart, I needed her too. Having something real to call my own, a pet that I could show much affection and who reciprocated, was beyond what money could ever have bought.

Also since the time we had lived in my grandmother's house, I had become familiar with a businessman who came knocked on our door all too regularly. His name was Wally Wilson, and every time he made an appearance, an awful scowl immediately covered my mother's face. Despite her antipathy toward him, my mother would nevertheless open the door, and he would come inside.

As I would eventually understand, this nuisance who always had a foul-smelling cigar in his mouth, his fedora pushed back on his head and tipped to one side, was an insurance salesman out of Garden City, and he came around when my folks were not current on their life insurance payments, which apparently was often.

Not long after we moved to the farm, Wally Wilson found his way there despite it being in the country, fifteen miles outside Ulysses. We kids had long ago begun mimicking Mom's expression when this man appeared. This day was no different. Not only was his cigar, an uninvited familiarity with us, a put off, he also loved to hear himself talk and was difficult to get to leave once he descended on us. When he was finally ready to leave that day, I sighed with deep relief as he got into his car. He got into the seat, pulled the door shut, and started the engine, talking all the while. He put the car in gear, still talking. He puffed on his cigar, then removed it from his mouth with his right hand, and lowered the hand to the steering wheel and hollered, "See you later," as he stepped on the gas pedal. As the car pulled away, we heard a horrific scream and then silence.

That bastard had run over my cat Precious. Thankfully her awful scream was managed with her last breath, and she was dead before I reached her. Her body was flat like a pancake, and I fell to the ground sobbing. From the deepest parts of me came stabs of pain so excruciating and panic so sickening I was completely overwhelmed. My little friend, my baby, my pet, my source of physical comfort, my unique companion was *gone* in an instant. That there was nothing I could do about this awful loss I had suffered so abruptly and unexpectedly at the hands of yet another gross, disgusting man was only the latest in a very long series of profound challenges I was left to deal with.

Living as far from town as we did meant we were not within the boundaries of the Grant County Unified School District. Instead we attended a country school named Red Rock. That school sat on state Highway 160, five and a half miles south of the farm where we lived. The children of farmers, including a good number of Mennonite youngsters and the children whose fathers worked at the two natural gas plants near Red Rock, comprised the student body.

I quickly felt comfortable at that country school. By and large the students were friendly, not nearly so aloof acting as those in Colorado had been. Most of my classmates accepted me quickly, and fitting in there felt as welcome as Colorado had to my sister Gayla. There were just as many cordial and approachable kids who were seventh and eighth graders, which further enriched my time at that school.

At school that year, I was batting a thousand on unfriendly male teachers. There was only one class to each grade, and the sixth-grade teacher was a man whom I came to regard with disdain. Not only did William Orth's face resemble that of a platypus; he also had possibly the worst cigarette breath I have ever smelled. I don't know if we students in his class were that badly behaved or if sixth-grade preteens are naturally difficult. At any rate, Mr. Orth often yelled very loudly and very sternly at us individually and collectively. Despite his less than affable demeanor, I nevertheless enjoyed my semester there very much.

Always enjoyable was the period at school that the band practiced. I was in my second year of band and played the French horn. Anything musical has always been close kin to me and has never failed to edify and grow me. When the teacher was talking to other players or working with another section on some part of the piece we were practicing, I was always well entertained by a boy named Greg McHenry, who sat to my left at the end of the four-man trumpet section. Always funny to watch and listen to, this boy took apart the valves and other parts of his horn incessantly and was regularly admonished by our band instructor, Ernie Lou McGuire. I laughed so heartily and so often at Greg's antics it was like a natural Valium that neutralized much of the stress of life that existed beyond the stage in the gym where our band held class.

The fun with the entertaining Greg McHenry continued every day on the bus going to and from school. Especially because of him and two brothers, Tommy and Ricky Longtin, and their silly antics and innocent mischief, time passed quickly and easily during our lengthy bus ride. Those three guys were so amusing and comedic I always looked forward to that part of my school day and the free entertainment.

There was another aspect of riding that bus that was not enjoyable at all and another time in my childhood it seemed like we kids were vying against the Dark Side. Our persecutor, the dark knight of Red Rock, was actually a Mennonite, and like the scary August Kissner several years earlier, Jacob Koehn's antagonistic attitude, needlessly strict bus rules, and mean-spirited behavior earned him his riders' contempt and badgering.

To begin with, Jacob's appearance was a put-off to us kids. He was tall with a very bushy orange-red beard. His eyes were blue, deep-set and beady, like a blue-eyed rat. The hat he always wore resembled the kind worn by Amish men in photos of that sect. I don't know if he disliked us kids because we weren't Mennonites or for other reasons, but his enmity was clear, and just as clear was his enjoyment at the sense of power he wielded over us youngsters.

The trailer and outbuildings where we lived sat a quarter of a mile off the road. The French horn I carried to and from school most days was large, awkwardly shaped, cumbersome, and heavy. Our antagonizing bus driver would not drive that quarter mile to the trailer, instead offloading us at the road. Of course, exercise is always healthful for children, and on days with nice weather, the walk from the bus was not as offensive. Daily, though, as he would open the door for us to disembark, a simultaneous sneer would spread across his face. Regardless of the cold, snow, mud, or load with which we might be encumbered, provoking youngsters was a one-sided game the loathsome man clearly enjoyed. As it were, all the other students' homes sat much closer to the roads the bus traveled, so for them, Jacob Koehn's sick delight was not as aggravating and burdensome as it was for us four Carter kids and in fact me in particular with my big horn.

As much fun and enjoyment as I had in the classroom and on the bus with classmates and other Red Rock students, I suffered enormously while trying to socialize in other ways that winter.

At one of the natural gas plants, there was a community building where dances were occasionally held for the sixth, seventh, and eighth graders. A record player with an accompanying stack of 45s, a table with punch and cookies, a few mothers who served as chaperones all made for a very exciting place to want to be.

Physically very mature for my age, I was greatly aware of boys and wanted nothing more than the kind of validating age-appropriate attention from a handsome, polite boy could have provided me. Except for the geekiest, homeliest boy in my third-grade class, there had never been a boy who had shown interest in me as a prospective girlfriend. That might not have been so hard to bear had that been the norm, but from early on in elementary school, little boys and little girls demonstrate interest in the opposite sex, and that was certainly the case at Joyce School. However, I was the girl with whom boys were readily drawn to as a friend but never as a girlfriend. Along with all the unhealthy garbage I carried around inside me, that sense of rejection from boys was a big part of the load.

To her credit, my mother had told me many times that I was old for my age, far more mature than my male classmates, and because of that, my plight would improve as I got older and was around older boys. Older boys would be more apt to be on my level and would therefore show interest in me. I was familiar with the desperate need within me to feel attractive to boys but had no comprehension how great that need really was.

I knew I was pretty. I had only to look in the mirror at the face that looked back at me and knew it was nice-looking. My mother also did her best to comfort me by often explaining I was a person with a broad frame and thick build, but that didn't mean I didn't look nice, and it didn't mean I was fat. Someone once told me I had more of my dad in me than he had, and my physical appearance was strong evidence of that claim, so I found Mom's insistence reasonable. I never thought my mother was lying; however, I was never able to figure out the painful fact boys had no interest in me. For lack of any other explanation, I had faith my mother's prediction would come true and older boys would be attracted to me.

More than anything, what we get the least of is somehow what we yearn for the most. Beyond my parents' attention and approval, followed by piano lessons, what I needed most in my life was the validation that healthy attention from the opposite sex might render. Because I had received perverted sexual attention by adult men and had had no healing from that, there was no way I could have responded normally had I indeed received any attention from any boy. Impossible to have understood at that time, had boys actually shown interest in me, my own desperation would have prevented normal interaction and could easily have led to paths of promiscuity and other vices exhibited by so many females who seek exactly what I did and for the same reasons.

The unrequited need for attention, affection, acceptance combined with hormone levels of teenagers manifests itself unequivocally in promiscuity, sexually transmitted diseases, pregnancy and its dilemmas, poor school performance, dropping out of school, and so forth. Through education, experience, professional help, and maturity, I eventually came to understand these elements of tragedy, but that realization took a long time. In 1962 as a newly pubescent young girl, I was about to experience rejection that clove my soul in a manner not even molestation had and more concretely laid in a course already destined to attract troubles to my life. One of the most painful experiences of my life occurred at this tender age.

Periodically at the Cities Service gas plant's community building, dances were held for the sixth, seventh, and graders of Red Rock

School. A record player, a stack of 45 records, mothers who functioned as chaperones, bowls of punch, and a table of refreshments all set the stage for youngsters to gather and socialize, dance, and gain a bit of experience with the emerging world of interest in the opposite sex.

As I prepared for my first (and last) Cities Service dance, I felt like a debutante about to be presented to society. Here was a most important opportunity for me to be around the all-important older boys in a social setting. The reassurances my mother had given me so long I relied on to get me to this evening. Now the time had come.

The evening of the dance I spent a good amount of time preparing myself before finally I was ready to put on the beautiful gold dress Aunt Tibe had bought me. I looked pretty. I was optimistic and excited. No, I was impatient and about to explode. I needed my vindication and my validation, and I expected to dance holes into my stockings while receiving my due. Little did I know if I had danced more than any other girl at the gathering, and received all the attention of all the boys present, that and a thousand other dances would not have been enough to begin to cure what ailed me.

As Gayla and I entered the brightly lit building, music was playing, and there were a couple dozen students already there. Immediately Gayla joined classmates of hers, and I did the same. Most of the kids were drinking punch, so I went to the refreshment table, and one of the mothers poured me a glassful. Eventually I found a chair on one side of the room and sat there with my punch, trying to watch my posture, make sure I kept my legs together and looked pleasant.

At first no one was dancing, but after the better part of an hour, there were a few couples dancing to hits of the early 1960s. Little by little, more of the boys found their way to the side of the room where most of us girls were sitting and feigning interest in conversation with one another. The dance floor was becoming busier as more couples joined those already dancing. There were lots of boys there with whom I had nice interaction every day at school, boys to whom I was a friend, even eighth-grade guys who surely would want the company of a mature girl such as I. I looked at the other girls who were not being asked to dance and could understand why no boy was interested in them, but certainly I didn't exhibit any of the characteristics that made them unappealing.

By the end of an agonizing, traumatizing evening, not one boy had steered himself anywhere near me. Not one of them wanted any of my company. I had bet it all on my mother's assurances about who would have interest in me and had rolled snake eyes. Mom had been completely wrong. As had been the case after Paul molested me and I risked all to tell my parents, I again sat breaking into pieces. Every time a different song played without anyone asking me to dance, I fractured again and again. No one noticed the death occurring right there in front of them.

At least my body did not betray me publicly that evening. Only after I was in the semiprivate cocoon of the family car did my trembling composure disintegrate, and my pain, confusion, feeling of worthlessness and utter despair about the present and future all created gushing tears that fell as swiftly and as profusely as the waters of a flash flood. I cried as if someone close to me had died. Actually, this is exactly what had taken place.

After arriving at the Stever Place, my mother spent a good while trying to console me, but her efforts were for naught. I appreciated my mother's attempt to comfort me and recognized the love she expressed witnessing her awful mess of a daughter. Long past the time in my childhood a good amount of maternal attention would perhaps have meant some healing, I was again completely, utterly decimated.

A very dark sense of acceptance engulfed me that night. Whatever it was about me that caused boys to completely disregard me as a desirable female I could not understand. That they did regard me thusly, however, was no longer deniable despite what my mother or any other encouraging soul might say to persuade me otherwise. The weight of that kind of realization on the psyche of a youngster steals a special kind of youthfulness from her. The further destruction, disfigurement, and debris that comprised the flood's toll inside me were situations with which I was already well acquainted.

To continue to subject my scary emotional health to such torture would have been an exercise only a masochist would inflict. For years afterward I never entertained the idea of attending another function like that dance. If emotional pain could actually kill, I would have been dead long ago.

One day that spring while riding the sadistic Jacob Koehn's school bus toward home, we kids saw smoke in the distance. As we traveled in its direction, we quickly realized it was coming from the Stever Place. Now extremely concerned and tense, I was afraid it was our trailer house on fire. Fearing for our parents' safety and that of our pets made the bus ride toward the fire seem like an eternity. Our stop was the last one on the bus route, so winding back and forth over the countryside that day to drop off other students first was agonizing. Finally, the three Longtin kids and the four Carter kids were all who remained on the bus, and by the time we dropped off the Longtin kids, I was nearly frantic. Fortunately at that point I could see the couple of miles to where we lived and was able to discern the trailer house was not what was afire.

Along the road that led from where we exited the school bus to the trailer and outbuildings sat a very large haystack comprised of first-rate Sudex feed for cattle. It was about halfway between the county road and the trailer, so from a distance, the close proximity was why the trailer appeared to be what was burning. The stack of hay was approximately fifteen feet high, seventy-five feet long, and thirty-five feet across, and it was this stack that was on fire. It had been burning for several hours, so by time we arrived there from school, it was fully engulfed.

There were fire trucks at the scene that had been driven the fifteen miles from Ulysses, as well as law enforcement officers, some farmers who had come to the sight of the blaze, and my dear father, who looked bewildered, sheepish, and completely off his game. I felt really sorry for him and was so relieved he was not injured or killed in the calamity that the loss of all that hay really didn't register with me for a while.

As it turned out, an attempt to be productive and useful had backfired on Dad. That morning he had sat about to burn weeds out of the ditches on either side of the road that led to the trailer. Unbeknownst to him, a feral cat whose home was in amongst the hay bales of the haystack happened to be in one of the ditches and caught on fire. At that point the terrified animal hightailed it toward its home in the haystack. As chance would have it, when the cat found the entrance to its straw home, it took the fire inside with it. There was no way Dad could access the cat's hidden chambers, and the haystack's fate was sealed. Obviously there was enough flame, oxygen, and literal tons of fuel to cause a fire that was to last for nearly a day and smolder for several days.

The situation was volatile enough that several firemen and law enforcement officers stayed through the night and part of the next day to be on hand in case the fire threatened to get out of control.

Lost in the haystack fire was $3,000 worth of hay and undoubtedly the poor cat. If the stack was insured I have no idea, although since it was the early 1960s, I doubt it. At any rate, I do not recall my grandfather being angry with my father, which helped make a serious misfortune a great deal less difficult to overcome.

After the fire was out and all the hubbub had died down, regularly riding or walking past that awful-looking mess roiled my insides every time I was forced to look at it. It signified things that were extremely powerful, deadly, and the way awful things so often happen to people who are simply trying to do good. It spoke so much of life as I had known it; attitudes, events, and surprises that devour so much in their wake and require one to start over from the ground up.

Thankfully there was no more upheaving drama that spring, and by time school was out, Dad was healed nearly enough to return to work. Though not earthmoving, one incident I happened to witness nevertheless left me with profound understanding and my mouth literally agape.

We had two Daschund dogs as pets, a male named Hercules and a female named Dutchess. As are most dogs of that breed, they were friendly and good-natured. One day I was outside, and from across the driveway, some fifty feet away, I saw the two dogs sitting in front of the very large doors to the wood-framed Butler building that served as the barn. The doors were probably twenty feet high and just as wide and slid open by means of rollers inside a track at the top. The dogs looked nearly comical; they were so small and low to the ground and appeared to be primly sitting for a portrait against this huge backdrop. They were so close together they touched and looked posed with their heads pointed in opposite directions, jaws lifted proudly. The profile shot they seemed posed for would no doubt have been impressive.

At any rate when I saw them, I called out to them. I coaxed Dutchess who immediately began to wag her tail but did not move even an inch toward me. This was unusual as she was a happy, gregarious dog and excellent companion to all us kids. I continued to call to her as I walked toward them and the barn, but Dutch just sat there as if immobilized.

Finally I was within a few feet from them and still calling to them. When I was nearly upon them, Dutch finally tried to move. She got up and tried to walk toward me. As she did so, Hercules also began moving toward me, only backward. I was trying to figure out what was going on, and as the dogs drew nearer, my mind put two and two together for a sum that was dumbfounding. The dogs were hooked together at the butt! I was completely speechless, although my mouth did fly open and gaped widely for several seconds. As much as I thought I knew about the facts of life, this was one fact about which I was completely ignorant. The concept of an erection was totally foreign to me, until that split second in time that I realized what was going on between these two dogs!

Remaining true to my distorted attitude toward all things sexual, after the utter shock of my realization wore off, I immediately became infuriated with the dogs and began kicking and screaming at them. Naturally the frightened animals tried to run from their assault but were having a hell of a time moving. After several yards of this awkward movement, Hercules's manhood/doghood fortunately unloosed itself from its reproductive positioning and fell onto the ground, and away they ran at breakneck speed. With me chasing them and still screaming at them, the canine lovers made their way to an outbuilding that was a bunkhouse of sorts that also served as my brothers' bedroom. The two frightened dogs disappeared beneath it to safety from their enraged pursuer.

Unable to get my hands on the lascivious dogs, I walked around aimlessly for quite some time, shaking my head in disbelief. The sight of Hercules's elongated penis dragging behind him on the ground I could not get out of my head. I thought to myself, *It goes inside. He had it inside her.* That idea seemed so gross and awful that it made me nearly gag. Further putting two and two together, I realized that it must work the same way with men and women. At that point I really was about ready to vomit.

I spent the better part of that day alone with my thoughts and the realization that had been visited upon me that day. Many times through the years I had seen dogs humping other dogs and really hormone-crazed dogs that would try to hump human's legs, but never did I realize the extent of their closeness when they were actually able to achieve coitus. I had seen puppies and kittens being born before so knew how baby mammals exited their mothers' bellies. As to precisely how they got into their mothers I was completely unaware—until that day on the farm. The irony of all this is that I was physically a young woman technically able to become pregnant and give birth, to become a mother myself. That the body and the mind develop at such differing paces is a mental chasm difficult to span.

Seventh Grade

By the time Red Rock School dismissed for summer, we Carters were about to move again. In the six months since Dad's nearly fatal accident, he had sufficiently recovered and was well enough to not only return to work but completely change his line of work. This Quixotic windmill Dad decided to chase would prove to be a much better idea on paper than in reality.

Reed Carter, the same uncle of Dad's who had taken him in as a teenager, had long since moved back from southern California to the part of Oklahoma where the Carters had originally homesteaded and had lived till the dust storms of the 1930s. As so many Oklahomans did during that ruination, Reed and other family members had moved to southern California in search of a new beginning. Reed was a master carpenter who continued his craft in his new surroundings, constructing houses one at a time, selling them upon completion, and living off the proceeds as he busied himself building the next one.

In Laverne, Oklahoma, Uncle Reed had constructed his own house a couple of years earlier. During this process, he built the garage first, in which he and his wife lived while he built the house onto it. It was while they were living in the garage I went to stay with them for a couple of weeks. My great aunt and uncle were very enjoyable and treated me very kindly. As a youngster, not yet a teenager, I thought living in the garage was an exciting adventure. It was new, neat, clean, sturdy, and showed off Uncle Reed's expert carpentry skills.

Uncle Reed was a tall, lean bald-headed man in his sixties with an extreme amount of nervous energy who loved bologna, a staple in his diet that we ate nearly every day I was there. He drove a Dodge

Valiant and was a huge Barry Goldwater fan. Both of these facts set him apart from most people I knew but seemed to fit well with his distinct persona. Uncle Reed talked a whole lot and did so loudly but lovingly and had a pet name for nearly everyone. His wife he called Lila, short for Delilah. He called my father Bobby. I was called Frannie, the name by which most of my father's side of my family affectionately addressed me. He was quite entertaining with his near-constant jabbering, and as an adult, my guess is that Uncle Reed might have gotten along easier with children than with adults. At any rate, when I stayed that while with them at their garage/house as a nine- or ten-year-old, I had pleasant memories and a fun time.

Uncle Reed clearly loved my dad very much and to some degree seemed like a father figure to him. Reed came to visit us fairly regularly for several years, and we kids always enjoyed those times. Cooing his sweet nicknames to all of us, entertaining us with his level of energy, and amusing us with his opinionated rants ensured his visits were enjoyable and memorable, and I for one delighted in the attention and obvious fondness he held for all of us. Other than being married to his cousin, Uncle Reed seemed pretty much like everyone else!

With my predilection and intense curiosity about that which was discussed only in lower tones, I was fascinated with Reed and Delilah's marriage. Aunt Delilah was also quite a nervous person, who nevertheless seemed to enjoy being around us five kids when they visited us. In looking at her and listening to her, one would never get the impression she had the kind of grit required to go outside societal, even legal dictates and break some important rules as she and her beloved had done. Even though they were rule breakers, they seemed to have suffered no visible retribution. I liked them very much, but without the feeling of safety and freedom to seek clarification from and pose questions to my parents about this family anomaly, I judged these old folks to be semi-outlaws to have married one another. I further wondered, if marrying your cousin was against the law, why my uncle and aunt hadn't been arrested. I was confused about how to think and feel toward this vexing situation but knew better than to risk garnering new disapproval from my mother and dad by asking questions about this situation that existed within our family ranks.

Common knowledge provided other information that was equally fascinating to me. As it was told, when Reed and Delilah became man and wife, Uncle Reed had had himself "fixed" to avoid having any children that might be mentally deficient or sickly. I had seen a couple of scary movies as a child that depicted insane asylums of long ago and the inhabitants thereof, and those scenes terrified me. To think Reed and Delilah could have had a child with an appearance akin to some of those Hollywood images and possibly be locked up in a dungeon or an institution similar to those portrayed cinematically was a powerful thought that I could not dismiss.

My experience around anyone with any kind of a disability was unsurprisingly restricted. In Ulysses I knew of two people who were retarded. Buzz Downing was one of them. He was a young adult who had Down's syndrome, although at that time he was referred to simply as being a mongoloid. With the physical characteristics of one with Down's syndrome, he did look different, and ignorance translated into apprehension, so no one had to tell us kids not to go around him. His two older sisters were close friends with my aunts Karen and Vicki, and one day I was with Karen at the Downings' home. I was completely unsure how to behave toward Buzz, which made me most anxious and nervous. One thing I did observe was that he was neat and clean and wore a well-ironed short-sleeve shirt and overalls like my dad wore. He did not look like the people in those awful movies and even seemed friendly. It was clear his sisters were not taken aback at his appearance or behavior, and they treated him like they would any family member.

When my aunt Karen finally concluded her visit with her friend Sandra, we left. I could not get out the door fast enough. I didn't realize it then, but it wasn't Buzz I was afraid of; it was my own lack of knowing how to conduct myself around a handicapped person that created the uneasiness that pressed me down. Again I had to think my own way through the questions I had about Buzz and what made him different. Innocent curiosity and the questions it produced had gotten me the cold, glaring looks of disapproval from my mother too many times. Going to Mom with questions was just too risky. Coming up with my own explanations to perplexities was a path down which I was accustomed to traveling by this time.

By the end of the school year at Red Rock School, Uncle Reed and Dad had hatched a plan that entailed us moving, not west to Colorado this time, but southeast 140 miles or so to Laverne, Oklahoma. We would move to Laverne, and Dad would work with Uncle Reed in the house-building business.

The idea of leaving Ulysses again did not appeal to any of us kids or to our mother. She wasn't as keen on Uncle Reed as we kids were and simply did not buy into the plan like Dad did. Despite our parents turning to us kids a couple of years earlier as the final authority on whether or not to remain married, our voices in moving hither and yon were not requested or allowed. Soon after receiving our final report cards for the school (as had been the case several times hitherto now and would continue so), Uncle Dale arrived bright and early one morning with a truck, helped us load our belongings, and moved us to our latest destination.

Coincidentally or not, in Laverne we settled into a garage to live. The garage sat next door to Uncle Reed's house, but unlike his house, our garage was probably as old as Reed was. Housing a large family that included three teenagers inside a decades-old garage was a far cry different from an older couple with no children occupying one newly built and comparatively quite spacious. Aptly we called this place the Garage.

The temperatures in Oklahoma that summer were miserably hot. Inside our garage home, we had a small swamp cooler, but staying inside was not only unpleasant in other ways, it was generally not allowed. Not much space remained beyond that being used to situate our furniture and life's necessities. Too many people in too small a place never exist without friction and its offshoots. Besides, Lonnie and I had an appointed job, and production was not negotiable.

On the lot of land that held our garage home also sat the old house that went with it. Reed and Dad's plan was to renovate the old house, and then we would move into it, but before we could even start work on the house, we had to affect a few necessary repairs on the garage to render it livable. The first priority was new shingles in order to put a halt to the leaking roof. My older brother Bruce soon went back to Ulysses to work, so we were down one pair of hands already. My older sister Gayla simply wasn't a person who would be useful in that kind of work, even if it had been possible to coerce her up the ladder. Stacy was too young to even consider using at that kind of a job. So it fell to Lonnie and me.

Except for the heat, I actually didn't mind the work. We pulled the roofing nails from where they had been placed long before and, once the old shingles were freed, tossed them to the ground. My mother grudgingly went along with our task of working on the roof, but it was another nail in the coffin that would eventually contain the entire Laverne fiasco.

As the old adage says, "The road to hell is paved with good intentions," which pretty much summed up Dad and Uncle Reed's plans about them being in business together. For reasons too long past to recall, Dad never did work in Laverne with Reed but continued to work in Ulysses while his family was a good three hours away in Oklahoma. The situation reeked of déjà vu except we were in Oklahoma instead of Colorado. On weekends Mom would hit the road with us kids to Ulysses, undoubtedly for respite from a situation she was loathing more each day.

When we made the move from the farm to Laverne, Mom brought along her few head of geese that patrolled our yard. One weekend while we were in Ulysses, Uncle Reed made an Alexander Haig-type decision. He misjudged his authority and made a command decision without actually being in command. His screwup was as wrong as it was bold and daring, and like Haig, it would cost him dearly.

Returning from Ulysses and driving up to our garage home, the place was too still. Mom got out of the car and immediately began looking for her geese, to no avail. After realizing they were indeed absent, she naturally went next door to see if Reed could shed any light on the whereabouts of her feathered friends. When questioned, Reed smugly informed her that, yes, he knew what happened to them. He said he had killed them all because they were nothing but a nuisance.

A wave of shock traveled through my mother. For an instant, she didn't trust the reaction welling up inside her because it was incredulous to imagine anyone having that much gall. Staring into Reed's uncontrite expression, however, she knew he was serious in his admission of slaughter. Mom's mouth pursed. Her eyes became narrow slits in her head as she glared at this audacious goose slayer. The blood in her veins ran ice-cold, and if looks really could kill, Reed would have dropped dead on the spot.

Then and there my mother told Reed Carter what she thought of him, to which he replied that if she would stay put rather than burning up the road back and forth to Ulysses, we would all be better off. Like one of the much-feared nuclear detonations during the Cuban missile crises only a few months earlier, Mom and Reed went ballistic, and nothing was left unsaid. The geese murders ignited the already-unstable situation, and the war was fought right there on Reed Carter's front porch. After all weapons had been discharged, there was nothing left but the nuclear winter that was to follow.

The miserable heat in Laverne and our living quarters were something loosely akin to another Oklahoma family's, Steinbeck's Jodes. These conditions and Dad's absence flew in the face of the plan he imposed on us and rendered it the pipe dream it really was. With the geese massacre and the subsequent mouth fight between Mom and Reed, our permanent departure from Laverne became imminent if not amicable.

Within a day or two, our faithful Uncle Dale was backing up his truck to our garage home to move us back to Ulysses. After making a short order of loading what we owned into the familiar truck, Dale got behind its wheel, and Dad hoisted Stacy up and into the cab of the truck and then climbed in himself in shotgun position. Mom, Gayla, Lonnie, and I positioned ourselves in our 1957 Chevrolet station wagon, and exhibiting the indignation and anger that was still raw, we rolled out of Laverne without so much as a wave as we drove past Reed and Delilah's house. At least we made it back home before school began, so as it turned out, the summer seemed some sort of a strange adventure that, thankfully, was more short-termed than long.

Between the farm ground where we lived while Dad recuperated from being crushed beneath his pickup truck and Ulysses, the highway passed through an unincorporated village named Hickok. My parents had spotted a rental house there, and after the Oklahoma goose chase / goose murder, we arrived in Hickok to begin anew.

Fairly new, neat, and very clean, this Hickok property was respectable looking and situated on a large corner lot that was complete with grass, a hedge at least five feet tall that bordered the two rear sides, and a concrete slab that paralleled the front of the house and perfectly accommodated our vehicles. The house was also unique because it did not sit facing either of the unpaved streets that intersected in front of it. Located at about a forty-five-degree angle to the highway and a stone's throw from it, the concrete parking slab was not originally a part of the landscape. Because the house sat at an unusual angle, I imagined there must be a really special reason the builder had oriented it so unusually.

Years later I learned there was little mystique or mystery to the uniquely facing structure. The house and property were owned by the farmers' cooperative and had originally been built as a weigh station for trucks hauling crops. At some point the operation ceased, and the truck scales were removed and replaced with the concrete slab that served as our parking area. I didn't know it while we lived there, but the co-op wanted to sell the house, and my folks rented it, hoping to procure financing with which to purchase the place.

Inside our new abode were a large living room, kitchen, and two bedrooms. The third bedroom that was to be headquarters for Bruce and Lonnie was a small detached structure located against the hedge at the rear of the lot. This small rustic wooden shack was comparable in size to a large shed and, except for being seriously cold through the winter, was a great man cave for my brothers. In fact, the boys liked it well enough to give it an endearing name. They called it the Sugar Shack, a term picked up from an eponymous song popular around that time. The Sugar Shack was roomy, private, and fun. Never able to be accused of being avant-garde at bestowing titles, we simply dubbed this house and its lot Hickok.

Lonnie and I would often scale the outside of his and Bruce's bedroom and, from our perch atop it, felt powerful, like we were rulers in some small kingdom. While overlooking our minions of Dutchess, Hercules, a few more geese Mom acquired, several chickens, as well as our feline citizens, we would eat sandwiches and drink Kool-Aid, sit and ruminate about whatever was going on at the time, and strategize about what we would do next.

One afternoon Lonnie and I were positioned on our perch, surveying the realm, when our gaze fixed upon the daddy of the flock of hens. This grand rooster was very large and colored gorgeously with purplish-black feathers over most of his body that reflected the light to the point it nearly dazzled. His comb and wattle were bright red, his hackles and spurs excellent specimens, and his carriage even more regal than ours as he would parade around keeping tabs on his harem. As proud a creature as he was, the impressive chap deserved a name, but since we didn't like him, that honor was withheld, and we usually referred to him as "that dammed rooster." The cock was also just as cross and aggressive as he was handsome and had assaulted Lonnie on more than one occasion, much like the ornery goat Daisy had done so many times to me years earlier. For whatever reason, that day Lonnie decided to give that rooster some of his own medicine.

As with most boys, my brothers were fond of throwing rocks. As is also the case with most of their gender, my brothers had gotten in trouble over the years for doing so yet had not overcome the tempting urge to launch stony projectiles from time to time. This proved to be one of those times.

Anticipating possible scenarios within our keep, Lonnie and I had seen to a store of ammunition that lay ready in case of a defensive need. Unfortunately for the proud bird, that day our cache of arms would instead be used offensively. The proud potentate of our hens was simply in the wrong place at the wrong time that fateful afternoon, and Lonnie made the offhanded decision to retaliate for prior assaults and floggings he had suffered courtesy of that *gallus domesticus* bully.

Lonnie began his assault by tossing a few good-sized pebbles toward the foul. The bird scolded my brother and was not intimidated. Lonnie selected a bigger rock and launched it with more velocity. It hit its mark on the chicken's back, and the bird reacted accordingly. Unfortunately for its own good, the bird was unafraid and did not seek cover or retreat to the chicken coop. Angered by the cock's defiance, my brother then picked up a half of a brick we had found somewhere and launched that toward his impudent vassal. Alas, Lonnie's aim was a little too accurate, and in an instant, the rooster lay dead on the ground.

Involuntarily my brother's eyes bulged and his head jerked in my direction as mine spasmed toward him. Both our mouths flew open simultaneously. What the hell! "Oh shit," declared my brother. Completely surprised by this turn of events, I was frozen in silence as my mind was whirring with thoughts of this assassination and its consequences.

We sat there for quite a while before we descended from our tactically superior position and hesitatingly approached the carcass as if we believed that bird was sinisterly playing dead and would leap up and assault us once we were close enough to it. No such luck. The rooster really was dead, by our hands. Nearly silently and automatically, we headed toward the house and our mother. Inside we weren't confident and arrogant like we had felt perched high up out of doors.

"Mom, the rooster is dead," I said in a small voice.

She turned toward us with her full attention.

The Spanish Inquisition could have been no more unpleasant. Putting our tale into words and saying them aloud gave an awful sound to the irresponsible vandalism we had just committed. The rooster was a grouchy old bastard but not to the degree he deserved to die because of his disposition and role in life. There was no real defense for our actions, so we stood at the court's mercy.

Our jurist glared at the two of us. About a year earlier, when this same officer of the court had busted me at the gas station in Florence, I was terrorized and traumatized, but today was not quite as full of terror to me. So much of major import had transpired since that misdemeanor I simply wasn't as rattled and full of fear. That does not mean, however, that I wasn't most anxious about what retribution Billie the Barrister might exact from us.

Finally, our magistrate pronounced sentence. She ordered us to make restitution by salvaging what we could of the once proud rooster. In the ice-cold, menacing tone our mother expertly wielded, she added that we had better not make a mess dressing out that bird.

Silently we left the kitchen courtroom and proceeded to the scene of the crime. Yep, the rooster was still lying there right where we left him, the brick right beside his head. After conferring, we fetched a rake and laid it over the rooster's neck. Legs far apart, I stood on the ends of the rake, and Lonnie grabbed the bird and began tugging at it, trying to separate its head from its body. No luck. That bird was one tough old boot, and we were acquiring a new appreciation of it size, bulk, and strength. Lonnie pulled and pulled again and yet again. He may have stretched the neck some, but it was attached just as securely as it had been when we started.

Time for a different plan of attack; no, forget the attack. Time for a different plan. We put the rake back and moved on to a crueler tool, Dad's ax. I had had more than enough by now. I was crying and whining while onward I went. Lonnie was thinking more of how we would get the damned job done and over with as soon as possible. Along with the ax, we returned to the crime victim with a piece of wood to lay its head and neck on, and finally we were able to guillotine the dead creature. I was awfully sick to my stomach, and what had been a great day a little earlier was now anything but fun.

That proud bird now lay in two pieces, and the new challenge was to remove all its feathers. Earlier that spring, we had helped our folks butcher chickens at the farm. They had managed to buy some chicks and raise them for food, so we had had recent schooling on how to proceed. With Mom overseeing us, we eventually got the job finished and slinked away with as much dignity as we could exhibit, extremely thankful she had not taken some of our hide as our punishment. We tried to stay as scarce as we could around Mom for a few days until the situation had blown over to a manageable level.

That old bird became the chicken in chicken and noodles, but not before our mother cooked it slowly for the better part of an entire day to get it tender enough to eat. Needless to say, that was not an enjoyable meal, but I knew better than not to eat it. Lonnie and I continued to spend a lot of time on the top of the boys' Sugar Shack, but experience influencing his behavior, he allowed the minions to go about their business without harassment.

Bruce was between his freshman and sophomore years of school that summer, had a job so was not at home much. Gayla spent most of her time inside or with friends she had made at the Mobil gas plant, which was now only a couple of miles east on the highway. As always, our little sister Stacy was with herself, either inside the house with Mom or playing alone outside. As a kid, I never gave much thought to Stacy. She was younger enough than I that playing with her would not have been fun, and I had my buddy Lonnie anyway. Most times we other kids thought life for Stacy was enviable because she was the baby, and in some ways, we were no doubt correct. I have also since realized elements of that status must have been just as challenging to her as any we older siblings had to navigate.

Not long after we moved to Hickok, Gayla and I ventured into the world of business via the Grit newspaper. I have no recollection if we made enough money selling Grit to line our pockets with any more than a bit of spending money. Far more important was the sense of freedom and independence we experienced while delivering the periodical to customers within a several-mile radius of Hickok. That our mother trusted my sister to drive the family car on our route speaks not only to the low cost of gasoline but some unfathomable sense of trust Mom extended to Gayla.

Shortly after Dad was able to return to work, he and Mom traded in the 1957 Chevy station wagon we owned and came home with a light-mauve Chrysler sedan. It was several steps up from the Chevy, with a push-button transmission, plush interior, carpeted floor, tinted windows, and other luxury extras that said this vehicle was a real ride instead of just a basic issue, meat-wagon workhorse like our station wagon had been.

Now Mom was allowing Gayla to drive around at the helm of this beautiful machine, and we certainly made the most of it. Before departing on our paper route, we would swing by the small grocery store in our village. The building was about the size of a present-day convenience store, and Mr. and Mrs. Patterson stocked the store with an abundant supply of the goodies any kid desired. After grabbing a couple of soda pops and potato chips or sunflower seeds, we were off. With Gayla at the wheel and me enjoying the front seat view of the world, we could have been delivering bags of bird droppings and I wouldn't have cared. I enjoyed every mile we traveled. I can only surmise my sister enjoyed these days as much as I did because her normally acerbic personality was a lot closer to pleasant.

Too quickly summer vacation was at an end, and the time had come to begin the school year. The reluctance to let go of those fun days comingled with my anticipation about starting junior high school. Not only was I ecstatic to be returning to school in Ulysses and the familiarity that scenario would afford, I was just as happy to be reuniting with friends I had known since kindergarten and the joy those relationships imbued in me. As a bonus, the idea of being a seventh grader made me feel bigger, stronger, more important. The idea of changing classrooms for each subject and having several teachers every day appealed to me. Why, that was the same way high school operated, and high-school students were practically adults.

I was one excited student as the bus headed toward Ulysses and Sullivan School the first day of school the fall of 1963. Sullivan School was where I had attended kindergarten in what seemed a lifetime ago, where I injured my head and was mortified as my teacher drove me home. This was the school to which we Joyce School fifth- and sixth-grade girls had been bussed a couple of years earlier to attend that awful mother-daughter tea and watch that disgusting film about menstruation. It was the same building, but between those memories and the present I had experienced, so much those recollections seemed light years ago, and in the sense of how I had changed, they had occurred in some other place. At any rate now I looked eagerly forward to whatever lay ahead as a member of the seventh-grade class of 1964.

I was assigned to the homeroom of Mrs. Dorothy Russell, who also taught language arts. I quickly perceived the students this educator preferred, those to whom she spoke in a warm, engaging voice and with whom she actually conversed, at whom she smiled and became animated and cheered on academically and personally. I was absolutely not one of those students. Fortunately, I lost no sleep over my status as one of the "outs" in homeroom, but that old crone, her cold demeanor and contrasting treatment of students I knew was wrong, and I regarded her with contempt.

In contrast to and because of so many of the negative family dynamics I was forced to tolerate at home, my personality craved the success, fun, respect, sensible expectations, and calm environment I normally experienced at school. Therefore, I was a student who was glad to be in class, understood my role, and achieved accordingly. Looking back, I realize I could have earned much higher marks toward a brighter academic future and possibly greater accomplishment, but unfortunately, mediocrity at school was wholly acceptable in my family, so I managed well in school with very little effort. The bar I reached for was whatever I established for myself. Fortunately, I needed the positives that above average behavior and work at school fed me. Unfortunately, I didn't have the maturity, foresight, or parental expectation to set the bar much higher for myself even though I had the ability to excel had conditions been different.

Thankfully that school year was largely routine and without major upheaval or turmoil at home or otherwise. The one profound event that did occur happened to our country, not just to me.

While in study hall in the library one November morning, I was enjoying myself, alternately studying and daydreaming, glad that it was Friday. At the front of the room, Mrs. Alma Bogue, our study hall teacher, sat at the librarian's desk, attending to her own work. As I sat there, I observed our principal as he walked into the room and over to the desk where Mrs. Bogue was sitting. He bent over and began whispering in her ear. I kept looking toward them. Mrs. Bogue's face dropped and looked completely serious. She turned very pale, reached for her handkerchief from a pocket in her dress, and began crying silently. Now my attention was riveted on her. In a few moments the principal stood erect, turned, and with drooping shoulders and an anguished look on his face, exited the library.

Mrs. Bogue remained seated and continued to weep. By this time, I was not the only student who realized she was very upset, and our curiosity and concern were surrendering to impatience to learn what news was responsible for this sad turn of events. As soon as our teacher had composed herself enough, she stood to her feet. She tried to project her trembling voice loud enough to get the class's attention and eventually managed to do so. She said she had an announcement to make to us, that she had just been told President Kennedy had been shot and killed. She added a couple more facts that were known, that he had been in Dallas riding in a limousine with Mrs. Kennedy and had been shot from a distance but that no one had yet been arrested for the murder. Lastly, she suggested we sit and pray for his soul, his family, and for our nation. Then she crumpled into her chair and began softly crying again.

Instantly nausea enveloped me, and I flashed back almost exactly a year earlier when we arrived in Ulysses that November evening and I thought for a few seconds that my dad was dead. This time it was our president, and there was no doubt he was dead. For me personally, for every one of us seventh graders, for every person in Ulysses and in the United States as a whole, another layer of our individual and collective innocence evaporated instantly, nevermore to be. I sat there completely silenced by the sickening news. I continued to watch Mrs. Bogue. Normally she was a stern-looking, no-nonsense teacher who was very professional and businesslike in her comportment. Now she sat in front of us exhibiting a totally different behavior, not even self-conscious that she was very openly emotional and engulfed in shock, sorrow, and tears. It was a memorable lesson Alma Bogue unknowingly shared with me that day.

My mother's strained upbringing, unattended hurts old and new, distrustful attitude spawned by countless insults, injuries, and betrayals of sorts formed a personality unwilling if not unable to show much vulnerability. As a child, I do not ever recall seeing my mother entranced in that soft, tender, transfixed look of utter affection a woman exhibits while momentarily hypnotized by the depth of the love she feels for her child. In those ethereal moments, a mother is unaware of anything except the absolute love she holds for her son or daughter and which extends even to a cellular level. Such moments are extremely powerful for both mother and the child fortunate enough to be aware of his mother's gaze. This look of love sates its target and infuses the child with a unique strength that only it can.

In my whole life I never saw my mother cry over a sad movie. My first recollection of the awkward discomfort I felt in this type scenario was before I was of school age. My parents had recently purchased their first television set, and I was seated beside my mother on our sofa, watching a movie with great interest. I don't recall what the story line was, but I do recall the movie had black people and angels in it as well as several heart-wrenching scenes. I became quite emotional, and tears flowed onto and down my cheeks. I would have liked my mother to put her arm around me or say something reassuring, but that just wasn't her style. At some point I glanced upward to check my reaction against that of mother's. She appeared emotionless while I was reacting with profuse tears. Immediately I felt the discomfort I would experience again and again over the years during such occasions because of our completely different emotional constitutions.

The same knot of anxiety would grind at my insides even as an adult when the movie scene dealt with religious or sexual depictions. My mother wanted absolutely nothing to do with church and religion while I was growing up and ignored its existence and the role it played in my life. Sexual scenes in movies were treated like the crazy scenario where someone passes particularly fetid-smelling gas, yet those nearby pretend not to notice.

I needed my mother to guide and parent me in all ways, but oft times her needs simply trumped those of her children. My mother was emotionally handicapped from her own injurious childhood and never managed much healing. Had she been able to significantly nullify life's pillories by inner healing instead of warehousing them for decades, life for her and all those in her sphere would no doubt have been exceedingly different. Unfortunately, my mother's situation dictated she be on guard at all times. Such a vigil exhausts, so it behooves ones so tasked to keep their world as small as possible and maintain as much control as possible, maximizing the chances of avoiding any further injury.

My father was very similar to my mother in being unequipped to deal with this part of his and his children's lives. My parents' emotional inabilities resulted in huge gaps in their relationship with one another and those with my siblings and me. The toll these gaps exacted on me grew as I did.

So on November 22, 1963, despite a horrible national tragedy, I was able to observe an otherwise very businesslike, composed Mrs. Bogue, who occupied an important position in my young world as a teacher, freely and naturally express deep, strong, powerful emotion without embarrassment. This side effect of an otherwise horrific event proved as edifying to me as our president's violent death was calamitous to our nation.

By this time my twelfth birthday was four months behind me. My mind had long ago finished distilling the incidences of sexual molestation that had been forced upon me in the past. The demons that accompany that kind of perversion had possessed me for years already. My identity as a fat, discounted, devalued female had long been solidified. The uncomfortable interaction and tenuous security that were the trademarks of the troubled relationship I endured with my parents from early on had left me deficient in vital ways. The intense need I had for positive attention, affection, and validation from my parents had yielded a kind of hunger within me that was insatiable. Shame, the cornerstone of my mental and emotional makeup, had become my essence. The instinctive truths I fought to believe about myself were present but regularly assaulted in a myriad of ways, and the resultant confusion was becoming more and more burdensome. I was a preteen seriously at risk in several fundamental ways, moving day by day into a world that would exacerbate all these preexisting conditions. There was no way these afflictions that were engrained throughout my childhood and were a large part of my identity could serve me well. Nor could I have ever imagined how much and in what ways they would cost me throughout my lifetime.

I have vivid recollection of a girl who was an eighth grader when I was a seventh grader. Her first name was Elaine. She had curly brown hair that seemed unmanageable, hazel eyes set deep and a little too close together, and an uncomely mouth and smile similar to the Grandpa character of *The Munsters* television serial. She was loud, somewhat histrionic, and most noticeably quite overweight. She often wore too-tight bone-colored jeans to school that compounded her lack of allure. All said, this girl was unattractive yet had dared to try to draw attention to herself. Almost right away I decided I did not like Elaine. It was bad enough she looked like she did. That she did not possess sufficient sagacity to preclude her behaving in a way that made her an even greater laughingstock made me want to slap Elaine in hopes of knocking some sense into her.

I had no idea then that what was most repugnant about this girl was that she reminded me too much of myself. Her excessive weight and total rejection by boys seemed almost like a misbehaving family member who manages to get himself in trouble publicly and embarrass the entire clan. I tried to completely avoid this girl, to keep her at bay mentally as well as physically. I regret being so troubled myself that I could not be kinder to a girl who was probably in as much pain as I was and most likely could have used a friend.

EIGHTH GRADE

When school was over in the spring of 1964, the village of Hickok became history. Again my parents were unable to secure financing to buy the place, so we had to move on. Mom located a house inside the Ulysses city limits on Durham Street, and we moved into town. This house was even nicer than the one in Hickok. It was perhaps thirty years old, neat, clean, and big enough for our family with a detached garage out back, which was a first for our family. The front and back yards were nice-sized without a single blade of grass anywhere on that lot. There were a couple of lilac bushes in the back and a big elm tree in the front as well as one in the back, so Durham Street was not completely barren.

Once again my brothers occupied the poorly lit, cool, cavern-type basement. Had we not been as glad as we were to have a three-bedroom place, we might have viewed the basement differently, but we were simply grateful to live in this place that did not stand out in the wrong way, was in town, and in a solid middle-class neighborhood. We three girls shared a bedroom on the back side of the house, our parents' bedroom was at the front of the house, and the bathroom connected the two. All around us were houses that were average, nice, and very nice. The neighborhood was definitely a step up for my family, and like all things that require little getting used to, I was happy to call this place home.

As soon as summer vacation began, I was fortunate to secure a job. A job meant money with which I could really enjoy the summer and outfit myself to begin eighth grade in the fall. As with my job cleaning my grandparents' laundromat years earlier, this employment opportunity arose from the ranks of my family.

My aunt Tibe and her family had moved into town from Big Bow, and she had become a business owner. She bought a place that sat midway through Ulysses on Highway 160, next door to Russell Binney's small grocery store, the same landmark past which we drove as we entered the land of Trailerville ten years earlier. Before my aunt bought the building, everyone in Ulysses called that place the old drive-in. Soon the old drive-in was going to become Tibe's Café, but there was much work to be done before my aunt could turn out her first meal there.

The first matter of business my aunt and I settled when she offered me my summertime job was wages. She said she would pay me seven dollars for eight hours of work, and she would provide me meals when I was at work. Record albums at Pitts' shoe store sold for around four dollars each, it cost fifty cents to get into the swimming pool, and a beautiful pair of saddle oxfords at the shoe store cost twelve dollars. I couldn't wait to begin work.

The old drive-in was quite filthy inside, and my aunt, uncle, their children, and I set to cleaning it. Many buckets of bleach water and tons of elbow grease were expended to get that old building sparkling quite literally from top to bottom. In the end, the stools along the counter gleamed like new, tables and chairs were sanitary and sat like neatly ordered troops, windows shone and passed the sun's inspection, and the kitchen was as germ-free as humanly possible. Outside, the parking area was free of cigarette butts, paper, gum, and anything else that would detract. Even the concrete steps leading into the building had been scalded clean and looked new. It had taken several days working morning to evening to manage this feat, but the old place had cleaned up well, and Tibe's Café was about to open for business.

My job was dishwasher / prep worker. Initially I began work at 6:00 a.m. and was finished with my shift at 2:30 p.m. My aunt was always an incredible cook, and the residents of Ulysses eagerly sought her café's offerings. Right away there was plenty of business, so I stayed busy all during my shift.

After the breakfast rush had ended and all was washed and cleaned up from that meal, my job was to make the green salad that would be used throughout the day. My aunt and uncle were good instructors, and I learned quickly and well. Salad was contained in three-gallon plastic dishpans, and each day I made up enough salad to fill two of them. Then I placed them on the appointed shelf in the refrigerator and covered them with a slightly damp dishtowel to preserve the crispness.

After completing the salad, my next job was to peel potatoes to be used for french fries that day. I had to peel enough potatoes to fill two three-gallon tins. This was no small feat, and I soon excelled at peeling potatoes really quickly with my handheld potato peeler. To this day I am faster at peeling potatoes than anyone I have ever seen!

There was nothing about my job that was difficult to understand or accomplish. My work ethic was strong, and I was grateful to have the opportunity to work and, with the wages I drew, make my life easier and more enjoyable. Neither of my brothers ever had trouble finding work. There seemed to be more jobs available that were suited for boys, and they generally paid more than anything a girl could find. I had been working on and off since I was age ten. Household jobs such as cleaning ovens, washing windows, doing ironing, stripping wax, washing walls were plentiful, and I was big and strong and willing to work. I had also done light housekeeping and, as I got older, began to babysit for several friends and family members whenever they needed me. But regular work on a consistent basis was much harder to come by, so the chance to work forty hours a week that summer before I started eighth grade was a golden opportunity for me.

After the lunch rush was over, my aunt would go out the back door of the café, walk the fifty feet or so to where her and my uncle's trailer home was parked, and don her wife and mother hat for a few hours. While she was inside her home working or resting, it was my responsibility to assume the additional role of fry cook for these hours. I comprised half of the afternoon crew, and a waitress up front was the rest of the team's complement.

Frying hamburgers, cheeseburgers, french fries, chicken fried steaks, Salisbury steaks, and breaded shrimp I managed well. I was honored my aunt would trust me with this much responsibility, and

I never let her down. Generally, there was enough business between the noontime and evening meals to maintain a nice pace without becoming overwhelmed or having no customers. When the evening customers began arriving in sufficient numbers, I would step out back and knock on my aunt's door and let her know I needed her back at the café. It was an arrangement that worked well and benefitted me in many ways. My aunt's trust and confidence in me were great compliments and proved well placed. I did very well at my job and enjoyed the pride and resulting self-confidence such achievement naturally produces.

There were many other things I learned about life that summer. With people from all over town hungry for my aunt's delicious cooking, I met many folks I never would have otherwise. I got to work right along with adults and was treated well by them and by the customers too, especially the regular customers. Like anyone else, my aunt Tibe had her faults, but her assets were what stood out to me most often that summer. She laughed a lot, had a warm personality the public enjoyed, and had an optimistic outlook on life in general even though she and her husband were struggling to make ends meet the same as everyone else. We laughed a lot as we worked side by side, and sitting down to eat as a group after the noon rush had subsided are warm memories I cherish.

We always sat at the table closest to the kitchen area and ate good food while enjoying the camaraderie of family and coworkers. Our lunch break lasted for twenty minutes or so and allowed our bodies a chance to rest; then it was back to the job at hand. The many things I learned there that summer served me well as I moved onward and upward and closer to my role as a working adult.

A couple of goings-on with coworkers that season served as additional poignant brushes with the adult world. The situations were gossip fodder, and that kind of titillation only served to make them more interesting. Nevertheless, the impact and influence these situations had on me as a thirteen-year-old were valuable to observe.

For a while my mother's youngest sister, my aunt Vicki, worked at my aunt Tibe's café as a waitress. As a young woman about to turn twenty years old, my aunt was still as pretty as she had been when she came to Colorado to visit us three years earlier. Her impenetrable mystique was even more powerful. She still lived at home with my grandparents but came and went as a grown-up. One time when she opened up the trunk of her '54 Chevy, I had seen an ice chest of beer that she always carried there and was awestruck. In ways Vicki seemed like some of the starlets on the silver screen. She seemed so self-assured and capable and so pretty all the guys paid attention to her. Even my dad's brother, my uncle Dale, let Vicki take his new Corvette on weekends and tootle around town in it. A new Corvette in Ulysses was no small thing, and with a beautiful young woman dragging Main Street in it, the scene was like something out of a movie.

My dishwashing workstation at the café stood behind a wall that was around four and a half feet tall. Atop that wall was a shelf approximately a foot wide upon which we sat dirty dishes and supplies. The other side of the wall was the route from the dining area to the men and women's lavatories. I had noticed my aunt Vicky exiting the ladies' room several times at work but had not thought anything about it. Other eyes weren't so naive, and one day when Vicki strode past while I was in the kitchen area with Aunt Tibe, my older aunt's comments nearly floored me. She blurted out there was no doubt good reason Vicki was spending so much time in that restroom; she was probably throwing up because she was pregnant! What?

I reeled from that assertion and felt a bit nauseous myself! When I was able to think, I found myself feeling sorry for my young aunt. I shuddered at the thought of her being pregnant without being married. I thought of how upset and scared she might be and the concern and disappointment my grandparents would experience when they learned of their youngest daughter's situation. This was really bad, and I didn't know how to react or what to say. I also felt angry with my aunt Vicki. Apparently, she had been engaging in sex. Not only was it wrong to have sex before marriage, according to what was taught in church, the chance of ending up pregnant with all the shame and difficulties that would entail made no sense to me. So many issues boggled my mind and further confused me the more thought I gave to them, but becoming pregnant out of wedlock was something about which I had absolute clarity.

I also felt disgusted by my aunt Tibe's hypocrisy for announcing Vicki's plight and using the acerbic tone and spiteful visage she donned as town crier. For years I had known my aunt Tibe had been in the same situation back in the 1950s and had given birth to my cousin David before she was married. I also realized the man by whom she got pregnant was a married man there in Ulysses, and the entire affair was scandalous yet something my dad's family handled in stride. My aunt Tibe was always forthcoming about the circumstances surrounding her firstborn's illegitimacy, and I never could figure out if she was bothered by it or not. Now she was disparaging my aunt Vicki without any right to do so. Even though I was very put off by my older aunt's attitude and behavior, of course I said nothing.

The other offense I took that day was not as simple to put into words, but the way it gnawed at my insides clearly related its presence. My aunt Vicki was the youngest of my mother's three sisters, and my aunt Tibe was one of Dad's three sisters. Despite her many good qualities, Aunt Tibe had an awful reputation for talking unkindly about folks and continually stirring up trouble with her mouth. This day she was again giving into her dark side, which was enough to endure, but to make things more difficult, she was talking about someone from the other side of my family. I am sure Aunt Tibe realized she was infringing on my familial loyalty, but her need to demean others was greater than any integrity and sensitivity she might have possessed.

In 1964, such pregnancies were not rare, but they were certainly looked upon and handled differently than they are today. No older than I was, I thought that besides being a drug addict, getting pregnant without being married was probably the worst thing I could ever do. In my life, order was something I needed, pursued, and valued with a kind of reverence. The kind of disorder drugs and pregnancy as a single woman would spawn would be antithetical to all I had come to want for myself. I wanted to go to college and have a career, I wanted to have a prosperous lifestyle and a good husband one day, and in the present day, I wanted no trouble with my parents. It was not difficult to know illicit drugs and pregnancy before marriage would take me on a very different path in life than I wanted to travel. Sadly, in only a short amount of time, girls my age would begin falling by the wayside, as precisely this life-changing scenario would begin presenting itself.

Before I had to quit my job to begin school that fall, my aunt's morning sickness had pretty much passed, and her uniform was beginning to fit differently around the waist. She had graduated from high school a couple of years earlier and had not gone on to college or a trade school. She had shown some interest in the military for a while but never had enlisted. When this cute young barber came to Ulysses months earlier, most of the young women swooned over him, and now my aunt was pregnant with his child. I could see she was in love with him, so by the time they were married in October that year, I figured things must have been turning out all right. My grandparents gave her a traditional wedding at our church and held a reception downstairs. My aunt Vicki was a beautiful bride and wore a lovely traditional gown accompanied by bridesmaids who were also dressed very nicely. I was glad her situation had worked out for her, and the family welcomed her new husband into our ranks. Regardless, that wedding surrounded by its accompanying circumstances reinforced the thought having to get married was something I was never going to do.

Another affair of the heart I watched unfold that summer was equally as interesting and powerful in ways. It involved a young woman named Janet who also worked at the café waiting tables that summer of 1965. Janet was the daughter of Russell Binney, the owner of the small grocery next door. She had graduated high school that spring and planned to leave for college in the fall to study to become a Spanish teacher. She had been an excellent student with very high grades and was just as friendly and pleasant as she was intelligent.

In the Ulysses community at that time was one family of Japanese Americans. Two brothers were both farmers, and one of the brothers was a bachelor who took his meals at my aunt's café. Shigaroo Akagi was small in stature, hardworking, and engaging. Every time Shig would come in to eat, he would sit at the table near the kitchen area, and he and my aunt and uncle would visit as they worked and ate. I came to like this warm, friendly man very much and looked forward to the times he would appear.

One hundred and fifty miles or so up US Highway 50, in Rocky Ford, Colorado, the Akagis had other family. A brother and sister, niece and nephew to the Akagis, both college students, came to Ulysses to work for the summer. My aunt Tibe hired the young woman Sharon Toshiro as a waitress. Sharon was hardworking, intelligent, and easy to be around. I enjoyed getting to know her and working with her. Her brother, Doug, would come to the café to eat, often with his uncle Shig, so I also got acquainted with this friendly, handsome young man.

At first I was very aware of the phenotype of these new friends. I had never been around Asian people of any sort, and the obvious differences in our appearances were new and novel. That newness quickly faded to the background as I got to know who they were, not simply what they looked like. So far in my life, most of the people in my world had been white. There were enough Mexican people in and around Ulysses that brown was nothing unusual either. I had never seen a black or Asian person except on television, so the ethnic exposure I experienced that summer made me feel more grown and left me knowing I had learned something valuable.

Another situation that developed that summer provided me a glimpse of the adult world that resounded with some of the taboos that had been imparted to me a good ten years earlier. As it were, Douglas Toshiro and Janet Binney were taking an interest in one another. Becoming acquainted through interacting at Tibe's Café, they enjoyed one another's company, and before long, Doug asked Janet for a date, and she accepted. As I watched this developing friendship through the eyes of one not even due to start high school for another year, I was excited for my two new friends and at the same time mesmerized. These two young people were several years older than I with many more experiences and comprehension of the world. Janet would be going to college while I was still in junior high school, and Doug had already completed a year or two of college. I knew they were not exactly adults, but they weren't kids either. And they were fixing to break some of the rules we all knew existed. I watched excitedly but nervously as their summer romance played out.

Doug Toshiro drove a fairly new Ford that was a two-toned peach-and-cream color. In my mind's eye, I can see Janet sitting in the middle of the front seat beside him, as couples did back then. I recall their smiling faces and relaxed demeanor with one another as they drove to her uncle's drive-in movie theater. One time they even took me along with them, and the three of us had a grand time laughing and joking and enjoying each other's company. I also remember feeling somewhat tense and on guard because I knew age-old rules were being violated, and such acts also exact a price to be paid. I was grateful and relieved the evening ended without anyone at the drive-in becoming ugly with Doug or Janet or me.

One afternoon that summer, my shift at the café had ended, and I sat waiting for my mother to pick me up. Something had come up at home, and Mom was not going to be able to come get me for a while. Doug had come into the café and, after learning the situation, offered me a ride home. Thankful for his kindness, I accepted his offer, and we departed for Durham Street. This young man was so intelligent, polite, and friendly the two or three miles to my home were pleasant and comfortable. My friend drove into our driveway and stopped his car. I thanked him once again and said goodbye and exited the vehicle. I was happy as I entered the house and glad to be home after another day's work.

My mother stood beyond the front door and living room, at the kitchen sink as I entered the house. The window above the sink looked out at the driveway, and she quickly asked me who had given me a ride. I answered that it was Doug Toshiro, the nephew to the Akagis. As was the case so often with my mother, her silent response spoke volumes. Her face wrinkled into a slight grimace. Immediately I felt defensive, as if I had again done something wrong. I knew exactly what the issue was even though my mother didn't iterate it, nor did I. Doug was not white and that was that. I assured her that he was just a friend and happened to be at the café and offered to give me a ride home. I also knew should the same situation arise again, I would be expected to decline his offer.

If there are degrees of such, my mother was not nearly as racially prejudiced a person as my father was, and I imagined her reaction to my friend Douglas was an indirect way of trying to avoid potential unrest were my dad to find out that I had a friend who was Japanese by blood. With interracial mingling unquestionably taboo and with World War II only nineteen years in the past, I realized most grown-ups in my world regarded Japanese with hostility whether they were American or not. But I had come to look at Douglas and Sharon Toshiro as friends I really liked and were as American as I was. At that moment, I detested Ulysses and its inhabitants, my parents, the whole world, for such inane mores. I was also reminded that in more and more ways, I was not a good fit in my family and even the community.

Even though I never found myself without a way home again that summer, had the same situation arisen, I have no doubt I would have broken society's code a second time.

That summer was productive, very enjoyable, and very beneficial. I purchased nice clothes in which to begin my eighth grade year. I had spending money with which I bought plenty of 45-rpm and long-play record albums. I went to the swimming pool often after work in the afternoon and always had a fun time there. Thanks to becoming a member of the workforce of tax-paying citizens at age thirteen, I had found a way to improve my situation significantly in a number of ways.

All too soon, though, that eventful summer was bygone, and it was time to start school. Working had increased me in several important ways, not the least of which was my weight. Too many restaurant meals and ice cream sundaes added ten pounds to my weight, and I tipped the scales at 165 pounds. That new high meant my internal sliding scale registering hopefulness about boys fell to a new low. This vicious stressor coexisted with a solid confidence I felt from having held and succeeded at a paying job.

Money generally made life a lot easier, and having a job proved to have other worthwhile benefits as well. Working elevated me to a noticeably different status domestically. Most noticeable was that I was not at home for eight to nine hours a day, six days a week. While home life was tolerable, it was oftentimes a crapshoot. Within our home, there were no dramatic tirades or loud, menacing arguments or drunken brawls that enabled the outside world to view our suffering and torment. In fact, it was the very absence of such undeniable indicators of distress and anguish that served to keep our family dynamics painfully manageable and hopelessly unaddressed.

In Ulysses, a new junior high school had just been completed, which meant that Lonnie and I would be going to school clear across town on Missouri Street. That amounted to a walk-in excess of a mile or so one way. In the mid 1960s, there was not the fear and danger associated with kids walking to and from school like there is presently, so we had a lot of fun with friends on the way to and from school. We would take detours as we liked, stop at the drugstores for fountain drinks and snacks as we crossed Main Street, and do a lot of socializing all along the way. Unfortunately, by this time the small electric piano Mom had bought three years earlier that afforded Gayla and me a way to learn piano had been sold off and with it a very large chunk of my heart.

In the fall of 1964, Hickok School was on the very east edge of town. Being brand-new meant everything in it was also brand-new. It was like a brand-new home, and I loved the scent of its newness, the spaciousness of the hallways and classrooms, the different architecture and color schemes, the whole shebang. Another incredible aspect of going to that school that year was that as an eighth grader, I was one of the top dogs! The school housed sixth-, seventh-, and eighth-grade classes, and the feeling of superiority, importance, and accomplishment I felt in a school where I was at the top of the totem pole was intoxicating. I thought, if it felt this good to be an eighth grader, it must feel exhilarating to be a senior in high school!

At Hickok School, my homeroom assignment was with the two physical education teachers, Ms. Jones and Mr. Pollum. I was fascinated with Ms. Jones. She was the first young teacher I had had since second grade, and she was very pretty, with an olive blush to her skin and almond-shaped green eyes that were striking. She was friendly and relaxed and much more approachable than the older women teachers I had had in years gone by. Not only that, Ms. Jones was more like I was. By this time, I had my full growth and was five feet, nine inches tall. Ms. Jones and I looked eye to eye in height, and we were also close in size. She was not short and not even petite. For the first time I had a teacher that was young, pretty, and large like me. Just as importantly, she looked very attractive even though she was bigger than most women. She wore a white polo-style top most of the time and white shorts and always had a whistle hanging around her neck. Feeling like it was too good to be true, this teacher also treated me very nicely. I could tell she liked me and, unlike Mrs. Russell the year before, acted interested in everyone and wanted everyone to succeed. Getting to be around Ms. Jones two hours a day, in home-room and in physical education, was another one of the pleasantries of attending Hickok School.

During the winter of that school year, I experienced a profound event that still seems as though it happened only yesterday. One of my friends at school was a Mexican girl named Viola Gutierrez. She was petite with dark-black hair, wore glasses with cat-eye frames, and was easy and fun to be around. Her parents rented my grand-mother's house on Main Street, so Viola lived in the same house I had during my second grade in school, the same house in which my dad's coworker had molested me. Through our friendship, I had become acquainted with her mother, sister, and other family mem-bers, who were always welcoming and friendly to me when I would stop by with Viola.

One cold Saturday evening, Viola was riding with her brother and sister on the way to Lakin, twenty-five miles or so north of Ulysses, to attend a dance. Her brother was driving, lost control of the car, and wrecked, and Viola was killed in that accident.

I didn't learn about it till I got to school Monday morning, and when I did hear the news, I was numb with shock. The death of my friend, a young girl who died unexpectedly and violently, was too much for my mind to process. Back then there was no thought of going home because of such news. There were no counselors brought in to talk to whoever might be upset. There was not even any men-tion of it over the public address system. There was just business as usual.

Ironically, that tragedy was handled at school in much the way things were handled within my family. There was no mention of it, no discussion about the girl, her death, her absence, or our feelings. It was almost like it never happened, and if it never happened, there was no reason to discuss it, let alone be affected by sadness and grief.

During math class in the middle of the day, the teacher did bring up the awful news, and I suppose he deserves credit for that, but what he said and the way he said it left me abhorred, and from that moment forward, I despised Mr. Carl Will.

After we students were in our chairs, books were put away, and we were ready to begin our lesson, Mr. Will stood up from his desk located at the front of the classroom. He started, "I guess you have probably all heard about Viola by now." He continued with two or three more sentences and then he finished. With emphasis on the word *she*, he concluded, "She won't be coming back to class." There was no expression of sorrow for her or any of her family or her friends. Even if they were meant well, his words were without sympathy and could have been referring to a cow out in a field. His poor delivery was worse than if he had said nothing at all. For a second or two, I actually thought he was going to chuckle, and I wanted to scream at him. Perhaps he was upset and was inept at dealing with his emotions, but it was an awful misstep and was instantly seared into my memory.

He paused a moment or two, then turned away from us, strode to the chalkboard, and without further comment or transition from the sad subject at hand, his talk turned toward math.

Viola was Mexican, a year or two older than we other eighth graders, from a family of no means who worked hard just to provide the basics, but they were generous, friendly, loving people, and her life was just as important as anyone else's. Because of the way the school did not handle the situation of losing one of their students, I was left feeling a kind of a distance from people of my own color and culture around this tragedy. The facts of it all would take a long time to digest and opened my eyes to more of life's value, its frailty, and the many harsh realities contained therein.

That day after school, I stopped at Viola's house on my way home. Her sister Mary answered the door when I knocked, and we embraced one another and began to cry. I told her how sorry I was.

She thanked me and told me to come in. I stepped inside, where I immediately saw Mrs. Gutierrez sitting on the sofa to the right of me. I was completely unprepared for what else I beheld. Viola's casket with her body inside it was to the left there in the living room. I had never even been to a funeral and had seen only one dead body years ago, a baby my aunt had lost at birth. Now to see my friend dead and lying in a casket in the living room of my grandparents' house was surreal. I was becoming overwhelmed when Mrs. Gutierrez took my hand and bade me to sit down beside her. We hugged one another and sat there crying as I expressed my condolences. She thanked me and said she knew I loved Viola, which made my tears come harder and faster.

After a few minutes she arose, took my hand, and guided me over to the casket. I felt like I was dreaming a horrible nightmare. I was saddened yet curious in a way. This girl I had talked and laughed with, with whom I had walked side by side only three days earlier, now lay there stone cold in a casket, dressed in what looked like a bridal gown. It was more than my young mind could really comprehend. Viola's body had no scratches or cuts or bruises that were visible. She looked like she might just be sleeping except there was an unnatural stillness and lack of expression that screamed of her finality. She really was gone, dead, her body forever stilled, her laughter and our talks now only history. Such things require time to seep down to the core of one's understanding, and the full measure of this loss was only beginning its descent.

I left that house much changed. A lot of life-changing experiences had happened to me in that house, today's sadness only the latest. Some fifty years later, I still visit the grave marked by the heart-shaped headstone with an eighth grader's photo fixed in it. Each time I do so, I feel a sense of timelessness as I also revisit the acute sense of loss and sadness I suffered so many years ago, when this friend of mine was jerked out of the lives of us who loved her.

By this time, I had become a teenager, and around me, boys and girls were becoming increasingly interested in those of the opposite gender. For so long I had felt like an albatross because of my very early puberty, but that was no longer the case. Most of the girls my age were wearing bras, and a good percentage had begun having their monthly periods as I had already been doing for two years. A large number of us eighth-grade girls had also begun wearing a bit of makeup, and our appearance was becoming more important, and in a different way.

Each day male nature was asserting itself as the boys our age also began to experience puberty and the abundance of testosterone that accompanies the development of secondary sexual characteristics. At ballgames, walking home after school, inside classrooms, down the hallways during class changes, my friends and classmates were beginning to exhibit the telltale signs of romantic interests. I felt vindicated and less alone as this collision of hormones, inexperience, nature, and insecurity combined into that primordial porridge where nothing is well understood, transparent, or comfortable. We youngest teenagers ingested this potion daily with the preordained outcome: a compelling force that propelled us ever nearer the opposite sex.

Since I had been swimming in this soup for a long while, I was a veteran at trying to deal with its burden. Being painfully self-aware mixed with ungraceful attempts to manage burgeoning changes in bodies, attitudes, and expectations left no student unscathed although some were better than others at fabricating and maintaining a facade that provided some protection against the travails of this new complexity.

Entrenched buttresses like good looks, favorable status, high-end clothing, pleasing physiques and builds, and envious talents like athleticism might mean one could possibly traverse this maelstrom with some self-esteem and confidence intact. Most of us, though, were left to discover our strengths and utilize whatever skills we might possess or develop, to provide the best chance at surviving this storm. We eighth graders were on the ascent portion of our journey, and we would encounter many pitfalls before our metamorphosis into novice adults was complete.

Even though I had been dealing with this vexing time of life longer than most of my peers, I was no more adroit than they. To the contrary, the weight of my juvenescence simply compounded the burdens my mind and soul already harbored. None of my load was being resolved to where it could be jettisoned. Inside I was like a teamster fighting to regain control of a runaway span of horses while being pursued by bandits in the dark of night, over road washed out by torrents and gales. Notwithstanding, I was expected to safely deliver the coach full of souls who had entrusted their lives to me. The torment I lived with was inescapable.

With each friend or classmate who rejoiced that so-and-so had walked them home from school or called them the night before on the telephone, I smiled with my mouth while wincing inside, choking over the awful presumption that I would be sharing no such story with anyone anytime soon, if ever. Bone-weary from life's grindings, I looked for something that would make me feel better about myself and possibly even look better.

I turned toward my aunt Karen. Always a loving, caring figure in my life, she also enjoyed working with hair. After consulting with Karen about a new look for me, the two of us petitioned my mother for permission to execute our plan. Undoubtedly my dad was away from home working, because I cannot imagine he would have ever conceded to my pleadings. My mother completely surprised me when she gave Karen the okay to change my hair color. Not about to take a chance on Mom having a change of heart, my aunt and I quickly set about peroxiding my strawberry blond tresses till they looked more Nordic. I was very pleased and excited with the outcome of our afternoon's efforts, and after my aunt rolled and styled my hair, I felt strangely powerful, quite mysterious, and beautiful.

A friend of mine had also worn down her mother enough that Mrs. Mildred Moore's daughter, my friend Debbie, also showed up at school that Monday morning with her brunette hair dyed nearly black. As pretty as I felt with my new hair color, a part inside me also realized I was pushing the envelope by this lack of adherence to some of the social mores in place at that time. That same part of me was a bit jittery, but I wasn't about to let anyone realize it.

None of the girls our age had dyed or bleached their hair before, so the attention we received was genuine if not favorable. Reactions were as varied as the shades of blond from which I had picked my color. Boys said very little, as if they were intimidated. Most girls said they liked our hair but asked how we ever convinced our mothers to let us do that. Others said nothing, which actually said a lot, but I figured they were jealous, were prudes, or stuck-up snobs. I was experiencing that adage about the wrong kind of attention being better than no attention at all. Besides, it wasn't any more uncomfortable than anything else I had had to live with for so long.

That afternoon when the time came for American history class, I entered the classroom as I always did and took my seat. Sitting at his desk, the teacher, Mr. Jim Farley, looked at me. At first surprise clearly registered in his face, but his gaze fixed on me, and the longer he looked, the darker his expression became. As disapproving as his expression was, he might as well have been yelling at me with words. My friend Debbie was in Farley's class with me, and throughout the period, if he wasn't looking at me, he was looking at her. He managed to present the lesson and conduct the rest of class, and I was relieved when the bell rang. I stood up to make a quick exit, but it wasn't to be. Mr. Farley called out my name and Debbie's and motioned for us to approach his desk, which we did. Standing side by side, our arms wrapped around our textbooks and the large three-ring cloth binder each of us carried, Debbie and I had not anticipated this turn of events.

"What in the world do you girls think you are doing? Why did you do that to your hair?" he posed.

Feeling somewhat chastised but also defiant, I replied, "It's no big deal, Mr. Farley. We just dyed our hair."

He then asked with a demanding voice, "Well, what do your parents think?"

By this time our teacher, who had been standing but leaning backward against the chalkboard with his arms crossed over his chest, his signature pencil wedged between the top of his right ear and his head, quickly shifted his weight to his feet and shoved his hands into both pants pockets so forcefully I thought I heard fabric ripping.

When I gingerly answered that my mother had given her permission, he seemed at a loss for words. He then looked toward Debbie, and his eyes bore into her, demanding an explanation. She cautiously told him her parents didn't care if she dyed her hair. Mr.

Farley stood there involuntarily shaking his head, as though it were a muscle tic over which he had no control. At thirteen years, I had some idea about the correlation between harlots and dyed hair, but I knew not everyone with dyed hair was a chippie, as Uncle Reed often called such women. Although he managed restraint in his words, Mr. Farley's body language screamed outrage.

Still alternating between looking confounded and incensed, our teacher cleared his throat and folded his arms across his chest, as if protecting himself from us. Whether more for his sake or ours, the bell mercifully sounded for the next class period to commence. I said to him, "Mr. Farley, we're late for science." Without a word, he picked up a pad of hall pass forms from the top of his desk. He paused a couple of times while writing our excuse on that form, as if intruding thoughts kept breaking his concentration. As he extended his arm to hand me the form, it was as if he didn't want to let go of the form so we could be on our way. His tense posture, squinted eyes, and clenched jaw told me there were things he wanted to say but was holding back. That was one time, however, that I didn't freeze up and become mute and immobile. My hand darted from my side and latched on to the pass as my body was turning away from him and his desk, toward the rear of the room and doorway. His censure was intense and unsettling, and in days of yore, I could imagine Debbie Moore and me possibly winding up tied to a stake as the main event at a public bonfire. The things kids do.

As the title of a Madonna song expresses, I managed to "live to tell" about this harrowing (hair-owing) experience that elicited strong reactions from different people, not the least of which was my history teacher. We girls dyed our hair in the spring, and not long thereafter, eighth grade was history. To this day when I look at my eighth-grade graduation photo, I see a beautiful young face with eyes that are illuminating portals to a gentle soul and which could easily melt a heart. I also see a wistful smile that contradicts itself with accumulated burden lying unresolved behind it.

The dishwashing / prep worker job I had at my aunt's café during the summer whetted my appetite for my own money to the point I could not go backward and not have any. As a sophomore in high school, Gayla was taking in ironings and babysitting to make money. In turn, she hired me to iron her clothes, and I gladly accepted the job. I also made money babysitting occasionally at first and more as time progressed. During high school, I did ironings too, cleaned houses, babysat for occasional jobs and full-time jobs during the summers. Work was salvation in several important ways and something I turned to more and more as time went past.

Spring came and with it went my grade school years. Hickok School staff conducted their official graduation ceremony, and that rite of passage surely put the icing on my cake. No longer shackled with an ordinal number identifying my grade level in school, I eagerly anticipated starting school in the fall as a member of the freshman class at the large, impressive buildings that comprised Grant County Rural High School. Graduating from junior high school imbued me with a sense of power and achievement, and I could barely contain the excitement I felt about how different my life might be as a high school student.

Because I had always earned good grades in school, I had no concern about the academic aspects of high school. Being a freshman among all the upperclassmen didn't bother me either. After all, my mother had assured me many times that I was mature for my age, and being around older boys would mean I was more likely to be noticed and appreciated by such guys. The scarred, scared part of me that was starving for attention, affection, and validation was becoming more difficult to fend off with every day that passed. The part of my soul where such needs were located housed a withered, feeble shut-in made nearly invalid by too many searing instances of disregard from boys whose attention I yearned for, from my parents whose own pathologies and troubles too often left only orts with which to nourish that part of me. Years of emotional famine had extracted a commensurate toll on my siblings and me, yet the manifestations of this hardship were as varied and distinct as our five personalities. I was a bit nervous about beginning high school, but my excitement about what lay ahead far outweighed any reservation I experienced.

Unfortunately, that summer I could not return to work at my aunt's café. During the course of the school year, their situation had changed. Her husband's mother had died and left a house, property, and farmland in estate. Consequently, they decided to move to Big Bow, ten miles or so west of Ulysses, and farm on that land. Much to my chagrin (and the folks of Ulysses), Tibe's Café was history.

That summer I earned money whenever the opportunity presented itself but was largely bored and dissatisfied that I had no forty-hour-a-week job, but at age fourteen, I was still too young to hold most jobs since age sixteen was the magic number for most businesses to consider hiring a teenager. Always happy to be able to spend time with either of my grandmothers, midsummer I went to my grandparents' farm near Lakin, a half hour's drive north of Ulysses. I adored my grandmother, and she always treated me like the feelings were mutual. She was cultivating an enormous garden that I helped her attend, and I got to see my aunts Tibe and Ruby and my half a dozen cousins when they would visit for the day.

My uncle Dale lived at the farm too, out back in the same old trailer where we had lived two years earlier while Dad recuperated from being crushed. After we left the Stever place, my grandparents had moved the trailer to the farm outside Lakin, and it was a place for menfolk to bunk as needed. After Dale had arrived home from work in the evening and my grandfather was in from the fields, family time was great. As with so many men, Uncle Dale showed attention via joking and teasing rather than touch or kind words. In its own way, that felt just as good because the love he expressed with his indirect style was heartfelt and consistent.

As my grandmother prepared the supper meal, the aroma of potatoes and hamburgers frying, homegrown vegetables heating up on the stove, garden-grown tomatoes and onions being sliced for use with the hamburgers would have made a vegan's mouth water.

From home-made juice for breakfast accompanied by pork my grandparents had raised and butchered, to fried potatoes covered with gravy, and homemade bread that had been toasted on both sides in a skillet then slathered with homemade jelly, meals from my grandmother's kitchen were as close to heaven as one on earth could get! The woman was an excellent cook of plain but delicious Americana delights. She had raised nine children, cooked for many hired hands and harvest crews, turned out many a meal in restaurants as a divorced woman in the 1940s, and any who sat at her table saw their appetites fully and deliciously sated.

The better part of a month I spent there was relaxing, productive, and edifying, the kind of times that result in precious family memories. With one appalling exception, my step-grandfather proved to be a lecherous old man who saw an opportunity to prey on a young girl and indulge his disgusting urges.

It was afternoon. I was in my grandmother's kitchen busy at the sink washing fresh vegetables we had harvested from her garden earlier in the day. She was busy doing laundry, and out the window above the sink, I could see her hanging wet clothes to dry. I heard the back door being opened and could tell by the very heavy steps and creak of the floor it was my grandfather. He stood well over six feet with a large frame and carried a lot of weight, at least four hundred pounds, give or take a few score. Soon he stepped into the kitchen and over to the sink where I stood.

"Hi, Frannie, what'cha doing there?" he queried.

"Just washing up these vegetables for Grama," I replied. He could see Grandma through the window too, and I am sure her absence cinched his decision.

He was standing so close beside me our bodies were touching. Immediately I knew he was up to no good. Instead of walking away or otherwise taking any action, I simply stood there, as I had done so many times in my life, frozen again. It was as if I were standing in a road with a car bearing down on me, knowing I was in mortal danger but unable to move a muscle, as if standing still might make me invisible and somehow cause the danger to evaporate.

My grandfather didn't evaporate, though, and for years thereafter, I punished myself thinking, because I didn't move, he must have thought I was all right with what he did. Looking straight ahead so he was able to keep sight of my grandmother, he moved closer and put his extremely big, heavy, smelly arm around my shoulders and pulled me snug against him.

"You know you sure are getting pretty and growing up," he said as he lifted my right arm from behind and slid his hand under it and around to the front of my blouse. "Yes, you sure are pretty." And his coarse, rough fingers began pawing my sizeable breast. He cupped my breast, felt for the nipple, and uttered an uncontrollable sigh. He continued rubbing my breast in a circular motion while emitting guttural sounds of sexual excitement. Finally he cupped my breast from beneath and gave it a slight squeeze. He was quite excited, and I…I stood dead still while he satisfied his lust sufficiently with the time he had at hand and loosed his grip around my torso. He said nothing further. Once again I died inside, as I had done years earlier at the hands of my uncle and my dad's coworker.

I don't know how this molestation would have ended otherwise, but thankfully, my grandmother finished hanging the clothes she was pinning to the line, picked up the basket, and began walking toward the house. Of course, when the excited predator whom I had always known as my grandfather saw his wife was nearing, he withdrew his hand from my breast, arm from around my shoulders, mutely turned, and walked out of the kitchen into the living room. He was sitting in his easy chair by time my grandmother walked through the living room toward me in the kitchen.

"Mama"—the term with which he generally addressed my grandmother—"I sure could use a glass of iced tea," he said to his wife. I continued to stare down into the sink at the vegetables, aware only of how cold the water felt as it ran over my hands. My mind was otherwise empty. I had flipped off the switch inside my head and tried not to think or feel. At the same time, that most wounded, scarred, ailing part of me retreated even deeper inside me, seeking a safe place to hide.

"Frannie, are you about done there?" I heard a voice ask as though it were far away. My grandmother was now at my side, the one opposite where a few moments earlier my grandfather had stood. In the other sink she was busy with the ice pick, breaking up the ice she had removed from a coffee can she filled with water and used to make ice for drinks.

"I'll be done in a minute, Grama" was my answer. She filled an empty twenty-four-ounce glass with ice, then poured tea she had brewed over it, turned, and carried the cold drink to her husband.

I finished the vegetables I had been rinsing off, laid them to the side of the sink, onto the wave work area where one could also place a drain rack for dishes. Then I walked into the bathroom, locked the door, leaned against a wall, and cried without shedding a tear. Eventually I slid down the wall and sat folded against it and tried to hang on to the numbness that was buoying me. Later, after I heard my latest molester leave the house, I rejoined my grandmother.

Ninth Grade

August 1965 was drawing to a close and starting the school year was just around the corner. Overall I was hopeful, actually depending on high school to be a far different social experience than the last few years had been. I was ready to enjoy this new experience, to participate in all the adventure it had to offer, and to reap the benefits of the effort I was ready to give.

Before school had ended in the spring, I received a letter from the debate coach at the high school inviting me to consider joining the debate team. That single letter flattered me greatly and affirmed that I was desirable in some regard. Me. Debate team. Wow. It never occurred to me *not* to join the debate team. It never occurred to me that a good number of my classmates had probably received the same letter without having the reaction I did. In the debate class were students from all four grades of high school. I really enjoyed being in class with the older students, and they all seemed to accept me and the one other freshman in the class. The resolution we were debating was one about collective bargaining and was very heady. Such language and format was completely new to me, but I dug in and listened to the lectures about the art of arguing and methods of researching the topic. I listened to the other students as they participated in practice debate rounds on the ministage in the debate room. When it was my turn, I gave it my best effort.

I was a member of the debate squad for two years. Although I was never a good debater and had a commensurate win-loss record, I benefitted greatly from the experience. One of the most impressive and enjoyable benefits of this experience was traveling to various towns to debate in tournaments. I was flabbergasted to learn the school would pay for us debaters to stay in nice motels and would pay for us to eat in restaurants. I felt so important and thoroughly enjoyed going, seeing, doing in a style that denoted support, respect, and comfort. Traveling most of the time in our coach's fancy car, spending time in close quarters with the seniors, juniors, and sophomores, interacting with students who valued public speaking, thinking through issues, and keeping up on current events empowered me. Laughing, joking, and having the camaraderie of team members strengthened me.

As well as debate, I was a member of the high school marching and concert bands that year and every year of high school. During my freshman year, I also joined the Pep Club, Y-Teens, intramural sports for girls, auditioned for and landed a role in the all-school play, played my French horn in ensembles, and participated in forensic tournaments doing dramatic readings. Overall I was exceedingly active in extracurricular activities and, with my studies, achieved honor roll status most marking periods. I enjoyed everything in which I participated and was earnestly investing myself in all with which I was involved. For a time, my heart floated upward, and I felt more optimistic about encountering life's favor in the steps I trod.

My mother was right about one thing. I did enjoy being around older boys. In band I sat second chair, first part that landed me squarely beside a young man who was a senior. Not only was he tall, dark, and handsome, he was an exceptionally accomplished French horn player who qualified by audition for a national high school band and had toured with them during the summer. Allen Williams was a celebrity of sorts in my world, a musician with a talent and mastery I revered. He was also quiet, soft-spoken, and without need to be loud, boisterous, or boastful like so many young men. Best of all, he seemed to like me despite my being only a freshman, so my days in band I floated through on a hormone haze. Allen did have a serious girlfriend, so my adoration of him was without romantic notions. Even if he hadn't had a girlfriend, he was so far above me the gap could never have been closed enough during that time of my life to allow that kind of daydream. I was quite content to simply be as close to him as playing my horn afforded. When that year ended and this Adonis graduated, his absence made my heart ache all through my sophomore year.

All around me boys and girls were showing more interest in one another and acting on that interest. There were dances held at the old high school gymnasium on a regular basis, and out of desperation, I did risk heartbreak and attended a few. Again I decided to heed my mother's exhortations and trust that older boys would recognize what the younger ones failed to see in me. Unfortunately, my mother's encouraging words were simply that, and the handful of times I attended school dances that fall and winter was simply more salt in my wounds.

The only boy at those dances who ever asked me to dance with him was the one whose invitation signified I belonged to that group of girls who didn't measure up to the standard of appealing boys. If no one except Inez Moreno asked a girl to dance, her status as an untouchable was clear. Since attractive guys deemed me an outcast to the dating world, I would be prospective only to a boy (Inez or his peer) whose standing, also determined by rejection by the opposite sex, indicated he was equally repugnant.

Unable to appreciate that like I, Inez might have been a person worth knowing, I loathed him as a loser. The sad truth is that the hearts of spurned, mistreated, overlooked people often grow hard and mean instead of more compassionate and empathetic. Their unmet need for validation, attention, affection, tenderness, and caring swells like a tumor whose destruction is uncontrollable. This insistent necessity consumes the souls and futures of the hapless and forlorn because that is the nature of disease.

Even sadder, to the opposite sex, I granted absolute dominion over my feelings and reactions. Their opinions and choices might as well have come from God himself, as much value as I placed in them. My logic seemed infallible, and once again, the burden of unbearable sadness, crippling disappointment, and unspeakable longing that coursed through my vessels was an obscene, deadly load I sustained every moment of every day. So many years and too many disasters would occur in my life before I began to realize a different truth and begin to heal.

Despite the pain of being a girl no desirable boy wanted anything to do with, one question persisted: why? What made me so unpleasing to boys? When I looked in the mirror, I liked the face I saw. I was big and somewhat overweight, but there were homely girls and overweight girls who had boyfriends. This perplexity truly baffled me.

The toll of such rejection and devaluation for so long by so many had already been enormous in my life. Below my surface, in my innermost core rested a cauldron. For fifteen years it had been the repository of life's bitterest gall. The countless tears it held was the broth in which the bile of unhealed and unresolved pain simmered into a toxic mixture that would make the grandest wizard's most potent potion seem like infants' Pablum. Like a gestating fetus, this brew took up more space each day. New injuries and defilements slid down the chute from the outside world and plopped into the vat to accumulate with all the rest of the gore. The romantic disregard exhibited toward me was the catalyzing ingredient of this brew of misery. After rendering down, what was left was the pure toxin of accumulating anger and an indescribable desperation.

During the fall of 1965, homecoming was not far away when one day I was shocked, repulsed, and elated all at the same time. A boy asked me to go with him to the homecoming dance! Mike Allen was a sophomore who attended the same church as me. He stood nearly six and a half feet tall and was very thin, which made him appear even taller than he was. He suffered from a pronounced case of acne and simply was not my idea of handsome or intriguing. I was taken completely by surprise when Mike asked me to be his date, and I kind of froze when approached. Inside I was screaming "Yuck, no!" but with my mouth and vocal cords I said yes.

To this day I have no idea if his actions were driven by a sincere interest in me or the simple desire to have a date for the homecoming dance, but I do recall that waiting for the week to pass until homecoming arrived was no less difficult than had I not been asked to the dance by a boy. Because I automatically assigned Mike Allen the same status as Inez at the dances, I was inconsolable. I kept thinking, *What if he tries to kiss me? What if he tries to hold my hand?* Being asked out by this young man reinforced my vile pathological belief system.

After the homecoming football game, I dashed the three blocks to my house and changed from my band uniform into the dress I was going to wear to the dance. Mike arrived on time, and my mother answered the door and invited him in. He came inside, and I hurriedly made my way from the kitchen into the living room where he stood. We exchanged greetings, and he helped me on with my coat. My mother wished us a good time, and we began to make our way to the dance, walking under the fall moon in the crisp, evening air of autumn the three blocks to the old gymnasium at the high school.

Mike was a polite and mannerly date. He tried to make conversation and did nothing wrong except be himself. I was not attracted to him, not interested in him, put off by his looks, and didn't want to be on a date with him, so nothing he could have done would have helped much. The fault for my unease was mine. I should have thanked him for asking me to the dance and graciously declined his invitation if the idea of going on a date with him was so insufferable. Although that sounds simple, I was as far from that kind of presence and good manners as east is from west. Mike Allen had stumbled into the minefield that constituted my emotional makeup and in which I was hopelessly mired.

Finally the dance was nearing its end when Mike excused himself, saying he would be right back. A few minutes later, he did return and announced that he had asked someone to give us a ride home from the dance. Instantly I was mortified, embarrassed, and fuming. That approach seemed almost like we were a charity case and went completely against my grain. How dare my date assume I would be all right with that approach to transportation? I walked to the dance and I was fully prepared to walk the three blocks home from the dance. His plan for transportation should have been handled before this juncture, and I was most offended at his lack of planning, even resources. Never having been in this situation before, I bit my lip and walked with Mike to the parking lot and to the car of the Good Samaritan.

The evening was getting no easier. The car was a two-door with bucket seats in the front, which meant Mike and I had to get into the back seat together. I could feel my pulse throbbing in my temples as my nerves frayed. The close confines of the car's back seat meant I had to sit uncomfortably close to my date, and I was very concerned he might try to put his arm around me or touch me somehow. During the short ride to Durham Street, my mind raced. I was sure if he tried to kiss me good night, I would vomit then and there. Traveling three and a half blocks seemed an eternity, but finally the car came to a halt in the driveway where I lived. Mike leaned forward and found the door handle, then pushed the door open enough that he was able to unfold himself from the back seat of the vehicle and get out. Then it was my turn, and he extended his hand to mine and helped me unfurl as well. In one fluid motion, I stood up, thanked him for a nice time, and was up the five steps and to our stoop and inside the house so quickly I doubt he even had time to utter "good night." As it turned out, that was my first and my last date during high school.

Despite a nearly desperate need for reciprocity from boys to whom I was attracted, I was my own saboteur at ever achieving what I wanted. I was also my own savior from the likely effects of getting the attention, affection, and validation for which I was starved. Through older eyes, I have given thanks scores of times that my life was devoid of any romance. Never having received sufficient attention or affection from my father, the one whose responsibility it was to nurture that part of me, I grew up looking to romantic attention as the magic bullet to meet my emotional needs.

The weight of my unmet need for recognition, attention, affection, and encouragement would have manifested in ways no teenage romance was meant to encompass or sustain. Any simple, lighthearted, fun dating life soon would have been crushed by the weight of issues not meant to be resolved through dating and attention from a boyfriend. All that I needed but hadn't received from my father as an infant daughter forward was snowballing in its urgency and debilitation.

This plague of suffering for young girls was nothing new back in the 1960s and persists in its consumption of countless futures and abilities of females altering lifetimes of mothers and offspring and interfering with achievements that might have been. I was only one of countless souls afflicted with this curse and its effects. Though I did not think about it all in these kinds of terms then, during my ninth-grade year, girls began dropping by the wayside due to this scourge.

One classmate with whom I had become friends my sixth-grade year, during my semester at the Red Rock country school, was the first statistic. As a young child, her mother had died, and life with a subsequent stepmother proved disastrous for Bonnie Allen. Petite, cute, intelligent, and outwardly jovial, she became pregnant during our freshman school year. A girl who should have been popular and successful instead became the girlfriend of a guy several years older, a guy whose name evoked only negative responses when mentioned, a guy regarded as trouble and one easily pictured as winding up in jail along the way, a guy most girls would have been repelled by rather than attracted to.

In a few short months, it had become common knowledge around school that Bonnie was pregnant by Art Epperson. In the 1960s, a girl in this situation was not common, and when it did occur, the reaction was quite different than in schools presently. Pregnant teenagers were looked down upon not only for engaging in sex before marriage but even more so for "getting caught." As a collective, we had been taught doing so was immoral and fell short of the Bible's teaching. Immoral or not, a pissant could figure out being pregnant without being married at any age would make life for the baby and the mother extra challenging and more difficult. The situation would embarrass and distress the families of those involved. Being an unwed pregnant teen was bad enough; being in that situation as a very young teen was even more scandalous.

Married or not, being pregnant as a teenager is a situation uniformly rejected as a good idea nowadays because teenagers are not adults, and babies need the benefit of adult minds and resources to maximize their chances of health and well-being. Teenagers having babies are a drag to families, communities, and societies. That truth was understood, and coupled with the accompanying stigma, the incidence of teenage pregnancy during the 1960s was seventy or so out of every one thousand. The majority of girls in this situation married before delivering their baby. A number of them were sent away with an accompanying tale meant to cover up the truth of pregnancy and to facilitate adopting out the infant when it was born. Through my high school years in Ulysses, I knew of no one who simply stayed in town and had their baby as a single mother, whether they were a legal minor or not.

Nevertheless, the drumbeat of this tragedy was always present, and despite the risk and stress of engaging in sex, there were those who did and those who conceived pursuant to that choice. Bonnie Allen was that girl in our freshman class of approximately ninety students. As disconcerting as my aunt Vicky's pregnancy had been, she was in fact a high school graduate and was a legal adult. Bonnie was three or four years from being either.

The utter shock I felt when I heard the gossip that turned out to be true caused my mouth to gape and stifled my voice. When I found my voice, I could say only, "Oh my god!" The shock eventually receded, and in its place I experienced a nauseating mixture of sorrow, anger, and disgust toward this girl with whom I had enjoyed sleepovers, laughter, and an edifying friendship during that difficult winter on the farm after my father was gravely injured. After my family and I moved to Hickok and I reentered school in town, I no longer saw Bonnie regularly but valued and missed her as a friend, a classmate, a peer. Now as ninth graders, our paths diverged abruptly, dramatically, and permanently. Not dead in the physical sense like my friend Viola the year before, Bonnie was nevertheless instantly transported out of the world of opportunity, advancement, upward mobility, and the hopeful possibilities that a half-grown teen should be looking forward to. She never reappeared. She was forever removed from the world of those of us her own age. To her former life as a member of the class of 1969, she was history.

Before her baby was born, Bonnie and Art Epperson were married, and the differences in the facts of our lives are things about which I can only speculate.

After the emotional gamut of the homecoming dance and first date, autumn gave way to winter. During the course of that frosty season, I developed an ardor for a classmate of Mike Allen's.

Duane Harbour was the fourth in a family of five boys. His three older brothers, in the age group of my aunts Karen and Vicki, were very good-looking, testosterone-rich young men of few words and reserved demeanors that made the young women of Ulysses all but swoon. Duane was also on the quiet side but without the sultry sexiness of his older brothers. He was a bit taller than I with a neat, clean appearance and the brightest red hair that made him stand out in a crowd. Even though it was always from a distance, I was drawn to his quiet nature, clearly exhibiting no need to be loud and gross and vulgar as so many his age were. I developed a serious crush on this sophomore boy.

One of my friends from debate class who was a senior was also on the yearbook staff. Aware of the crush I had on Duane, she surprised me one day with a photo of him she had appropriated from among photos in the yearbook work area. Other than Duane actually showing interest in me, nothing could have been more appealing. I carried that black and white photo in my wallet through the end of my tenth-grade year, fantasizing how he would approach me, how it might feel to hold hands with him, how it might feel to know he was thinking about me or looking for me in the hallways during class changes, or buying me a box of Valentine candy. It was a world of hope full of delights and scenarios I rehearsed in my head over and over, what to do if he ever tried to kiss me or ask me on a date. Just in case, I wanted to be ready and not blow it.

One afternoon in the spring of 1966, I was walking from my grandmother's laundromat past Joyce School, where I had attended elementary school years earlier. On the west side of the school in the playground area, there were several high school-aged boys playing a game of basketball. Immediately I caught sight of the bright red hair and my heart leapt. As I continued to walk between the tall chain-link fence cordoning off the playground and the curb of Central Avenue, I sensed Duane was actually looking at me, and my heart began to race.

Any other girl probably would have walked as slowly as possible without looking obvious. Not I. As badly as I wanted to catch his eye and hopefully his attention, I reacted with utter panic. I felt almost terrified as I realized Duane had apparently excused himself from the game and was advancing in my direction. The fence ended up ahead where the playground met the school bus parking garage. At the rate he was moving, he would arrive at the garage about the time I did.

I wanted nothing more than for this dream boy to approach me, and now it seemed he was in the process of doing just that. So many times in my life I had frozen in place when I should have run. This day I ran when it might have behooved me to stay put! Suddenly I began walking as fast as I could, even breaking into a quicker gait several times until there was nearly a block between Duane and me. Naturally my behavior communicated a message to this prince. What was he to think? Eventually he stopped, turned around, and walked back toward the schoolyard and basketball game. He never made another move toward me, understandably.

I was beside myself with disappointment, anger, and confusion. Of what was I so afraid? Why did I become completely unnerved? How was I ever going to change? This inner part of who I was, was perplexing, exasperating, and kept me tethered to a puzzle to which I could not find the key. Ironically it was the antithesis of who I was in all other ways.

Being a debater and competing in forensic competitions were building confidence within me. I had roles in two school plays that year and enjoyed performing in front of audiences. More than once I participated in activities that called for me to speak at a podium in front of the entire student body and faculty and did so easily with few nerves. Band and ensemble competitions never made me very nervous. At school I was very involved, well-known, and well liked even though I was only a freshman. I was competent, enthusiastic, outgoing, and engaging in my role as a student, club member, family member, and friend. I had many male friends and acquaintances but none who was interested except as a friend.

As a girl longing for romantic interaction with boys, I was inept, paralyzed from an incomprehensible lack of confidence or innate sense of how to conduct myself, how to encourage or ignore advances, how to be a girl. This quandary within me would occupy more and more of my thoughts and feelings without any resolution. Over the course of time, this inner overgrowth would act like a malignancy. It would create intense pain that was ever present as it ate away at vital parts of my psyche, stunted normal emotional functioning, and increased a fear and starvation that exerted more and more control over my all aspects of my life.

In the fall of 1965, I began a close friendship with Vickie Keller, a girl I had known since we were in kindergarten together. As freshmen, we had several classes together and would often work on Algebra homework together. I knew her mother from Brownie Scout days, and our parents were acquainted, so a familiar classmate for years was becoming an actual friend. Vickie's dad owned and operated a vehicle repair shop, and her mother did the office work at the business. Vickie was the second of two children, her older brother two years her senior. Because of the nature of her father's business, access to cars came easy, and after successfully completing driver's education at school that year and gaining her driver's permit, Vickie soon had a car. This status translated into a great deal of freedom and privacy for us two girls.

One of the activities we engaged in privately was experimenting with smoking cigarettes. In my mind, my lopsided logic held that if I were putting a cigarette in my mouth, I probably wouldn't eat as much and hence lose weight. Of course, losing weight was the key and prime requisite for a decent life. This being the case, I would be stupid not to smoke.

For several weeks I felt smug and grown-up but lost not one ounce of weight. I never liked the awful taste smoking left in my mouth, I never could inhale without choking and then coughing violently, and except for the idea of losing weight, I really didn't want to spend any of my money for cigarettes. There were too many things to spend money on that I actually enjoyed. I never became hooked on cigarettes and gave them up after a short spell, moving on to some other means of trying to lose weight. My girlfriend took to cigarettes like a fish does to water and wound up a rather heavy smoker.

Vickie's life and surroundings were a lot different from mine. With her dad a successful business owner and having only two kids to provide for, income level and its disbursement was a far cry from that of my parents. Though not fancy in any way, the Keller home was comfortable and plenty large for four people. In the living room was a beautiful spinet piano, and Vickie took lessons from one of the best piano teachers in town. I didn't envy Vickie about her material possessions except for the piano and her being able to take lessons. She was a resistant student and practiced very little, and I resented her not valuing her good fortune.

One activity the Keller family enjoyed was cooking steaks on the grill. At my home the word *steak* meant round steak that my mom would roast slowly several hours to tenderize and serve as delicious Swiss steak, which we never failed to enjoy. One evening at Vickie's house, her parents invited me to stay for supper, and I gladly accepted. Her dad Floyd was grilling T-bone steaks and said I should stay and eat with them. We had no barbecue grill, nor did anyone else I knew. I had seen my aunt Tibe prepare many steaks on the grill at her café but had never eaten one. That evening courtesy of my friends' parents, I ate my first mouthwatering, delicious beefsteak and from that experience learned about one of life's real pleasures. The baked potato that accompanied it, already delicious with salt, pepper, and butter, was made more so by another part of the meal that was also a new taste for me: sour cream. This fine dairy product I had heard about but had never come closer to than seeing it sitting on the shelves of the dairy case at the grocery store. The creamy richness it added to my potato combined with a bite of my juicy, tender steak was one of the most enjoyable mouthfuls I had ever chewed. Vickie and her family enjoyed their meal but, as it was one they ate regularly, could not have savored or relished it like I did.

After everyone was finished eating, the cleanup was also quite different than at my home. The dirty dishes were rinsed with running tap water and then placed inside the dishwasher to be washed and sanitized. Once the machine was loaded and Vickie and pushed the on button, we wiped down the table and countertops, and that was that. Because there were seven in my family, there were always a considerable number of dishes to be washed after a meal. Not only did the plates, tableware, and drinking glasses constitute at least a couple of sinks full to be scrubbed, rinsed, and stacked, the pots and pans to prepare enough for seven people were routinely a formidable undertaking to clean. At my home, that chore was permanently assigned to Gayla and me, a fact that made the idea of eating away from home even more alluring.

Another piece of property the Kellers owned was a motorboat. It was clean and bright with a motor that seemed enormous to me. With this boat in tow, they would go on vacation each summer, stay in rented cabins, and enjoy weeks at Lake of the Ozarks in Missouri, five hundred miles or so to the east. While preparing for one of these trips, Vickie asked me if I would like to go with them. My eyes bugged out and my mouth flew open. Of course, I would like to go! As soon as I could speak, I asked her what her folks would think about that idea. She said they had already said it was okay, if my folks didn't care.

Within a few days I was in the back seat of the Kellers' beautiful new two-toned Pontiac Catalina sitting beside Vickie, her parents in the front seat. Both were heavy smokers, and the entire car pretty much stayed a haze of cigarette smoke. Although smoking regularly otherwise, Vickie was not yet bold enough to light up in the presence of her dad and mother.

Behind the car, the beautiful boat was in tow. It sat up high and rode proudly, as if it couldn't wait to reach water, and for several days anyway, relish its marine environment instead of marking time on a trailer under a carport.

This trip was exciting in different ways. I had never been on a real vacation, I had never been to a huge lake like the one in the Ozarks, and I had never been around a boat. What had me most captivated was the idea I was going to get to learn to water ski. I could hardly believe it was true. Vickie had known how to ski for several years and assured me there was nothing to it. I was waiting with bated breath to be gliding across the top of the water while being pulled by this powerful, beautiful boat.

Once we arrived at the lake and had begun settling into the cabin the Kellers rented, I saw some familiar faces a small distance away. The Walters and Munson families were set up nearby. These three families had vacationed together here before. Everyone was jovial and upbeat and welcomed me. I had no trouble fitting in and had a good time getting to know these people better during that week of leisure and relaxation.

The only disappointment of the trip was that despite much effort, I was never able to water ski. Everyone was very patient with me and helped me every way they knew, without success. Not being able to get the hang of water skiing was very disappointing, but I nevertheless enjoyed a week of truly memorable fun with folks kind and generous enough to include me and a vacation that enabled me in widening my horizons, gaining precious memories, making new friends, and seeing more of what the world and this life could offer.

Vickie and I remained friends through high school and two years of college to follow before life took us our separate ways. Those years often saw me spending time at her home and her passing time at my home too. Some of Vickie's ways irritated my mother a great deal, and though Vickie liked to be at our house, my mother wasn't fond of her presence. Because I realized that I was also edgy when my friend came around. Since she always had a car, we normally left in it and were free to do pretty much as we pleased. I frequently wondered why Vickie even wanted to come to my house. It wasn't as though I enjoyed being there any more than was required.

Things at my home were tolerable, but there was always tension. Dad was at home sometimes but just as often was away working. Long ago I had learned his presence was simply something on which I could not count. The natural gas pipeline jobs on which he worked took him to places near my hometown but also to points within bordering states and farther, for different periods of time. Whether it was sacrifice to be away from his family so much or a lifestyle that he sought consciously or otherwise, the older we kids got, the less our father was around.

Mom always went through the motions of homemaker without fail. She cleaned the house, laundered and mended the clothes, managed the finances, shopped for groceries, and cooked three times a day. She handled a lot of responsibility and labor routinely, solving problems and making decisions without batting an eye. She was faithful in the execution of her duties, but she was seldom joyful. Her (and Dad's) expectations of us kids had not changed from the time we were small children. Never spoken aloud, I knew good and well that I was not to cause trouble of any sort, not to ask questions that would make them uncomfortable, and to handle the invisible parts of being human the best way I could figure.

Bruce, Gayla. and I were now teenagers, and soon those ranks would increase when Lonnie turned thirteen. Gayla and I merely tolerated one another, Bruce was fairly easygoing as long as things went his way, and toward that end, he surrounded himself with minions with wills and minds that bent with little resistance. For peons unable or unwilling to subordinate themselves to Bruce, the affiliation was always short-lived, and the expatriate looked elsewhere for a new band of brothers with whom to forge a friendship. Lonnie and Stacy made few waves, so on the surface, our family functioned as well as most. But all really wasn't so well.

Bruce had always struggled in school and, although he was now attending high school for the fifth year, had not earned all the credits he needed to graduate in the spring. His attitude and position embarrassed me. He was the oldest and needed to set a good example for the rest of us. He needed a high school diploma, and that he wasn't trying harder to earn one showed something was wrong with him.

In the mid 1960s, special education departments didn't exist. Whatever my brother's learning problem was, I don't know, but even if it had had a name back then, the either-or view of the world with which I was being raised would have precluded me having a different opinion. I didn't have much respect for Bruce, had no shared interests, in fact had very little to do with him other than occupy space under the same roof, eat at the same table, and enjoy the presence of some of the boys he brought around.

Gayla was a junior in high school and had started dating a boy named Jerry Mills. She had dated several other boys during her high school years but had not had a steady boyfriend until she went out with Jerry. Dating was not easy for Gayla, not because of her looks or personality, but because of her attitude regarding her family and its location on the socioeconomic scale. When a boy would call at our house to pick her up for a date, my older sister insisted our mother keep us other kids strictly out of sight to avoid embarrassing her. Our nomadic way of life and family economics caused Gayla a lot of stress. Her full intention was to have a much easier lifestyle as an adult. She possessed a sound work ethic, made good grades, so I had no reason to doubt she would attain what she desired in life. She was also attractive to boys, so I figured finding the right man with whom to work toward success should pose no problem either.

Jerry Mills quickly became Gayla's steady boyfriend, and it wasn't long before she was wearing his class ring. She got acquainted with his family and liked them very much. In her need for a higher social rung, Gayla considered Jerry and his family acceptable. She may have been falling in love with her boyfriend, but Gayla unfortunately found out the hard way that at home, she was still very much expected to follow rules that had long ago been silently but surely codified.

During the fall of her junior year of high school, Gayla skipped school one day to go with Jerry to an out-of-town football game. A group of students/couples went and had a fun day goofing off, thinking they were stealth in their escapade. Alas, however, the teens tarried after the game. When my sister failed to make it home from the game in the correct amount of time, her fate was sealed. Unfortunately for her, Dad was actually at home and was waiting for her when she came through the doorway. Upon interrogation, Gayla admitted the truth, and Dad was quick to administer punishment.

Dad stood nearly six feet, two inches, generally weighed around 240 pounds, and was thickly and powerfully built. Most men would not have wanted to tussle with him, so watching him set in to his five-foot, six-inch, 120-pound sixteen-year-old daughter was a sight forever branded in my memory.

He went into the kitchen, retrieved the flyswatter, and returned momentarily to the living room armed with his enforcement. He held the swatter upside down, the metal handle portion poised to grab flesh and inflict severe pain at our father's behest. Face-to-face with my sister, Dad quickly grabbed the front part of her upper left arm and in a fluid motion jerked her body about forty-five degrees and simultaneously began whipping her backside from the middle of her back as far down as her knees. He walloped her at least a half dozen strokes, all of them landing squarely hitting their targets. This horrifying scene of punishment was carried out in the living room with us three younger kids and our mother watching. It was brutal, and even to the senses of a fourteen-year-old, the punishment was far too severe for the crime. Gayla was wailing so loudly it seems unlikely the neighbors didn't hear the painful cries her thrashing was producing.

Even though I didn't care for my sister any more than she did for me, I was profoundly sorry she suffered the beating she endured. Dad could be terrifying, as this latest example served to remind. The immediate and grave punishment given Gayla was a very stark reminder of the ever-unspoken but understood rule in our family not to cause trouble. She had welts and bruises on her thighs, her rear end, and her back that made me cringe in fear and seemed to take a really long time to disappear.

Down but not out, after the whipping she endured, Gayla nevertheless told our father if he were ever to lay a hand on her again, she would leave, and he would never see her again. Regardless why not, Dad never raised a hand to my older sister again, and a year and a half later she was a high school graduate, pregnant, soon-to-become Mrs. Jerry Mills and a parent herself.

We lived on Durham Street a relatively long while. For two years I called that address home. It was another house my parents tried to buy but were unable to secure a mortgage. Shortly, though, they would see another chance at home ownership, and it would work out in their favor.

TENTH GRADE

O n US Highway 160 heading east out of Ulysses sat the drive-in theater. Situated on the north side of the highway, this icon of fun summer evenings was the edge of town for many years. A few years earlier, on the south side of the highway, lots had been measured off, and people were moving mobile homes onto them. The street on which these homes sat was Texas Avenue, or as my father referred to the area, Tortilla Flats. Mom's sister Karen and her husband had purchased one of the lots and were living on it in their mobile home. The lot and mobile home next door to them came up for sale, and Aunt Karen told my folks about it being available. My parents applied for a loan with which to buy the property, and this time they were successful. After twenty years of being renters, their status was about to change.

This area being developed was new, neat, and clean and housed no trashy-looking mobile homes. Texas Avenue ran a bit less than a quarter of a mile with maybe a dozen lots on either side of it. Besides our relatives, we knew several of the Texas Avenue residents: two coworkers of my dad's, a family who were friends of mine (including one daughter, Clementine [Meza], who had taken care of me in the hospital when I broke my arm five years earlier), and older brothers of one of my classmates and their families. Having my aunt Karen and my five-year-old cousin Tammi next door was a special treat for me. Always having enjoyed my aunt and adoring my five-year-old cousin, all in all I was happy to be where we were.

After school released for the summer in 1966, we departed Durham Street, which was located almost to the town's western boundary, and moved lock, stock, and barrel across town to Texas Avenue and home ownership.

Our new home was a modest trailer. It was twelve feet wide by sxity feet long, with a bedroom on either end of the trailer. The bathroom was between the rear bedroom and the kitchen. Between the front bedroom and the kitchen were a dining area and living room. My parents occupied the front bedroom, and we three girls and Lonnie occupied the one in the rear.

Into that small bedroom we moved two sets of bunk beds, one wooden and the other metal. The metal set of bunks had been given to us sometime along the way by our grandpa Van. They were rumored to have come from the military, an alluring bit of information. Although new enough to us, these bunks were old, and the resiliency of the springs was more like a septuagenarian with a lot of arthritis. Atop them the four- or five-inch-thick mattresses were no doubt as old as the bed frames, and sleeping there resembled stretching out in a hammock. We kids were young and strong and managed to emerge from our racks each morning without difficulty. The challenge for Lonnie and me, who slept in the top bunks, was not to sit up, as doing so would have meant slamming our heads into the ceiling, so close were the quarters. Quickly we learned to slide sideways out of bed in the morning. Life lived so closely was not offensive. We kids were simply happy our folks were buying instead of renting this place, and we would not have to keep moving from house to house.

With two sets of bunk beds sitting on either side of that room, there was just enough space remaining between them for us kids to climb into bed, one at a time. The front wall of the bedroom housed the closet, built in with four doors. Beneath the doors were four segments of two-drawer sections. We were each allowed the area behind one closet door and two drawers that were a foot or so wide, perhaps eight inches high, and as deep as the closet was. During warm weather, Mom packed away everyone's cold-weather clothing and reversed the process seasonally. With this practice in place, each of us was able to store our clothing in our allotted space.

Space was limited enough between the two sets of bunk beds that only one of us at a time could access our clothing. Neither the closet doors nor the drawers could be opened fully to stow clothing or retrieve it, without coming into contact with the bunk beds.

Functioning within our bedroom required paying attention. To enter there, we took a step or two, following the door as it opened into the bedroom. At this point we would then step sideways to the right two or three steps, navigating the space between the foot of the first set of bunk beds and the closet doors. The next move required us to make a ninety-degree turn to maneuver between the two sets of beds. Whichever bed was the destination determined which direction we turned. If we needed to get into the closet or drawers, more careful maneuvering was required. The extremely cramped quarters simply meant we had to cooperate to function. We soon became accustomed to what worked and learned to make do.

Floor space was as valuable as real estate on Park Avenue. Bruce was odd man out and slept in the small living room area on the couch that made into a bed. This was not a hide-a-bed sofa but one where the back slid forward and down and rested parallel with the floor, rendering the seat portion perpendicular to the floor. Pushing this obelisk forward a couple inches farther released a hinge whereby the seat then laid down beside the couch's back section, both of which comprised a bed of sorts.

Bruce's clothes were hung in the closet of the front bedroom along with those of our parents. Where anything was kept that belonged to any of us but wasn't a necessity I do not remember. Perhaps such items remained packed away when we moved into the trailer. I didn't find this living situation offensive because Dad's plan was to build an addition onto our trailer home that would more than double our living area. Such an addition would mean sufficient space to live comfortably, and most importantly, whatever we had would be ours rather than a landlord's property. The sacrifice necessary to achieve the stability of a home and property my parents would own was worth it.

Each summer I looked forward to visits from relatives who would return to Ulysses on vacation. Seeing my mother's older brother, Uncle Gail, his wife, and their two children was always enjoyable. My uncle worked for the Bureau of Land Management so moved around during his career with the federal government. Gail had served in the navy during World War II and had gone to college on the GI Bill afterward, where he majored in forestry. He was the only person on either side of my family who had gone to college, and I respected him very much for that achievement. My aunt Lil was very pretty and demure. She always dressed nicely, was well coiffed, with skillfully applied and flattering makeup, a standard to which I aspired. She played the piano well and understood a lot about music, exhibited a passion for singing, all of which further raised the esteem I felt for her. She was soft-spoken, had soft, elegant-looking hands that exemplified how she presented overall. She was not prissy or prudish in her classy looks and refined behavior; that was simply who she was.

My uncle and aunt's children were younger than I. Their daughter Janet was near my sister Stacy's age, and their son Randy was even younger. I had fun being around Janet and watching Randy, who was an extremely inquisitive kid who liked to take things apart to see how they operated. His parents always had their hands full overseeing Randy, and observing their interaction was often amusing.

During their vacation that summer, my uncle and aunt invited me to go home with them for a while, to Rawlins, Wyoming. I was excited at the prospect and quickly accepted their offer. Always interested at what lay beyond flat, hot, windy southwestern Kansas, I enjoyed the drive through Colorado and on north to Cheyenne, Wyoming, then west to Rawlins.

In Rawlins I played on a softball league and felt welcome by the folks I met there. I did well playing ball, and as always, the recognition I received and the value I was to my team served my starving sense of self-esteem well. Like several of my other aunts, my aunt Lil saw I was beyond my years physically and made good use of that. That summer I had my first experience washing storm windows that were as difficult to reach as impacted wisdom teeth. Cleaning those windows from hell was a two-day saga with me as the heroine and eventual but war-weary victor. I did not mind working and enjoyed whatever money I earned doing so, but after that experience, I swore I would not wash anybody's windows again if they were constructed like these bastards.

One day I was witness to a blow-up of sorts that left my mouth agape and completely confounded my sense of who my aunt was. It was mid-July, windy and hot in Rawlins. My uncle was at work, and Aunt Lil, her children, and I were all in the house seeking relief via air conditioning. Cousin Randall, who was about to turn nine years old the following month, was simply being himself. He reminded me of a young "absent-minded professor," very intelligent but less astute socially and with interpersonal relationships. Randy had an old, large radio of sorts he was busy gutting and trying to reassemble, kind of like a Frankenstein radio he had dissected and was putting back together but not necessarily like it had been originally. His mother instructed him to move his mess down to the basement, where it would not be cluttering up the living room or a tripping hazard. She repeated the instructions two or three times with the same results: Randall was either in his own world or was ignoring his mother.

Right up to the point of explosion, my aunt Lil was herself: dignified, composed, very ladylike in the classical sense. One second she was her normal self, and in the same amount of time, without warning, she let loose. She yelled Randy's name in her loudest voice and moved across the room toward him. I was in the hallway about to enter the living room and witnessed the forceful steps taken by a woman whose patience meter had expired.

From stately to fierce in an instant she was upon Randy, kicking at him, yelling that she had told him to go downstairs and meant what she said, slapping at his back, then kicking again, while Randy, whose attention his mother finally had, began writhing on the floor, trying to deflect her feet and hands. A chubby kid with the graceful movement akin to a harbor seal out of water, Randall alternately rolled, tried to crawl, dragged himself a lunge at a time across the floor, whimpering with alternating expressions of shock, confusion, and desperation that he "was going."

Aunt Lil's soft canvas sneaker had been launched from her foot during one of her kicks in the air toward her son. The doorway to the basement was now just a few feet from her feet, and like an ace soccer player working the ball, Pele Lil Elliott maneuvered her son toward the goal. Finally within shot, she positioned herself above her son and, still yelling, executed a free kick to her son's arse that sent it through the doorway onto the top stair.

"Ooh, agh…gee…Mom…"

Again with her foot, not a kick but a push, and Randy's arse plopped onto the second stair.

"Umph…oh…golly, stop, will you."

With the mumbling blob curled up on the stairs, his mother summoned a final surge of strength, and her bare foot found his buttocks one last time. "Next time do what I tell you!" yelled a shrill voice just before the door to the basement slammed shut.

Randall's pride had suffered a decent blow, but beyond that, nothing was injured. I had never been more surprised by anyone or anything in my life than I was that day my aunt finally had to talk to her son in a language he understood. Even though I was dumbfounded when this reserved, gentle woman suddenly went commando that afternoon, I began snickering simultaneously because the entire scene had a surreal comedy to it. As the day and month drew on, I could hardly cease thinking about Lil and Randall's bout and the funnier it became. That incident also reminded me never to assume someone who is quiet and reserved by nature can't get just as upset as anyone else.

Even though that memory has given me many good laughs throughout my lifetime, an awful story that made the news that July while I was in Wyoming terrified me and continues to give me cold chills to this day.

The morning of July 15, 1966, started as any other ordinary summer day, until the television was turned on. Newscasters were relating a breaking story, enumerating the facts known thus far regarding the murder of eight student nurses in Illinois.

The young women had been slaughtered some time during the night. The viciousness of the killer and carnage the perpetrator had created were incomprehensible, not only to my teenage mind, but to the entire nation's. Again I tasted the acrid fear that welled up from the deepest parts within me, the same reaction that expressed itself nearly ten years earlier when the Clutter family had met their grisly deaths. That such evil human beings exist was a thought upon which no one could dwell too long without being overcome with fear, sadness, paranoia, and anger. But when crimes this unspeakable periodically do occur, as individuals and collectively we cannot avoid the unnerving evidence that there are such monsters that walk among us. Even the adults in my life were deeply shaken by this bloodbath. Some cursed, some prayed, some shook their head in disbelief, some wept; all were deeply affected. When children witness adults trembling, the gravity of a situation is felt even more so.

How could someone devolve into a being this evil? How many murderers did it take to orchestrate such a heinous, diabolical butcher of so many young women who, ironically, had been preparing for a career in which the core principle was to care for other human beings?

As always, when such unsettling events occur, we became especially cautious about locking the doors and windows there at my relatives' home. Feeling unsafe and heartbroken over this obscenity, for weeks thereafter I was simply spooked. Literally looking over my shoulder was a precaution I adopted. Entering a dark room became something I couldn't muster the courage to do. Thinking about the horror and pain the nursing students must have suffered before they lost consciousness all tortured my mind in waking and sleeping hours. The entire massacre and ongoing publicity about it helped make me very anxious and uneasy.

Even when the authorities arrested and eventually convicted the killer, I remained very troubled by aspects of the mass murder. The one student who survived did so by rolling beneath a bed. I fretted as to how that young woman could ever live normally after enduring such a horror story. Seeing the families of the victims on television and their clear brokenness broke my heart too in sorrow for them. I wondered how any of them could not be driven mad thinking about what their loved one had had to endure at the hands of the murderer. The whole thing exhausted my mind and spirit. The horrible story being broadcast that July morning became a specter that was pregnant with questions to which there simply were no adequate answers.

My visit with my uncle and aunt and my cousins ended the first part of August, when my mother came to fetch me. Lonnie and Stacy were with her, and after departing Rawlins, Wyoming, we headed east across Nebraska, then south to central Kansas. My dad was working on a pipeline job in Hutchinson, Kansas, and we were going to visit him for a few days.

When working away from home, Dad would rent a place to stay. In Hutchinson that summer, he had located a place on the far eastern side of town that was affordable. Zinn's Motel consisted of perhaps ten individual efficiency apartments built around three sides of a quadrangle and facing inward. The driveway ran in front of the cottages, parallel with the structures. The business office / manager's apartment sat on the front side of the courtyard, bounded on either side by the driveway and the highway to its front.

Zinn's piece of real estate had long passed its peak and needed a major overhaul. The apartments looked tired, worn, and outdated but were not yet ramshackly. Inside Dad's unit was a room with a worn sofa against one wall, a heating stove against the front wall, and a door on the far side of the room, behind which were the commode, wash basin, and shower stall. An interior wall separated the dwelling into two rooms, and behind it was the cooking stove, sink, small table with two chairs, and a bed in one corner. The place was actually inviting in a way. Like a pair of new shoes that are more comfortable after they have been broken in, this little shanty must have been built fairly sturdily to hold up as well as it had, for probably thirty or forty years.

Dad was glad to see us and enjoyed us being around a few days. He told us the old lady who owned and ran the place was nosy but harmless. A couple of his coworkers were also staying there, so he had neighbors of sorts. Dad's unit was one positioned along the south side of the property. Diagonally to the west lived a nigger guy, as my father referred to him, who seemed to live alone. Dad had seen the guy coming and going, oftentimes carrying a paper bag about the size of a pint of liquor. We were told to "just stay away from him" and behave ourselves while we were there.

The next day while Dad was at work, Mom left to find a laundromat and wash the dirty clothes that were piling up. She took Stacy with her, while Lonnie and I remained behind. I was sitting on the sofa reading comic books. I had opened the door to encourage a breeze to come my way. The sagging screen door did provide a barrier to flies and mosquitos and allowed me to see the comings and goings within the court. In a few minutes I heard the sound of car tires slowly rolling across the gravel covering the driveway. I looked up and recognized the car of the black man my dad had instructed us about. This neighbor pulled alongside his apartment, turned off his car, and got out. I had not seen him before, nor had I ever been around a black person, and I was curious. The screen door afforded me the ability to look out without someone being able to see me doing so. The man looked to be in his midtwenties and was quite tall and lean, which made him appear even taller. His skin was very dark, and his arms and legs seemed extraordinarily long and graceful. He was dressed neatly in slacks and a polo-type shirt. He was clean-shaven and walked with his head held high. In his hand was a small paper bag, just as Dad had mentioned. He walked across the drive-way to Mrs. Zinn's apartment and knocked on her door. Although I could not see her doorway, I could tell when she answered her door because I could hear them conversing. In a couple of minutes, the man reappeared, crossed the driveway to his apartment, and entered.

"They really do look a lot different than we do," I marveled to myself. I was inquisitive about black people. I wondered how their hair felt and if they really did smell differently than we did. I wondered how it would feel to look into a mirror and see a face covered with black skin instead of white. Knowing my questions were going to remain unanswered, I soon returned my attention to my comic book and continued enjoying the latest adventure of Superman as he battled Lex Luthor.

Probably twenty minutes later, I was still reading when I heard the gravel crunching again under the weight of another car. I looked up to see a fairly new Buick sedan parking beside the black man's car. The driver shut off the engine and opened his door to get out of the car. On the other side of the vehicle, another man emerged then shut the car door. They were both around the age of the other man, but they weren't as lean as he was. These two guys were thicker, and their strength was obvious. Their short-sleeved shirts revealed really well-defined muscles, as if they might be boxers. They were talking between themselves as they walked to the door, opened the screen, knocked on the door, and entered the apartment of the black man.

I didn't know exactly what to think. Being around something so new and different was a bit intriguing but unsettling at the same time. Exercising a distinct feeling of caution, I arose from the sofa, walked to the door, and fastened the latch on the screen door, then shut the wooden door and locked it as well.

Back home in Ulysses a few weeks later, my sophomore year in high school was approaching quickly. Much of the excited anticipation with which I had begun high school a year earlier had faded. I remained active in debate, but absent much success, this would be my last year to participate on the squad and in forensic speaking contests. I continued to enjoy music by being a band member, and that year I began studying the German language and culture and found it very interesting and satisfying. I also enrolled in a one-semester typing course, designed for anyone not needing the longer vocational typing course. I was bound for college, not secretarial work. As it turned out I easily excelled at this new skill. The requisite English and science classes I tolerated but without any real interest or joy.

I went about the business of school without standing out. I continued to make grades high enough that I was on the honor roll more often than not. Inside, however, my emotional struggle was raging. My unrequited interest in boys created more and more drag on my spirit. All around me I witnessed boys and girls engaging in traditional mating rituals. Between classes, at school functions, in the movie theater, in cars dragging Main Street, there were more and more of my fellow students who were experiencing all degrees of romantic involvement.

On any day while I was in high school, there was some boy I would be fantasizing about. Most of these young men who had caught my eye were upperclassmen, which meant I was not in the same classes as they. Passing through the halls between classes was an exercise in trying to catch a glimpse of that certain handsome face with whom I was currently smitten and then, like a snapshot memory, behold it over and over again. Like a powerful drug, watching the boy whenever I was able produced a kind of euphoria inside me. With no reciprocation, no hope of any of the boys to whom I was attracted ever showing interest in me, the cycle became more painful each time it repeated. I was growing more and more weary inside but was powerless to stop engaging in this pseudo life in which boys were a part. Having had a physically mature body for four years already and enduring the hormone storm that engulfs all healthy adolescents, I was a peach ripe for the picking. Coupled with my lifelong unmet need for affection and attention, I was sorely troubled, emotionally quite ill. Turning off all those drivers or even slowing them down was impossible to do by myself, and the notion of significant help from any source in that day and age was as fanciful as my wish for a boyfriend.

That year another fellow student who had also been a good friend wound up in the same predicament as Bonnie Allen found herself a year earlier. Debbie Moore, the friend with whom I spent a lot of time in eighth grade and who was my partner when we dyed our hair, was pregnant. I was saddened and infuriated at the same time. I was quite confused about many things, but regarding winding up an unwed teenage mother, my thoughts were logical and precise. I could not understand why Debbie would do something so wrought with life-changing risks, would chance becoming the butt of jokes and ridicule, and would bring embarrassment to her parents, brother, and two younger sisters.

I had known her mother since early elementary school, as she was another parent who was one of my Brownie scout leaders. My father worked with Debbie's father on pipelines, and during my eighth-grade year I had spent a lot of time at their house and always enjoyed being there. Now all too soon Debbie was soon to become a wife and, shortly thereafter, a mother. Her soon-to-be husband was two years older than she. I knew his parents and family too and observed all these people through my lens of strong emotion. Nevertheless, in the spring of 1967, along with a handful of their family and even fewer friends, I sat in a pew at the Catholic Church in Ulysses and witnessed my fifteen-year-old friend and her boyfriend become man and wife.

Very pregnant Debbie was nevertheless outfitted in a pretty white wedding gown, much like the one my friend Viola had been buried in during my eighth-grade year. Viola was also Catholic, and I found myself uncomfortable thinking about her, her dress, Catholics' odd ways of doing things, that I was actually inside a Catholic church the first time in my life, for knowing Debbie was not Catholic but was now becoming one because her husband was Catholic, for smiling when inside I felt like I needed to flee. All told it was a stressful occasion, and something that was meant to be joyous was only sad to me.

Not surprisingly, Debbie did not return to high school. Two of my friends had fallen by the way in the same manner, and I alternately grieved for both of them and the opportunities they had lost but also shook my head in disdain at what I perceived as a lack of morals and certainly a lack of sound judgment.

Outside of school, life on Texas Avenue was busy. Dad was working with a friend of his deconstructing the oldest building in Ulysses, Binney's grocery. The store was squarely in the middle of town on Main Street. Going inside Charlie Binney's store was like stepping into a time warp. The old wooden building harked back to the time my grandparents were children. Charlie Binney, always sitting near the cash register, was a friendly old man. His sister, Catherine, one of my mother's elementary school teachers, was always there with her brother and was the usual cashier. This old building felt and smelled like days gone by. It was long since past its prime, but its uniqueness and mystique imbued it with a character that was undeniable. Now, however, its days were numbered, and my father would be half of the team to raze this old friend.

Dad was not going to be paid in money for his work tearing down the old store. What he was going to receive for his efforts was the lumber that constituted the structure. As the store came down, its component pieces were hauled to our lot in Tortilla Flats. With that lumber, Dad was going to build the addition on to the trailer in which we lived. In a way we would be living in the old Binney building, and that idea was sentimentally appealing. The addition was going to be the same length as the trailer and a foot or two wider, so our living space would more than double when the effort was completed.

Before my father could begin to build the addition, however, the lumber from the old grocery store had to be cleaned up. What that meant for us kids was pulling nails from the boards. It was our job after school to go outside and work at this task, which was a love/hate effort. Pulling nail after nail after nail was boring. There were several five-gallon buckets sitting on the ground, spaced in intervals beneath the long planks of wood and beside the sawhorses on which the lumber rested. Before this phase of refurbishing was completed, those buckets and more would be full with all the nails we pulled over the course of the fall. Before the weather turned cold, the old Binney store, a sentinel connecting present day and days long past, had finished its watch, and where it had stood was now a vacant lot at the very heart of Ulysses.

The idea that life can be defined as a series of changes and even transformations aptly describes the fate of the old building in which we had conducted a lot of business through the years. In only a short while, the wood from the old store was transformed into the frame, walls, floors, and roof of our home. As we kids generated usable lumber from the old store, Dad trimmed the ends that were not salvageable and sorted the boards by length and width. This process was tedious but productive, and it was an especially joyous day when my father actually began constructing the addition to our trailer.

Through the fall and winter, Dad put to use any and everything he had learned about carpentry as a teenager from his uncle Reed, and rather like the experience with Uncle Reed and garage living a couple of summers earlier, we managed to live in very close quarters for the better part of a year, until construction on the rest of our home was finished. The addition was nearly like another trailer house. It was the same height, was rectangle in shape, simple but sufficient. At the front of the addition was a new living room from which an opening matched up to the front doorway of the trailer. Inside the trailer the former dining room and living room area became only a dining room. Toward the back end of the trailer and its rear doorway, Dad constructed another matching opening that connected the hallway in the trailer to the hallway in the addition. Entering the hallway of the addition, then, one could go left to a bedroom, forward to a second bedroom, or right and back ten or twelve feet to a small laundry room. Off the laundry room was a doorway leading to a porch and the backyard.

Before the school year was over in the spring of 1967, my family was enjoying what seemed an enormous amount of space provided by the addition to our trailer. Gayla graduated high school in May. and our newly enlarged home easily accommodated all the family and friends who came together to celebrate my sister's accomplishment. With the additional space, I no longer felt like we were a bunch of sardines packed snugly in a tin. Now my brothers shared the front bedroom of the trailer, Stacy and I occupied the rear bedroom that had barely managed to house the two sets of bunk beds earlier, and Gayla had one of the bedrooms in the new addition. Our parents occupied the fourth bedroom.

I felt very proud of my family's ability to make do with such little space as we had done in order to work toward a better living situation. Now we had a new, neat, clean add-on, and there was enough living area not to feel cramped. Dad did the finish work on the inside after we had moved into the rooms of the addition. After completing the work on the inside, he began work on the outside. He put up chicken wire in preparation for stuccoing the outside of the addition. He ran concrete for the small porch off the new front door. Not a square inch of this home was fancy; there was no crown molding, plush carpeting, fine draperies, beveled countertops, expensive tile, or other such amenities. Not one time, though, did I ever regard our home with a feeling of lack because it was absent such features.

What did occupy my mind was the fact that we owned this place, we had as much space or more than we had ever had, it was all neat and clean, and I was proud to be able to bring my friends to my home that was becoming more and more attractive each day. The home my family and I were able to build reflected and compounded our understanding and willingness to sacrifice and work to achieve important goals in life. Not only were our characters enriched by the experience, but we also had a home that we could call our own. My heart was full of pride and thanksgiving in a way that could never be repossessed.

During the latter half of that school year, an evangelist named Ford Philpot came to Ulysses and held services in our high school gymnasium. Each night of his crusade I attended with my grandmother Bea. Mr. Philpot was an excellent speaker as the full gymnasium indicated, and his message was always stirring.

Even though I had had an extremely emotional time at my church's altar while in the fifth grade, I nevertheless felt so burdened inside that by the time this evangelist offered the altar call and urged attendees to come and be saved, I figured I must not have been saved after all or I would not still be feeling so awful inside. My chest felt ready to explode, my blood pressure surged upward, and I could feel my pulse inside my head, neck, and chest. I was unable to hold back my tears, which came profusely, rolling down my cheeks before falling onto my dress. I stepped into the aisle and made my way down the stairs to the floor of the gymnasium. I turned to the left and walked most of the distance of the basketball court till I arrived at the platform on which stood the guest evangelist, his podium, microphone, and speakers, and which served as the altar. I knelt down with the person who greeted me as I arrived at the altar. She asked me the appropriate questions, whether I believed in Jesus Christ as my personal savior, whether I was sorry for my sins, and whether I was willing to claim Jesus at this time. In between my sobs and gasps for air, I answered yes to her queries, at which time she prayed with me.

Again the toxic emotions I lived with daily were all in my throat, about to suffocate me. I was racked with awful feelings of worthlessness, hopelessness, guilt, shame, and many others that I thought were products of my sin. As was the case at the altar scene five years earlier, I wept bitterly. When I was finally able to compose myself, I stood with all the other people who had come forward to the altar, and Ford Philpot commended us for having publicly proclaimed Jesus as our savior, reassured us all of our place in heaven, exhorted us to grow in Christ, and then closed the service with a final prayer. Confused as to whether or not I was really saved five years earlier, I felt safer thinking surely I was saved now if not before.

In the days following, I did my best to live a Christian life to the degree I understood that commitment. I knew my sins had been forgiven. What I didn't know was why I still felt so rotten. A few months later I was more dejected than ever. I was missing the Christian mark often enough I believed myself to be an utter failure in the realm of religion. The persistent bleakness I contended with every hour of every day continued growing within me as surely as my two class-mates' babies had grown inside them.

Emotionally, home was becoming a place I could barely stomach. For whatever reason, my mother was increasingly unpleasant to be around, and it seemed she enjoyed having me there no more than I enjoyed being there. One afternoon I approached her for permission to go with my friend Vickie to the movies that evening. With no thought, my mother instantly, nearly automatically, replied no. I then asked her why not, to which she answered, "Because I said so." This scenario of our parents' apparent automatic negative answer repeated itself often with us kids, and it was frustrating beyond measure. I shot back at my mother that I would ask Dad when he got home and he'd let me go. Bad decision. My mother's eyes narrowed until they were slits in her head where eyes had once been. She pursed her mouth in such a way that I believed she was about to spit at me. In a moment, with her voice pinched more tightly than I had ever heard it, my mother hissed at me, "You may have your father wrapped around your little finger, but you don't have me."

My mother's face was contorted with anger. Her scowl was intimidating and awful looking. At that moment I was struck with a realization that left me chilled to the bone. My mother was behaving like I was her competition instead of her daughter. Her words and body language clearly conveyed her disdain for me. At that moment I felt not like this woman's daughter but merely another female she regarded with contempt. Not only was my mother not my friend, she seemed to consider herself my adversary. Something fundamentally changed with her behavior toward me. I felt very injured, frightened, and rejected. Sadly, I also felt a kind of power I hadn't before that was confounding and scary.

Mad as hell, my mother hurriedly made her way to the living room, and I stormed out of the kitchen into the hallway, on into the hallway of the addition, and finally out the back door. There was a stoop out back several feet square. I stood there for a minute or two, mightily upset, wishing I had somewhere I could go to escape. I generally spent as much time as I could away from home. School functions, friends, even relatives were people and place with whom I felt better and welcome. Still, the time I was at home was generally heavy with a continuous tension that was life sucking.

On the back step of our house I felt nauseous and needed to vomit. I sat there and cried for a good while. I was already a miserable person, and the row I had just had with my mother felt dangerously unnatural. I had no idea how to go about fixing my situation with my mother or any other aspect of my life. I wanted to run away from everything. Alas, there was nowhere to run.

When the school term ended and summer vacation began, life took a decided turn for the better. Gayla had secured a job waiting tables at one of the cafés in town. The Hav U 8 eatery proved to be a blessed relief from some of my stresses. The business was owned and operated by Mattie Mae Stegman. Mattie was over six feet tall with not an ounce of fat on her body. Her skin was a beautiful brown that reflected her Native American heritage, and her face was equally pretty. Mattie's voice was not at all loud but authoritative, and she liked to laugh. I found her easy to be around and could tell she liked me too. Years earlier I had been around this impressive woman. While in elementary school, she was in charge of our school cafeteria. Her build, carriage, and good looks I remembered from those earlier days. Now she was in business for herself and needed a dishwasher.

Through my sister I learned I could probably get a dishwashing job if I went and talked to Mattie. I went to the Hav U 8 the same day and was hired on the spot. My work experience at my aunt Tibe's café three summers earlier served me well, and I handled my job easily. I liked the entire crew of workers at the café and enjoyed going to work. From the safety of the kitchen, I observed the interesting activity in the front of the building where the customers were served. A round window in the swinging door that separated the serving area from the kitchen was as close as I wanted to get to the work up front.

I worked the early shift, arriving by 6:00 a.m. The kitchen area was divided into three sections by two walls in the shape of an upside-down T. The grill, steam table, refrigerator were to the left side of the configuration. The dishwashing area was to the right, and in the third section, at the back of the building, were the back door, storage shelves, and Mattie's pie-making area on the wall opposite the back door. She baked several pies each day as well as managing the employees and the myriad of tasks involved with day-to-day operations. On the floor at one end of her pie-making counter sat a big gold flour tin that was perfect in height and diameter to serve as a seat when Mattie took a break. She talked with me a lot, instructed me about all things pertinent to my being good help in the kitchen, and I enjoyed my work environment a lot. I could tell Mattie valued me not only as good kitchen help but also as an individual, and that knowledge felt precious to me.

After I had been on the job most of the summer, Mattie jolted me with a suggestion she made that eventually turned into an ultimatum of sorts. During a lull after our lunch rush, my boss came from her work area into mine and said she wanted to talk to me. I stopped what I was doing and turned toward her. She surprised and alarmed me by telling me she didn't want me as the dishwasher any longer. I thought I must be getting fired, and instantly Mattie's hand went to my shoulder, and her dark piercing eyes looked straight into mine. "I want you to go to work out front, Fran."

My eyes widened and my mouth flew open involuntarily. What? To me that was both great and awful news. I was not being fired, but I absolutely did not want to work out front. I loved peering through the round window of the swinging door that separated the dining area of the café from the kitchen. There were always good-looking guys coming in to eat that I really enjoyed ogling from the safety and distance of the kitchen! There was no way I could imagine myself able to be as close to them as a waitress had to get. The feeling I had was one of near panic, exactly like the one that caused me to behave so poorly when Duane Harbour had shown a hint of interest in me a couple of years earlier.

I pleaded with Mattie not to make me do that, to let me keep washing dishes. She would not budge. She tried to assure me that I needed to get out of the kitchen and that I would do just fine as a waitress out front. She promised me she would keep a close eye on me and would teach me all I needed to know, but that was little comfort. The appetite for my own money that I had acquired long ago first working in my grandparents' laundromat was so engrained I eventually yielded to Mattie's plan for me.

I had never been more afraid of anything in my life than I was the morning I had to report to work as a waitress. As with most fears, this one evaporated in short order when I faced it. In fact, I quickly realized I enjoyed interacting with the customers very much and rapidly got command of the skills involved in my new job.

True to Mattie's word, one day she showed me how sincere she had been in the promise she made to me. At the counter of the Hav U 8, there were at least a half dozen of the stools that are standard fare in diners. All but one of the stools and every one of the tables was taken when another customer entered, walked past the end of the counter on which the cash register sat, and sat down near it on the unoccupied stool. I did not recognize this latest customer. He was dressed in business attire, and I figured he was probably a salesman.

As I waited on him, I detected nothing out of the ordinary. I greeted him, served him a glass of water with enough ice in it to make it refreshing, handed him a menu, and went about my business. When I saw he had laid down the menu, I returned and took his lunch order, and when our cook hollered "Order up," I quickly picked up the plate of hot food and strode the dozen paces or so to the waiting man. A couple of minutes passed without incident. Then without warning, the man's behavior changed completely. He bellowed toward me, "Hey, girlie, come here!"

The Hav U 8's seating capacity was perhaps thirty to forty, and at mealtime, the place was usually full. That day was no different, and when the man on the stool yelled, his tone was so loud and fierce the whole place fell quiet.

I hurried the few steps to where he sat, but before I could make an inquiry as to what he needed, the guy blew up completely. He screamed that the food was no good, yelled how dare we serve slop like this, and with his volume steadily increasing ordered me to "put this shit in the goddamned trash where it belonged." As I had done so many times in the past, again I simply froze in place, unable to speak, unable to move, completely shocked and decimated.

About that instant I heard the swoosh of the swinging door to the kitchen, and before the unhappy customer uttered one more syllable, he was peering up, high up, into Mattie's very dark unhappy face. Her imposing height, carriage, and near-instant appearance rendered the villain mute. Mattie, however, was anything but mute. Her words were clear, concise, and to the point.

"You listen here, you old bastard. You don't talk to this girl or anyone in here like that. You get your sorry ass out of here, and don't come back."

The man, who had only a few seconds earlier been loud, profane, insulting, and full of himself, was now a picture of meekness. Without a sound he reached toward his pants pocket for his wallet but was again interrupted by the formidable, commanding woman whose ire he had provoked.

"I won't take your money, you old son of a bitch, but you will apologize to this girl," Mattie said in an icy, resolute tone.

The dining room was altogether quiet, and all eyes were riveted on the showdown at the counter. Time seemed to stand still. Like in a Western movie at the gunfight scene, Mattie was waiting for the would-be bully to make his move.

Fortunately, the man chose not to escalate the situation and instead hesitatingly mumbled an apology to me. He had no sooner voiced the final consonant of his apology when Mattie hissed at him, "Now you get out of here, and if I ever see you in here again, I'll call the law." Wisely avoiding more reproach, the man did exactly as ordered.

As if perfectly cued, in near unison, all the customers turned back toward their plates and resumed a good meal that had been rudely and surprisingly preempted. As for me, I was stunned, and my cheeks were as red as if the guy had slapped me with his hand instead of his words. I had been sniped, but the attacker had been instantly and properly reckoned with. Mattie had championed me without even having to think about it. She valued me enough to put the abusive creep in his place. That day I felt a sense of self-worth that I had never felt before. Whether she realized it or not, this strong, loving woman had given me a gift that day that was priceless.

Summer seemed to fly past, and soon I had to make a decision that was telling. I was thinking about whether or not to continue working at the café after school started. I was used to earning money. In the past, I worked odd jobs cleaning house, doing ironing, babysitting, and anything else that might enable me to earn a bit of spending money, but the idea of continuing to have a regular paycheck was greatly tempting, and in the end I yielded to it. I discussed the idea with my mother, and she agreed to my working if I could manage it and my schoolwork.

ELEVENTH GRADE

About to begin my junior year of high school, my attitude regarding school was sorely diminished from even a year earlier, and the polar opposite of what it had been when I started high school in what felt a lifetime ago. I was no longer on the debate squad and had quit most of my other extracurricular activities. I went to school joyless, attending only because I had to do so in order to graduate and get away from home, my hometown, and the situations and associations there that I had grown to loathe. My work environment was enjoyable, predictable, and rewarding in ways beyond just a paycheck, and that was where I preferred to be.

However, going to school and working afterward until 9:00 p.m. at the café left little time or energy for homework or anything else. One day in American history class, I was resting my head on my crossed arms on my desktop, nearly asleep. The teacher called on me, and I didn't answer. When he realized I was dozing, he became angry and threw a blackboard eraser at me. It hit my desk beside my head, chalk dust settling onto the right side of my face. Groggy and a bit dazed, I raised my head in embarrassment. The teacher remarked that I had better stay awake in his class, and if I couldn't, I needn't bother to attend. I felt humiliated and weary.

Not surprisingly, my grades reflected my situation, and I knew I could not continue to work so much and do well in school. Before Thanksgiving, I had given up my job, unhappy now because the benefits garnered from working were no longer in place to help sustain my pocketbook and emotional state.

Gayla and her boyfriend, Jerry, had married in August and were expecting a baby in the spring. Their lives were changing quickly and dramatically because soon after their wedding, he was drafted and went into the army. When her new husband left for military service, Gayla moved back in with us and would remain at home until Jerry returned from Vietnam in the spring of 1969.

It was not easy trying to get used to the idea that my sister, only two years older than I, was now a married woman. I, on the other hand, had been on exactly one date, had never been kissed by a boy, and had no idea what having a boyfriend felt like. This contrast in our experiences made my sister's status seem odd, and the situation grew more so as Gayla's pregnancy became apparent. She now considered herself grown and a superior to Lonnie, Stacy, and me. She and I argued frequently, and tensions grew even testier with the stress that accompanied Jerry's deployment to Vietnam in the spring of 1968. For more and more reasons, being home felt like a punishment rather than a refuge, and the tension therein continued ratcheting upward.

At school, a steadily increasing number of my close and casual friends and students in general now had boyfriends/girlfriends or were dating on occasion. Some of my friends became scarce in my life because as dating relationships grew, they spent less time with other girls. There were plenty of students like I, who did not date, by choice or otherwise. I realized I was not the only student who never dated, but that knowledge provided no consolation whatsoever.

As a member of this group of unrequited castoffs, I judged the others harshly, labeling them the same caliber as I had Mike Allen. I held most of them in disdain, and even to those I gave a pass, I could nevertheless understand why no one wanted to date them.

My attitude toward myself was one of astonished confusion. I absolutely could not understand why not one boy had any interest in me. What trait or quality made me incompatible with dating? I was well-known around school and well liked but was always a girl the boys wanted for a friend, not a girlfriend. Living with that scenario as it unfolded time after time took a brutal toll on my already frazzled emotions, and no matter how I tried to keep my mind elsewhere, I could not quit thinking about my plight or apparent inability to change it.

I entered high school weighing 165 pounds. With my five-foot, nine-inch height, I thought that number on the scales wasn't that bad, until I realized other girls as tall as I was were 25 or 30 pounds lighter with clothes sizes that matched accordingly. Nevertheless, by the time I was ready to begin eleventh grade, the scales were even less of a friend, the little lines rolling all the way to 180 before they stopped moving. I tried diet pills handed out by the awful Dr. Dodson. I tried counting calories. I tried a brand-new product called Ayds, which consisted of a type of caramel wrapped in cubes. This new fad was supposed to fill up one's stomach if you ate two of them twenty minutes before meals. All I lost with Ayds was the money I spent on several boxes of the weight loss cubes. I ate enough diet Jell-O and cottage cheese that, afterward, I ate neither again for many years. The final result of all my dieting through high school was that my weight continued to rise, slowly but steadily.

To her credit, my mother continued to try to comfort me and assure me that better days were to come. As she had assured me in junior high school that things would get better once I started high school, she now insisted college would be when things would turn around for me. Mom reasoned there would be older guys, even grown men, and they would be more apt to consider a girl's qualities as well as her looks. Mom would remind me that I was mature for my age, and high school boys simply were not as mature as I was. I wanted to believe her about college possibly being a happier experience for me, but I did not know how I was supposed to get by another two years until I was out of high school and in college.

I had four or five friends I hung around with on a routine basis. One of them, a girl I had known from early grades onward, had always been seriously obese but during our tenth-grade year had dieted severely and faithfully to the point she looked completely different. She met an older guy through a recreation center for teens and young adults that had recently opened downtown. Through the fall and winter that year, they became very serious, and at the end of our junior year, they married. But during the winter of 1967–1968, I spent a lot of time with Gary Ward and Selayne Tilson.

The three of us would often ride around in Gary's black Ford. As often as not, I drove and they cuddled in the back seat. Frequently we found ourselves at his apartment watching television, talking, making something to eat, or otherwise spending time. Whether we were in his car or at his apartment or with these friends or a number of others, drinking alcohol was becoming an automatic part of recreation and socializing. Although I did not realize it, drinking was for me a means of self-medicating the emotional pain that was eating me away inside. No doubt another time or setting would have found a youngster with such unresolved issues abusing illegal drugs, exhibiting promiscuity, or other reckless behavior that helped numb their pain when abused or rejected. For me, drinking alcohol simply meant getting drunk. At sixteen, the rot within me was of major proportion, and the choices I was making to try to cope with my affliction came with great potential for horrible consequences.

One Saturday sandwiched between afternoon and early evening, Gary, Selayne, and I were dragging Main Street, as was customary in those days. The boy on whom I currently had a crush was a year ahead of me in school and had probably never thought about me one way or another. We saw him in his car, and I let out a squeal. With good intention, my friend Selayne said to her boyfriend, who was behind the wheel that day, "Gary, stop that guy and ask him if he'd like to go riding around with us." I protested vehemently, instantly feeling the familiar terrifying panic that lived inside me and took center stage whenever there was possibility of contact with someone I wanted to notice me.

My protest fell on deaf ears, and the next time we saw my heart-throb's car approaching, Gary stuck out his arm and signaled the driver to go around the block. We turned right at the corner, pulled into the parking lot of the Christian Church, and waited. I was so nervous I thought I might upchuck. Had I not been in the back seat of the two-door car and unable to get to the door handle, I might have opened the door and simply run away, as I had done years ago with Duane Harbour. Unable to do that, I prayed that the guy would blow us off and continue alone.

Like a trapped animal, my eyes were riveted on the intersection half a block away, waiting to see what this boy I thought so gorgeous and desirable would do. In a few seconds, I spied his car as he slowed to obey the stop sign. My heart was pounding hard in my chest, my adrenaline screaming danger and giving me the energy burst I would need to flee. But I didn't flee; Selayne was adamant that we were going to see this through and would not let me out of the car. And then the car at the stop sign turned, in *our* direction! I thought I was going to pass out from my body and its systems reacting so intensely.

My Adonis pulled into the church's parking lot, rolled up next to us with his window a few feet away from Gary's. He put his car in park and rolled down his window. He had dark hair and dark eyes, was close to six feet tall, and nicely proportioned. Gary said hello, gave his name, and asked the teen if he wanted to ride around with us for a while. I thought I was hearing things when he said okay. He got out of his car and slid behind Gary into the back seat, where I sat, nearly apoplectic. He said hi to Gary, Selayne, and me as he got comfortable. I responded in like, feeling its beat each time my heart pumped.

Gary maneuvered the car back to Main Street, and as darkness began to fall, somehow it became somewhat easier to try to relax a bit. My two friends in the front seat were doing their best to keep conversation going, with little help being afforded from the rear seat. I was too nervous, and our guest seemed a bit disinterested, at least in their conversation. As it grew darker outside, he slowly inched himself in my direction. I realized what was happening, and I was thrilled.

When it was apparent the boy and I were occupying the same half of the rear seat, Gary reacted in kind and headed south out of town, drove a couple of miles, and turned off the highway onto a dirt road. After a couple more minutes, he pulled off the road into a field. As if I didn't realize what we were here for, I kept making attempts at polite conversation. Gary and Selayne immediately embraced and began making out in the front seat. Gary had left KOMA out of Oklahoma City playing on the radio, for which I was grateful.

What this handsome young man was thinking I will never know, but with a testosterone-rich attitude undoubtedly leading, likely compounded with a "why not" sense of opportunity, this boy reached out and put his arm around me. Romantic movie scenes that include displays of fireworks exploding are not necessarily that exaggerated. I felt like I was exploding inside and was full of bright, beautiful colors in all kinds of fantastic arrangements.

Actually, being this close with the latest boy who had somehow caught my attention felt just as good as I imagined it would. He was so handsome, his hair was combed forward rather like the Beatles and looked like a crown on his good-looking head, and the cologne he was wearing heightened my senses even more. I became completely aware of the differences between the sexes. The hair on his forearm glistened in the moonlight, his hands were clearly masculine, and when he took my left hand into his left one, I really did swoon. Completely oblivious to Gary and Selayne, the car, the field, the entire world, I was rapt in the first romantic moment of my life.

The guy who was my current heart's desire drew closer to me and began turning toward me. I could feel the warmth of his body through his shirt as he snuggled close. With our hands still interlocked, he gently moved his face toward mine. I was about to be kissed by a boy for the first time. Time stood still, and for a few brief seconds, nothing or no one else existed; it was as if I was a star on the big screen, and my leading man, the epitome of masculinity and handsomeness, was about to make his move. With a natural sense, I closed my eyes at precisely the right moment and felt his soft lips touch mine.

I couldn't believe how incredible kissing felt. Thoughts about how enjoyable it would be often captivated me, but in my wildest dreams I could never have imagined how pleasurable kissing would be when it actually happened. For a half hour or so that fall evening, I experienced the thrill of physical pleasure, the excitement of being touched and kissed and held buy a guy to whom I was very attracted. During that brief interlude, I thought perhaps I was going to join the human race instead of being only a spectator. For that same short time, I also believed I was probably the happiest girl on the face of the earth.

After a bit, Gary turned on the ignition, and we four headed back to town. I felt different somehow, almost womanly. That evening I had ventured with a guy to an exquisite place I had never been before. Fortunately the boy tried going no further than kissing, which raised my opinion of him even higher.

Back in town we stopped and got soft drinks before dropping off my prince at his car, after which my friends took me home. It was a Friday evening, and I walked on air the entire weekend. Based on our physical encounter, I assumed perhaps this young man would want to get to know me more, so I expected I would hear from him. Why, I might even have a boyfriend. Finally, as a sixteen-year-old junior in high school, maybe my life was going to improve, and not an instant too soon.

At school the following Monday morning, I was still drunk on the memory of Friday evening. Over the weekend, I had relived the romantic scene over and over in my head. I could think of nothing else. Sadly, nothing inside me was quenched. Instead, Pandora's box had been jostled enough that my strongest, most aggressive needs were storming that chamber of my soul, which barely managed to contain them.

Long before our encounter in Gary Ward's black Ford, I had figured out Mr. Wonderful's class schedule. Acting on that knowledge, I positioned myself in the hallways during class changes so the chance of passing one another was maximized. In fact, a couple of times that day I did see him, but it was clear he was not looking for me amongst the stream of students.

I assured myself his attention was legitimately elsewhere, that I was just having a bit of bad luck that day. That evening I prayed our telephone at home would ring and it would be him at the other end, wanting to talk to me. No call came.

Tuesday, Wednesday, Thursday, and Friday were repetitions of Monday. In my gut, I knew the sum to which this silence tallied but could not reconcile myself to the truth. For a short time a few days earlier, I had actually felt pretty, desired, noticed, and hopeful. I had had a taste of one of life's sweetest offerings. My physical senses had been aroused like never before, and the gaping hole in my heart had shrunk a bit by the feelings I experienced. Now the newly hatched hope I had clung to for several days evaporated, and the dark wasteland through which I wandered stood before me once again. How could I go back to hell?

That brief, euphoric encounter was all I would ever experience with that boy. I shuffled along, the truth about my handsome Romeo setting in more each day. He was an opportunist, and my conduct would have made an emotionally well person shudder. But then, I was an emotional cripple whose sickness prevented me from thinking straight, behaving appropriately, or thinking realistically. Inside I felt flat, the pain dulled beyond depression into despair, the same old unanswered questions and unmet desires snuffing out the little light my soul had managed to generate that dreamy fall evening.

Not a word of all my latest suffering did I share with my mother or anyone else. The experience and all its elements were mine alone with which to cope. The risk of sharing my sorrow with my mother was too great. She might feel empathetic. Even if she did so, there were no reassurances to be had. Or she might turn me over to Dad for acting like a slut. I needed no more of a load to try to manage. I was going through the motions of life but was succumbing to the burden I bore.

One evening a few weeks later, I crumpled under its weight. That Saturday evening, I was home, as were my parents and all my siblings save Bruce. We had finished eating supper; Gayla and I were washing the dishes and, in the course of doing so, began arguing anew. Like the music in the shower scene of the movie *Psycho*, her voice and words were harsh and piercingly discordant. Inside me, something began to give way.

Hearing the noise in the kitchen and tired of the friction between Gayla and me, Mom stormed in from the living room. Her face was twisted into a severe frown, and in a shrill voice, she demanded to know what was going on. To me it felt like gasoline had been thrown onto a fire, and her attempt at intervention wound up only escalating the ruckus.

At eighteen and sixteen years respectively, Gayla and I were no fonder of one another than we ever had been. This tension and disagreement was nothing new. As with so many things in our lives, the growing disdain we held for each other had never been dealt with, so it continued to fester. Coupled with the disappointment I had suffered over the last week, this latest row with my sister became the straw that broke the camel's back.

Mom yelled at us girls, demanding we be quiet. I could no longer be quiet, about Gayla or anything else that was eating me away.

I needed to scream! Mom, on the other hand, was simply expressing with other words, one of my parents' cardinal rules that was clearly understood though never iterated: make no waves.

This episode with my sister and mother was nothing unusual or especially dramatic, but my reaction to it proved a real start. Like an automobile rolling around on bald tires, this latest argument with my sister and our mother's reaction to it turned out to be the moment my may-pops blew out. I shoved past my mother and sister to the back of the trailer and the bedroom Stacy and I shared. I flung myself onto my bed, thinking that somehow I had to escape this mess that was my life. Within a minute or two, I arose from the bed with an idea that was practically eventually inevitable, given the degree and duration of my misery.

I stole the few feet from my bed into the bathroom, closed the door behind me, and locked it. I opened the medicine cabinet, grabbed all the aspirin and other over-the-counter medicines lined up on its shelves, and took the bottles to my bedroom. Mom and Gayla had gone the opposite direction and into the living room, so I silently stepped the few feet back into the kitchen and filled a glass with water.

I took the water into my bedroom, took the lids off the pill bottles, and began swallowing them by the handfuls. I genuinely hoped there were enough pills in the bottles to kill me once I managed to ingest all of them. When no pills remained, I lay down upon my bed and waited for their effect.

Whether it was chance or divine intervention, my mother behaved completely out of character by coming to my room. Whether it was to yell more at me or to see about me I do not know. She knocked lightly on the door as she opened it and called my name. "Fran," she said at the same moment her eyes beheld the several empty pill bottles. Her familiar frown crossing her face instantly, my mother demanded, "What did you do?"

I looked up at her and said with relief, "It doesn't matter, you aren't going to have me to push around anymore."

She whirled around and dashed out of the room, yelling my dad's name in a tone eerily like it had sounded that evening nine years earlier when I revealed to her that I had been molested.

"Bob, come here. Get in here. She's taken pills."

In a few seconds, my parents appeared in my room. Before they said anything, Gayla appeared behind them. I began screaming at the top of my lungs.

"Get her out of here! I don't want her near me!"

Mom shot Gayla a look, whereupon my sister gingerly exited my room. My parents picked up the empty pill bottles and shook their heads, as if doing so would render this scene a dream.

"What in the hell is going on?" my dad yelled and, in the same breath, said to my mother, "Go start the car."

The pills had been in my stomach long enough I was beginning to feel sick, when Dad reached for both of my upper arms and practically stood me up by himself. I was completely serious about escaping the increasing and unrelenting pain I endured every day. I had tried all I knew to slay the monster that unfailingly dogged me, but instead of relief, the monster was growing bigger and stronger. If death was the only means to rid myself of this cruelty, I was ready to welcome it.

At the same time, I was spent and had nothing left within which to protest. One thing that was still strong was my fear of my father, and because I was causing Mom and him trouble right now, I believed he might beat me before doing anything else. With a smirk I thought that if he whipped me, at least it would be the last time he would get to punish me. As it turned out, Dad's interest was getting me to the hospital as quickly as possible, and I offered no resistance as he continued his vise-grip hold on my upper left arm, guiding and steadying me as we walked through the trailer, into the built-on living room, and out the front door. It was dark, and the November air was chilly as my dad inserted me into the back seat of the green Chevy sedan that was the family car. Then he got into the back seat beside me, and with Mom behind the wheel, we made the five- or six-minute drive to the same hospital where I had come into the world.

We pulled behind the hospital where the emergency room was located, and even before Mom turned off the car's engine, Dad had me out of the vehicle and within a few feet of the building's entrance.

We walked into the emergency room, and Dad immediately said to a nurse standing just inside, "She took pills. I guess she wants to kill herself." Mom quickly caught up to us, and we three proceeded to the treatment room as the nurse had instructed.

The nurse immediately motioned to Dad to bring me across the room to the examination table and told me to have a seat on it. A nurse's aide had been summoned and was in the room with the nurse. Dad had retreated across the room and was standing near the door with Mom, out of the way of the women who were attending to me. Talking back and forth to my parents, the nurse got sufficient information from them and excused herself to go to the phone, while the aid took my vital signs and stood by. In a couple of minutes, the nurse returned with orders from the doctor to initiate treatment for this scenario.

The treatment consisted of my having to drink pints full of very warm, very salty water as quickly as I could. After swallowing several nauseating mouthfuls of the mixture, I began heaving, each esophageal contraction more forceful than the previous, and effectively emptying my stomach of its poison. As soon as my body would begin to calm down, I was made to drink more of the salt water till I resumed upchucking. I began to think there would be no end to this cycle, but after six or eight rounds of it and many pills having made their way back up this muscular tube, further retching was fruitless, and that ordeal was over.

I was admitted to the hospital for the night for observation. No sooner had I been put into bed in a room than my grandmother Bea appeared. She looked very upset and worried, and for that I felt badly. She hugged me and told me she loved me, and I knew she meant it. My parents were also in my room and remained nearly silent, occupied with their thoughts. In a little while our pastor, Reverend Harold Taves, entered my room as well.

I was glad to see Brother Taves. He was an extremely gentle, loving, soft-hearted man, and I could tell it pained him to see me so unhappy. He talked some with me and then prayed with us. He had begun to converse with my folks and my grandmother when the doctor walked into my room. Dr. Dodson spoke with the four of them briefly and then turned his attention toward me.

The same doctor who had told me six years earlier while seeing me for my broken arm that I needed to lose weight had been called in to the hospital to evaluate me. He was frowning and looked perturbed as he approached my bed. Without addressing me by name or making eye contact, he began asking questions pertinent to my physical condition. When those were addressed, he inhaled deeply, looked up at the ceiling while holding his breath for a few seconds, and then exhaled slowly. He looked into my eyes and asked, "Honey, why did you do this?"

Looking back at him, tears beginning to roll down my cheeks, I said, "Because I want to die." Naturally that answer prompted his next question.

"Why do you want to die?"

"Because I don't want to live anymore," I responded.

At this point the doctor began his lecture. With an impatient attitude and demeanor, Dr. Dodson enumerated obvious reasons to be happy and thankful in life and to want to go living. He chided me for upsetting my parents and family and exhorted me to stop making mountains out of molehills. Ending his spiel, he said I could go home the next day if I had no problems through the night from having taken as many pills as I did. Then he turned, walked toward the door, briefly spoke again with my parents, and left the room.

Dr. Dodson's scolding only made me sink lower. If I agreed with what the doctor had said, having called this attention to myself seemed selfish and needless. As I had at the church altar six years earlier, I began sobbing uncontrollably. I wept so hard I nearly choked trying to breathe. Pus exited my body in the form of tears. My mother came to my bedside and stood as if she wanted to help but knew not what to do. Right behind her, my grandmother appeared, weeping silently. She called my name and assured me things would be all right. She held my hand and stroked my hair and wiped my wet face.

My mother took me home from the hospital the next day. While not appearing to be angry with me, my mother was nevertheless behaving in a manner I had never seen before. There were none of her cold glares or her suspicious scowls that so often etched her face. She said very little as we left the hospital and drove home. I was out of words too so just sat silently, exhausted inside and out.

With my mother, my suicide attempt proved to be a turning point in our relationship. From the time we arrived home from the hospital, she took a different approach with me. I went to my bedroom and was about to lie down on my bed when my mother called my name. I returned to the small dining room in the trailer portion of our home where she stood. She told me to sit down, that we needed to talk.

For quite a long time that day, my mother and I did talk about why I was so miserable. Nothing I said was new to her or me. Despite my talents, abilities, interests, and successes, I was completely baffled and tormented by boys and everything that subject encompassed. Each day attention toward and from the opposite sex was becoming a larger part of life for young people my age, and it seemed I had been utterly rejected by all young men except those I deemed least desirable.

Not only did I not understand boys' rejection of me, I also didn't understand my desire for their attention since I was so afraid of it. There were two or three boys during my high school days whom my mother insisted were interested in me, but as with Mike Allen two years earlier, I viewed them with utter disgust. Tellingly, any boy who did show interest in me, I deemed a creep or dud, but because I viewed myself so differently from such boys, my status as a romantic leper was inexplicable.

Whether or not Dr. Dodson recommended follow-up care to my parents I have no idea. Even if he did, it didn't happen. Within my family, some changes did occur, however. Mom's concern for me helped change her attitude toward me enough that being around her was a lot less stressful. Gayla, whose own life was becoming more challenging with her husband due to go to Vietnam about the time their baby was to be born, backed off enough that our arguing fizzled to a tolerable détente. Bruce was gone most of the time working, dating, or pursuing other interests of a twenty-one-year-old young man and was a minor character in my life. Things between my two younger siblings and me had always been copacetic and continued to be. I didn't realize it then, but Dad was on his way to considering me a nutcase. Always adept at off-putting, he became even more distant in all ways after my breakdown.

Ironically the biggest factor comprising the emotional conundrum exhibited daily in my life was the one about which I was completely unaware. I had no idea how central my father was to my emotional turmoil and could not know decades full of traumatic tolls would pass before I would be able to dissect the quandary I experienced regarding boys and men, how I had come to be on that destructive course and the role my father played in this deadly pathology. At sixteen I was still very much a youngster in ways and held my parents in high esteem simply because they were adults. As such, there was a lot of their behavior and attitudes I had not yet begun to question. Though I did not understand it then, both my parents had issues brought with them from their own childhoods that were busy wreaking havoc on each of them and their children in turn.

The first love affair a newborn soul is meant to experience is the one with its opposite-sex parent. Regardless how that relationship goes, this vital interaction sets the stage for subsequent relationships in that person's life. As long as I can remember, I realized my father showed love for me. He did so by providing for my basic needs of food, clothing, and shelter. He guided me by establishing expectations he considered important or necessary. A few times he expressed a tenderness that was more powerful than any of his threats of beatings. Even when he disciplined me with corporal punishment, I never doubted that he loved me.

As comfortable as I have always been with the knowledge that my dad loved me, the idea of him being in love with me, or either of my sisters, is altogether foreign.

The actions of one in love (sans the sexual component) are distinct and powerful. The couple involved desire and enjoy one another's presence and company, demonstrate affection with loving touches, chosen pet names that are cooed at one another, and are preoccupied with thoughts of their beloved. Often gifts are presented, and each other's delight is as precious as the purest gold. This experience of feeling special and valued and the safety to express and receive love individually is crucial to the healthy development of every child. This first experience with such personal, powerful feelings lays the rudimentary groundwork for such relationships in the future and imbues the child with the emotional nutrients required to develop a healthy sense of self-worth, self-image, and safety that are fundamental to any relationship and especially romantic ones.

Such relationships begin to manifest themselves when a girl becomes interested in boys and continue throughout her life. Alas, the absence of such a relationship also manifests.

Not only did I lack that cornerstone experience with my father, such misfortune, coupled with the perverted experiences I suffered at the hands of sexual predators mentioned and omitted herein, produced a macabre emotional offspring. That those predators included family members exacerbated a scenario already heinous. Through the years, those harsh realities had been fermenting inside me as my physical body grew on the outside. Absent intervention or mitigation, much of my future was nearly predictable.

In my early years, I was well on track adoring my father and being in love with him. In one of my earliest memories, when I was approximately three years old, I got off my chair at the supper table and walked the few steps to my father's chair, where I pulled up my shirt to show my daddy how well I had eaten, knowing my full, protruding belly would please him. Over the years I much preferred hanging out with him whenever he was home and trying to involve myself in whatever he was doing. I would assist him tinkering on our vehicles. Washing auto parts in gasoline, fetching tools, functioning as his gofer were fine with me, as long as I got to be near my dad and feel like I had his approval. Not infrequently, my mother would exhort him to be careful and remind him, despite the fact that I was large and strong, he was not to have me do work that was too heavy for a girl. I dismissed her caution altogether. I was determined to win over my father, and if that meant working like the men did, so be it. Most telling was the idea that I felt I needed to win over my father.

Later, in high school, I enrolled in German class because I believed the phrases of Deutsch Dad had picked up during World

War II and often used signified his value of that language, and my learning it would raise his opinion of me. I was ever vigilant in figuring out what would please him so I might reap the reward of behaving accordingly, a constancy that conversely reveals the frailty of the relationship.

With Mom's shift in attitude toward me after my suicide attempt, I was given a new and valuable resource: someone to talk with about what bothered me. She didn't know how to change most of what was dragging me down, but she could work on changing her attitude and behavior toward me and chose to do so. A significant part of my life that had been very onerous was changing for the better, and none too soon. What a pity my father didn't follow suit.

Another change that was a positive in my life occurred in the spring of 1968. My grandpa and grandma Elliott became our next-door neighbors. Grandpa's health was beginning to fail, so they sold their home, property, and business to my aunt Karen and her husband, who lived next door to us, and swapped houses. My relationship with my grandmother Bea had always been edifying, and to have her living fifty feet or so from me proved to be a sustaining benefit.

For a couple of years, I had been corresponding regularly with my aunt Betta, Mom's younger sister who lived in Seattle. My aunt was outgoing and warm with a lively sense of humor, and I had been corresponding with her regularly most of the time I had been in high school. Her husband, Bill Humphries, had enlisted in the navy years earlier, and she had moved to Seattle when he was stationed there. They had divorced eventually, and soon after I started high school, she married again and had a third daughter. Even though she and my cousins Angelique and Val had not lived in Ulysses since the late 1950s, Aunt Betta and her girls visited home regularly, and the family bonds remained strong.

During most of that winter, I felt as bleak within as many of the season's days were without. Nothing felt effortless. To navigate each day took intentional effort. The depression I could not shake was the lens through which I viewed the world. It was like riches to a pauper then when my aunt Betta invited me to return to Seattle with them after their visit in the coming summer.

Having such an exciting experience to anticipate helped my mood considerably, and I thought the school year would never end so that journey could begin. I shared my news with Mattie at the restaurant, and she shared my excitement. She told me I could have my job there after school was out, and I could work until I left with my relatives for Seattle. I was thrilled with her generosity and understanding. Waiting to return to work at the café also made the second semester of the school year drag as slowly as time does for a child waiting for Christmas.

Knowing I would work a couple of months before going west also solved the question of how I would get home when it was time to return. I told my mother I would save my wages and, with them, purchase a plane ticket and fly home. I had never been on a plane, and the idea of actually flying in a passenger jet all the way from Seattle, Washington, to Wichita, Kansas, was a very heady idea. Realizing that I must pay for my ticket myself was also a very important idea. It was a reminder that if I worked, I could accomplish things that were important to me and enjoy the rewards of my effort. This idea was already deeply rooted in my psyche long before I graduated high school or reached the age of majority and was one of the most important assets I had going for me.

Aunt Betta had married well when she wed Uncle Ed Niederer. He was an educated man, outgoing, kind, and generous. He was an executive with one of the natural gas companies in the Seattle area, and their home and standard of living reflected his hard work and success. In the den of their home was a well-stocked wet bar that fascinated me while putting me a bit ill at ease. All that liquor in a home, a bar with a sink and running water and barstools to sit on, the whole works, was completely foreign to what I was used to. My parents occasionally drank beer, but alcohol was not to be found in our house on an ongoing basis.

Another feature of their home that was equally fascinating and completely alluring was their swimming pool in the backyard, or as Granny Clampett would have called it, their cement pond. In the front and back yards, the lawn truly was green, organic carpeting, and my aunt had so many beautiful blooming plants and flowers planted it seemed almost like a jungle.

To see in person that some of my very own family was living in such a big, lovely home that had all these fancy extras was a notable experience. During my life, I had been in one other home that might have qualified for this one's league. A lifelong friend in Ulysses lived in such a place, and my mouth nearly gaped every time I was in it. Now I was staying in as beautiful a place for the rest of my summer vacation from school. and I loved it! My new uncle asked me if I would like the job of tending the pool while I was there and offered an excellent wage for doing so. He did not have to ask twice.

Uncle Ed instructed me on all the how-tos of my new job, and I had much fun vacuuming the pool, cleaning the filters, monitoring the chemicals, cleaning the deck around the pool, and in between enjoying much swimming, diving, and playing in this divine novelty. I was having such an enjoyable time I had to pinch myself to make sure I wasn't dreaming.

My aunt took me sightseeing to the Space Needle, to the wharf, and one evening she and my uncle took me to see Bill Cosby perform. That was the first celebrity or TV star I had ever seen in person, and the expansion of my world left me drunk with gratitude, excitement, and anticipation of an adult life filled with such things.

I also celebrated my seventeenth birthday in Seattle that summer. My relatives presented me with a beautiful cake and expressed their gladness in having me in their home with them for a time and how I would be missed when I returned home to Ulysses.

Getting to know my new uncle and two-year-old cousin Tiffinie was easy and fun. Spending time with my aunt Betta was edifying, as her warmth and attention toward me made me feel special. Getting to be around my cousins Angelique and Val was a great deal of fun and allowed us to strengthen the bonds that had existed from the time they were toddlers in Ulysses. All too soon it was time for me to go home, and plenty of tears flowed as we all said goodbye at the airport in mid-August.

The flight back to Kansas was not disappointing. The sights and sounds of air travel and all it encompassed were new and very interesting. I had a window seat and took photos of the clouds far below me. The experience of flying left me feeling enriched and somehow important. Exiting the plane's air bridge at the gate, where my mother and younger sister Stacy waited for me, felt surreal, almost like I was in a movie, and I soaked up the feeling of being important and in the spotlight, even if it was for a very brief time.

SENIOR YEAR OF HIGH SCHOOL

What had been an educational, fun, rewarding summer was too soon *vorbei*. After a nearly unbearable winter and spring, I was able to cautiously entertain some hope again. I had one year of high school remaining, after which I would leave Ulysses for college and planned to never look back.

Being a senior in high school was elating. Finally, after twelve years of schooling, I had achieved a status long yearned for and felt a sense of importance that was intoxicating. Some of the teachers relaxed, and their attitudes toward us seniors were noticeably different than toward the lower classmen. I had plenty of credits accrued and needed only my required classes to graduate. Even though I knew I was going on to college, I indulged myself that year and took Gregg shorthand with a dozen or so other girls in my class. My sister Gayla had taken shorthand, and what looked like scribbles was always something about which I was very curious. At any rate I thoroughly enjoyed learning to take dictation and how to transcribe it, and I was excellent at it to the point I competed in business contests and did very well as a novice at this new skill.

In band, I sat first chair of the French horn section, and I felt proud and capable as the section leader. As a freshman three years earlier, I had sat there beside Allen Williams. That time seemed so very long ago. I felt weary and much older in many ways now. But perseverance had paid off, and the sense of accomplishment and status as a senior helped smooth my path that entire school year.

As it turned out, my senior year of high school would pass quickly enough. My grandfather Elliott's health was continuing to fail. Not long after the fall semester had begun at school, Grandpa Bill was diagnosed with bladder cancer and would soon enter Bob

Wilson Hospital to live out his final days. The family quickly formulated a routine so Grandpa would have a family member with him at all times. Grandmother was in and out during the day and slept there in a small bed set up for her by hospital staff. My mother and aunt Karen sat with their father during daytime hours as their responsibilities allowed. With everyone working together, the load was efficiently managed.

I went to the hospital nearly every day after school to visit with my grandparents, and it was not long before I was apportioned the evening shift. I felt honored to be included in this important adult undertaking and did my best to ensure my grandfather was comfortable and got whatever he needed. For a couple of months until he died in January 1969, I got to know Grandpa Bill more than I had in seventeen years. Always a bit gruff and quite reserved, my grandfather changed as death approached. For nearly fifty years of marriage, my grandmother prayed for her husband's salvation through accepting Christ as his Savior. Her prayers were answered, and before he died, Grandpa allowed our pastor to lead him to the Lord. Thereafter, nearly every day he would have me sit in the easy chair facing his bed and read to him from the Bible. He would sometimes ask me to pray for him, and though not done smoothly, I did my best to talk to God on behalf of my nearly eighty-year-old grandfather. Never have I been more honored to be included nor learned more about living and dying than those ninety days or so in the winter of 1969.

It was a sunny but cold day the day we buried my granddad. I wept so hard at the funeral my nose began to bleed, and I thought I was going to faint. On the drive south on Colorado Street to the highway that led out of town to the cemetery, I remember being furious with the rest of the world for going about their lives. My life seemed strangely suspended in time, and to see others driving and moving around as if nothing were amiss seemed disrespectful, and I wanted to scream at them to stop and be still.

Always at ease and closely bonded with my grandmother, after my grandfather died, I stayed next door with her most of the time. She appreciated my being around, and I felt steadier being there. Her piano, with which I had fallen in love as a small child, always beckoned, and Grandma never tired of hearing me play. We talked much about many things; doing so was always comfortable and felt natural. My grandmother displayed no uneasiness about any subject, allowed my curiosity unfazed, and talked with me as one woman to another, as often as she did as a grandmother to a granddaughter. My grandmother and her home were refuges from the angst that was so much a part of me, and in turn, she valued my presence, my company, and provided much guidance and support to a young woman struggling mightily with life's challenges.

A friend of mine who was also my sister Gayla's sister-in-law secured a job at Cantrell's Pharmacy and worked there as an after-school job. With her help and encouragement, I was hired soon after Grandpa died. Our duties were basic, and I enjoyed my job. Again I felt important. I had grown up going into Cantrell's pharmacy and going to church with the Cantrell family. Wearing the smock with my name tag on it, patrolling the aisles that were my charges, accurately handling money at the cash register, interacting with the steady stream of customers were all responsibilities I took seriously, wanting my employers to be glad they had hired me. I worked enough hours weekly to keep spending money in my pocket and buy things I needed without having to work too many hours, as I had tried to do at the café a year earlier. The four members of the Cantrell family and two other women who worked there all treated me very well, and it is always with fondness that I recall my workdays spent there.

Life takes some interesting turns in helping us learn needed lessons. Besides Jane Mills and me, Don Cantrell had hired a third teenager: Mike Allen. Three years had passed since Mike had asked me to the homecoming dance. He was even taller and thinner now, his acne was well under control, and as a coworker, he was reliable with a good work ethic. Mike generally displayed a sense of lightheartedness and was routinely entertaining. The three of us worked well together, and I came to value Mike's friendship and personality. I was truly sad when the days of working at Cantrell's came to an end shortly after I graduated high school in May 1969.

During the summer while I was in Seattle, my parents bought an antique piano from someone. It looked to be around turn of the century in age, was stained very dark, stood close to five feet tall, and on the few keys that hadn't been stripped, was covered with real ivory. This piano was extremely heavy, and I was kind of concerned that it might fall through the floor of our living room. I was ecstatic at our good fortune, and with what I remembered from the few piano lessons I received while in fifth grade, and what I knew of music after eight years in band, I could actually play the piano surprisingly well.

As soon as I began working at Cantrell's Pharmacy, I decided I would take piano lessons and pay for them myself. I talked with Sister Alta Lighty from our church, and she agreed to take me on as a student. Instead of a half-hour lesson, I paid for an hour lesson, hoping to progress as far as possible before I went away to college. I was joyful beyond words for being able to study piano since I had wanted to from the time I was a small child.

At school I would get a pass each day from study hall, go to the old part of our school complex that housed the music department, and use one of the practice rooms to practice my assignments. At home I became quite unpopular because I would play the piano until and unless my mother yielded to sibling complaints and made me quit for a time. I wanted to do very little other than practice piano. Playing music made me feel alive inside and hopeful about life. I could express my emotions through my fingers, and through them a healing flowed from the piano, out through the keys, into my body, and poured into my spirit, which devoured the mystical, healing potion, only to want more.

I took the ACT test and scored well enough to qualify for college, and Hutchinson Community Junior College (HCJC) accepted me as a student for the fall 1969 semester. Despite lack of serious, focused studying, little expectation from my parents, and achievement commensurate with my potential, I finished high school in the upper fourth of my class of '87, with a solid B average. My attendance record glaringly reflected my downward spiral through high school: as a freshman I missed three days of school, as a sophomore I missed five days of school, as a junior I missed fourteen days of school, and as a senior I missed over four weeks of school or 21.5 days.

When I applied for a $1,500 scholarship from Grant County, I could think of no reason I wouldn't be one of several selected to receive that assistance toward bettering myself. When those deciding the recipients passed me by and favored others, the last nail was driven into the coffin of my loathing for the place where I had been born and raised and all it signified to me. Months later when one girl who was given the scholarship dropped out of HCJC even before completing one semester and returned home to Ulysses, I seethed all over again.

It would have been very helpful to receive the scholarship funds without the burden of having to repay that money. Nevertheless, I was fortunate because my uncle Dale Carter, next to my father in age of his siblings, made me a grand offer. Dale had never married and, being without children, had decided to offer help to his nieces and nephews who were interested in going to college. I accepted his help and will be forever in his debt. When school began in the fall, I received a monthly check from my uncle in steady, clockwork fashion. After college I was to repay him, so there would be money there for the next one of the family to take advantage of. With no interest charges involved, I was fortunate in more than one way.

I was proud of myself when I walked across the stage at my high school graduation. I felt just as relieved to be done with that part of my life since graduation also meant in a few short months, I would be able to leave the hometown for which I felt little save disdain. I would be able to begin distancing myself from so many of the memories connected thereto and unpleasant, painful associations that would always be synonymous with the word Ulysses.

I was duly honored at graduation time with a reception Mom held at our home. Many family members and friends attended, and my accomplishment was well recognized and saluted with impressive gifts and congratulatory gestures. True to pattern, my father was away somewhere on a pipeline job and did not attend this important milestone in my life.

First Year of College

The summer of 1969 was a historic season. Not only did I turn eighteen years old that July, but five days earlier, the USA landed men on the moon, and Neil Armstrong became the first human being to place his feet on extraterrestrial soil.

Born in 1889 and having died six months earlier, my maternal grandfather never believed landing a man on the moon could be accomplished. I have continued to wonder what his reaction to that astounding feat would have been had he lived a few months longer. That my grandfather's life spanned the days where horse-drawn buggies were the travel norm, to the imminence of landing men on Earth's satellite and safely returning them to Earth, is a big thought that became an indelible impression on my mind.

In my personal life, equally historic and significant events were transpiring. I was preparing to leave for college. My grandfather Elliott had had a fourth-grade education. My father, the eldest of nine children, had a tenth-grade education, while my mother's formal education ended during the spring term of her ninth-grade year. I was the third of five children. My older brother never earned a high school diploma. My older sister graduated high school in May of 1967, married two months later, and was a mother by the time she was nineteen. Her life and college were divergent courses.

Undisciplined to the point I resisted serious studying, I nevertheless believed a college degree was my best chance to live an adult lifestyle that was far different from the one I knew growing up. My desire for steady and sufficient income that would provide stability throughout my life meant pursuing higher education, which I figured was the course with the best odds of achieving my goal. This realization I had grasped years earlier while still in elementary school.

So the question in my mind was not if I was going to go to college, but where. A college education would be my ticket upward from the chaotic meanderings of my family during my early childhood and the tenuous hold on the lower middle-class rung of society's ladder that I had known during my life thus far. I did not fault my parents for the socioeconomic level at which I had been raised. I simply wanted to rise higher.

Other than teachers and local professionals, my uncle Gail was the only college graduate I had personally known while growing up. He had gone to college on the GI Bill after he was discharged from the navy, in which he served during World War II. I couldn't wait to depart my hometown in the same pursuit and put as much distance as possible between all the pain, confusion, small-mindedness, and frustration I had come to associate with southwest Kansas. I hungered for more: more knowledge, more freedom, more culture, more affirmation and validation. I was full of hopeful anticipation that if I worked hard, I could acquire what I needed and sought.

Getting prepared to leave for college was exciting in itself. Aunt Tibe made me an offer relative to my approaching status as a college student that affirmed and delighted me. She said if I would do my share by helping with her housework, cooking, and other chores, she would make me clothes to wear at college. The time, money, effort, and skill involved in that gesture indicated how much she valued my enrollment in college and me. That summer I spent two or three weeks at her house in Big Bow, the unincorporated whistle stop village about ten miles west of Ulysses. In August when I departed Ulysses for college at Hutchinson, Kansas, I did so with some beautiful garments in my suitcases that were made by an excellent seamstress and lovingly crafted so I could look very nice while trying to improve my mind and my lot in life.

I had navy blue bell-bottom slacks with a matching vest and lavender gypsy blouse, a plaid orange-and-gray wool-blend shift, a lemon-yellow knit A-line dress that was very slenderizing to my somewhat overweight figure. There were other pieces in my new wardrobe, but these were the stars, and the pride with which I donned and wore them still excites me as I recall those historic days in my life.

I felt pretty, intelligent, confident, and special as I began my classes and stepped out in pride and eager anticipation, dressed smartly, proud of myself, and very thankful to my uncle Dale Carter and my aunt Tibe Dahlquist for how they had been willing to help me.

Friends since the time I lived at Pearl Carter's across the alley from her castle-like home, Zana Wheeler and I decided to be roommates and, with the help of our mothers, had found an upstairs apartment in an old Victorian home in Hutchinson owned by an octogenarian named Gunda Hiebert, who had immigrated from Norway to America as a child. Mrs. Hiebert lived downstairs, and we girls would occupy the large, sunny apartment in the upstairs of her home. Zana was going to attend Hutchinson's business college and pursue a secretarial certificate while I was enrolled at HCJC.

It was with great elation and anticipation that when the day finally arrived, I departed Ulysses for college over two hundred miles to the east. Our mothers accompanied Zana and me and were as excited as we girls while getting us settled at Mrs. Hiebert's. When I actually began attending classes, I had to pinch myself to make sure I wasn't dreaming. I, Frances Carter, was going to college. That knowledge felt wonderful. Each day as I walked the couple of miles to school, I did so with great pride and a sense of excitement and adventure. Life was definitely getting better.

Although our friendship ultimately survived our attempt to live together, Zana and I were not equipped well enough to live together as roommates, and well before the end of the first semester in Hutchinson, I sought another place to live. Another friend from high school, Vickie Keller, was also attending HCJC and lived only five minutes by foot from campus. She and around ten other girls roomed together in a very large, stately old home whose owners lived there too, while they rented out the bedrooms of their house and oversaw the functioning of that busy, pleasant place. Vickie's bed was one of three in the basement area, and there was no problem fitting in a fourth one for another girl.

Chores were divided up and monitored by our house mother, Mrs. Maybelle Fountain, and her husband, Gerald. The duties were posted in the dining room and operated rather like a duty roster in the military. The house was full of people always coming and going. The atmosphere was enough like a family to be very supportive yet enough of a business arrangement to allow freedom and growth while contracted responsibilities ultimately determined success or failure in this arrangement. Actually, the entire setup ran very well, and I recall little friction or irresponsibility on the parts of any of the bevy of young females living there with a middle-aged couple.

Through a bulletin board at the college that existed for postings of work opportunities, Vickie had gotten a part-time job working for a mail contractor. My friend drove her boss's pickup truck, traveling one of the two routes under contract. Vickie's job was to pick up sacks of sorted mail from the Hutchinson post office around five o'clock or six o'clock in the morning and drop them off to the corresponding post offices in the small towns surrounding Hutchinson. Traveling these routes involved forty or fifty miles on the outbound leg. After completing the route, Vickie would drive back to Hutchinson, attend classes as her schedule dictated, and after classes again drive the route, this time picking up the sacks of mail from the secure anterooms at the rear of the post offices and transporting them to the Hutchinson post office for sorting and processing.

The mail contractor was a woman named Elizabeth Hendricks, who was about ten years older than we girls. Through Vickie, I became acquainted with Liz, and not only was hopeful about a job possibility, I also enjoyed her friendly attitude and intelligence. This new friend was a very different-looking person. In fact, in some ways, parts of her body didn't seem to match the rest. Because of painful and debilitating arthritis in her hands and legs, her joints were over-size. Walking had become challenging to the point there was no grace in her movement, and the disease process had left her wrist bones enlarged enough that her forearm joined her hand without a hint of contour. Her movement was generally stiff and jerky, and pain was her constant companion.

Still, she was formidable. Liz was outspoken and seemed unable to comprehend speaking any way but loudly. Although right around five feet tall, this elfish woman was a person who would never be overlooked, ignored, or otherwise disregarded. She was very intelligent and obviously liked having Vickie and me around. Not often without a cigarette in hand, she laughed easily and genuinely.

Quickly and just as easily she expressed other, darker emotions. Liz flabbergasted me when she related that as a child, her mother had taken money from adoptive parents to relinquish Liz's two brothers. With Liz, though, the mother could not find anyone who was interested in adopting the little girl, let alone someone that would pad the woman's pockets too. So as Liz told it, her mother simply gave Liz away. Fortunately for Liz, she was given to her maternal grandparents and was raised in a stable home by grandparents who loved her.

Even though Liz had neither children nor the kind of challenges and concerns that come along with them, she nevertheless seemed fraught with worries, including financial difficulties, a marriage that was not working, and a husband whose work on construction jobs meant he was away most of the time. Liz seemed to embody a life of struggle that had left her weary and world-worn at a young age.

Not long after Vickie went to work driving the mail truck, Liz offered me a job too, and I jumped at the chance to earn a bit of money. I felt important carrying US mail back and forth to the outlying towns, and compared to several of the jobs I had done in my life, this one was a breeze.

I was enjoying my classes at school, I enjoyed hanging around with Vickie and Liz, I enjoyed driving the mail truck and earning a bit of spending money so had no complaints except the one that never went away: I might as well have been invisible to the opposite sex.

At the college, I did see men who were clearly older. There were veterans going to school on their GI Bill, other men who were not necessarily veterans but were adult students. In my classes, there were guys who seemed fairly mature, were handsome, and who chitchatted with girls and expressed that open-ended interest that allowed the possibility of going to the student union to sit and talk or saving face by acting nonchalant if girls did shut them down. As had been the case all seven years since I had experienced puberty, there were boys who talked with me, a couple with whom I was very comfortable and considered casual friends, but not a one who was interested in me as a potential date or girlfriend.

I was banking on at least a few college guys finding me interesting enough or pretty enough or whatever it was a girl had to be to get noticed by a guy, to provide the antidote for the malady that had deprived me of emotional health nearly all my life. I had absolutely no comprehension of what was driving me or why. I only knew I felt incomplete, voraciously hungry for something, and was truly dominated by this obsession and the anxiety and depression that were its progeny. I was even further from any kind of an understanding about the implications of this awful misery. As with scores of other diseases, without arrest or cure, its strength would grow, and its effects would swell. Ungirded by lack of understanding or treatment, how could I know my future was virtually predictable and almost certainly perilous?

During my second semester at college, I silently acknowledged the undeniable realization that HCJC was going to be no different from the dance at Red Rock School had been, the dances at Grant County Rural High School had been, or any of the other soul-gashing disappointments of hopeful expectations had been. After my attempt to end my own life a couple of years earlier, hope was a precarious four-lettered word. I had healed enough that I held on to a wee bit of that pernicious temptation of hope, but the result was turning out to be absolutely no different than ever before.

Even though that repeating scenario in my life had not changed, some things had. I was on my own with important responsibilities that I was handling well. I was in a different town where there were more people, folks from a lot of different places I found interesting. I was in an academic womb, and each day I was developing, learning more about subjects I found indeed interesting and from people I looked up to and who treated me like an adult. Life was tolerable.

One of the most different aspects of being in college was going to school with black students. With no black people in my hometown during the 1950s and '60s, I had seen black people only on a few television shows and most often in the news during the civil rights struggles of the 1960s. At HCJC, the situation was different, and there were black students in several of my classes. In particular was a girl in my Spanish class. She was soft-spoken and always had her schoolwork ready and well prepared. She dressed nicely and was always pleasant. If she had been white, I wouldn't have looked at her twice; however, not only was she not white, her features were very black in the classical sense of the word.

Akin to an innocent young child, I was extremely curious about Leslie's physical appearance. Her very kinky hair she always wore fastened at the top of her head in a kind of topknot. Her skin was very dark brown, and although her mouth was not large, her lips were very large. They were as dark in color as her skin, but they turned outward enough that part of what was visible was very pink, like the inside of her mouth. I knew staring was not polite, but I did it, a lot, whenever I thought Leslie wouldn't notice me doing so.

At Mrs. Fountain's house, one of my housemates was another black girl named Donna. As outgoing and jovial as Leslie was quiet and reserved, Donna was easy to be around at home and never seemed to be uncomfortable with the fact she was the only ethnic person in a large household of white people.

One of the girls living at Mrs. Fountain's hung around nearly exclusively with black students and dated black guys. She and her dates would often hang out in the living room and watch television or study together. Despite all the racial tension in our country, at Mrs. Fountain's house, on my college campus, and within my living quarters, I never witnessed or heard about that sort of ugliness. Now living in a diverse world, I was experiencing an additional kind of education than what I was receiving by reading books and listening to professors' lecture, and as implicitly important.

Late that year, my grandfather VanHoozer was killed in a farming accident. He had been operating a piece of equipment that cut the tops off sugar beets. The beet tops had become clogged in a section of the machine. My grandfather got down from his tractor and tried to clear the obstruction with his hands, without turning off the piece of machinery. When the tops cleared, the machine lurched. Van was somehow jerked forward and was impaled on a sharp part of the machine. Alone in the field, he bled to death.

Understandably, I had never liked him after the day a few years earlier when he had fondled my breast as I stood at the kitchen sink in his house. When my mother phoned me and told me the news of his death, I inwardly smirked. Again, I felt the same satisfaction I had at ten years old when my uncle Bud died. Both he and Van had molested me, and in the end, both had suffered horrible deaths. Luck or fate had denied them easy deaths, and I thought their suffering amounted to justice of a sort. I was smug with a bizarre sense of vindication.

For my beloved grandmother's sake, however, I was broken-hearted. I went to Ulysses and immediately sought out my grandmother Valta. We clung to one another, and my heart broke all over again to see how devastated she was. My dad and his siblings were going to accompany her to the funeral home, and when they got ready to load into cars, my grandmother, still holding on to me, said she wanted me to come with her to the mortuary. I said, "But, Grama, I'm just a grandkid." She said she didn't care; she wanted me to ride with her and (uncle) Dale. Uncle Dale got behind the wheel of my grandparents' big green Electra 225 Buick, and with my grandmother in the middle of the front seat and me to her right, we set off to make funeral arrangements.

As with my grandpa Bill nearly a year earlier, when he lay in the hospital dying, I had been trusted with adult responsibilities and treated as such by my grandmother Bea. Now my other grandmother was honoring me the same way. That they valued my presence and were somehow strengthened by it was an awesome realization for me. That neither grandmother called on any of their other grandchildren during those trying times of heartbreak clearly showed their high regard for me. I didn't completely understand why my grandmothers felt that way toward me, but clearly they did, and that knowledge infused me with a supershot of self-esteem that I scooped up and deposited in my heart's safety deposit box. Kept there safely, I could take it out periodically to remind myself it was real and benefit anew from its rare beauty and healing qualities.

Back at HCJC, one of the female students who received one of the Grant County scholarships I had unsuccessfully vied for had dropped out of college before completing one semester. Again, I smirked and swore that if I ever became rich or famous, Grant Country would never be allowed to erect a proclamatory sign at its city limits with me as its subject. Neither would I ever endow one red cent to that awful place. Years would pass before I could acknowledge and understand the anger I felt for my hometown and all that was involved and associated with growing up there. Asking anyone for help of any sort has been extremely difficult for me from an early age. Yet as a senior in high school, I swallowed my pride and asked the good citizens of Grant County for help to go to college, citing academic achievement as one reason I deserved the scholarship that was available, and I was denied. I knew I would never give them a second chance to deny me.

One midday late in February 1970, I was walking between classes at school. There were many students on that busy sidewalk, and as I moved along, I saw another girl from Ulysses coming toward me. As we met, she put her hand on my forearm and pressed me off the sidewalk to the grass. Uncustomarily not offering any kind of a greeting, Kathleen Davis simply asked in a somber tone, "Have you heard?"

I responded quizzically, "Heard what?"

With obvious sadness she reported, "Dexter got killed in Vietnam." Dexter was Duane Harbour's first name!

My legs began to wobble, and I struggled for air. The boy with the beautiful red hair with whom I had been so enamored for nearly half of my high school years died a violent death at nineteen, thousands of miles from home.

A mere five years later, our national leaders would pull out of that country after having had US troops there since the late 1950s. They would thereby cede to the Communists all the ground and resources of South Vietnam and nullify the ultimate sacrifice more than fifty-eight thousand of our military men had made with their very lives. That decision also meant the Vietnamese people who had also fought against the Communists were doomed as we simply abandoned them. Duane's death would ultimately prove gratuitous. Now fifty years later, I still mourn his death and grieve for all the living he never got to do. One of my own life's regrets is that I was never able to actually know him.

Midwinter that year, Liz made Vickie and me an offer that was especially appealing and one we quickly accepted. Liz owned a really large Victorian home in one of the older, stately parts of town and lived there alone except on occasions few and far between when her husband was in town. She offered us girls our room and board. We would have to pay nothing, just work on the mail routes as we had been doing. We would no longer be paid a wage, but she did say she would give us a fair amount of spending money with which to buy necessities and miscellaneous items.

It was not easy to say goodbye to Mr. and Mrs. Fountain and all the roommates we enjoyed there, but I figured if I could live somewhere without having to pay rent, the rate at which I was accumulating debt would slow. We moved into Liz's house while the weather was still cold and settled in quickly. Liz's home was old and in need of serious repair on the outside, but inside it seemed like a castle to me. Originally built by the Gano family, whose name still adorned many elevators in Kansas at the time, it was a place where people of the upper crust would have lived. To a person like myself, who had grown up in the houses I had, this house was palatial in size and features.

On the ground floor was a formal dining room, with tapestry and rich paneling on its walls, a servant's staircase whose idea fascinated me, huge pocket doors between the study and the living room, a wraparound porch on the outside that was as large as the trailer portion of my parents' house on Texas Avenue. The original carriage house sat at the rear of the property, while authentic French doors opened from one end of the living room to the backyard. The winding staircase had been used in a movie a few years earlier and beckoned to the craftsmanship of bygone days.

The bedroom I chose had an attached bathroom. With a ceiling probably ten feet high, the room was cold feeling from the tiled walls and tiled floor. An ornate porcelain bathtub presided as a focal point. Beside it was a built-in tiled shower, and across the floor to the left of the sink was something with which I was completely unfamiliar. At first I thought the fixture was one of those things the French women were said to use to wash their private parts, a bidet. Liz would later explain to me it was a sitz bath and what it was used for. After that I gave it little thought except to tell myself that people who could have something that fancy must have had the money to have anything they wanted.

The bedroom I would call mine was approximately fifteen feet square, at least the size of the living room in my parents' home. A full-sized bed sat against the inside wall of the room and reinforced the regal dimensions of everything in the house. Compared to the bunk beds I had slept in for so long, this aspect of my new bedroom continued to make me feel incredibly fortunate. Complete with a bureau and mirror and a five-drawer chest of drawers in it, I had so much space all my worldly possessions were stored nicely with empty drawers to spare. Between the bedroom and bathroom on the outer wall was a walkway perhaps four feet long with what looked akin to a camping trailer slide out of today. Long, narrow windows had been built and provided a view toward the front and rear of the property outside and the driveway that ran from the street in front to the alley behind. I felt no less than a princess. I felt I had made a giant leap forward. To have this much space all to myself was practically unbelievable. With only three people living in a house that was so behemoth, my new situation seemed like a fairy tale dream from which I was afraid I would awake.

I fell in love with the house instantly. Because of its size and age, Vickie was spooked and afraid to be there alone, but not once did I ever experience any heebie-jeebies or similar sensations. I only felt warmth and security, like a very large mother who existed only to see to my comfort and safety.

Perhaps because there was so much space that nobody need get in anybody's way, perhaps because I was living in a kind of fairy tale world, or perhaps because Liz seemed to appreciate the life a couple of eighteen-year-olds brought to the place, we three got along well, and the rest of the winter and spring passed quickly and easily.

Because the mail routes involved driving roughly two hundred miles six days a week, purchasing gasoline was a daily part of the job.

Liz had a credit account at a gas station, so filling up the truck's gas tank simply meant signing the charge ticket. Because we patronized this station nearly every day, we had become acquainted with the men who worked there.

I developed a crush on one of the guys at that gas station, and if he were there when I pulled in to get gas, I would nearly swoon. His name was Charlie. He was blond-haired with blue eyes, almost as tall as me, and was a Vietnam veteran. Charlie was clearly several years older than me, but that only heightened his appeal. He drove a bright-blue Karmann Ghia, and as in high school, I indulged in a lot of fantasizing about riding around with Charlie in that cute sporty car. For all the good my hopes and fantasies did me, Charlie might as well have been a figment of my imagination or an apparition my subconscious had produced during a dream. By summertime I was so frustrated that I dreaded going to the gas station. Each time I did I was reminded that for reasons I could not identify or understand, I was invisible to men when they were "looking" at women.

The fact that buoyed me the most was that I had already completed one year of college. My grades were good, and I was looking forward to beginning my second year in the fall. However, paralleling my decline in high school, after moving to Liz's house, I had nothing more to do with college except attending classes. I attended no more football games, didn't go to the student union unless I had business there, and spent no time studying in the library or anywhere else on campus. I had gotten acquainted with a girl in my Spanish class and had gone to church with her several times, which I also quit. Including the possibility of a romance, the social life in which I had hoped to fit at college turned out to be another pipe dream, and I began to withdraw.

SECOND YEAR OF COLLEGE

L iz was friends with a woman around her own age whose name was Sue. Sue was going to school, about halfway finished with her studies to become a registered nurse. She had two little girls around five and seven years old. The older girl had blond hair and blue eyes and was of average height and weight. Her younger sister was quite different in appearance. This child was equally pretty but in a very different way: she was a black person. Although I was familiar with the word mulatto, I had never encountered one. Again, I was fascinated by my expanding world.

I inquired of Liz about the little girls' fathers. She explained that Sue was divorced from her older daughter's dad, and the little one's dad was already married to another woman. She added that his wife was black, and they had five children. My mouth flew open so wide. A bit farther and my jaw would have certainly dislocated.

Despite the depraved instances of molestation I had suffered earlier in my life, naivety was nevertheless one of my distinguishing characteristics. I held a kind of childlike belief that overwhelmingly people behaved as they were supposed to, and though I believed there was evil in the world, most of what I had seen of it had been via television or movies, not firsthand. Immoral behavior was something not unusual with Hollywood stars and other celebrities, but on a hometown level, expectations were generally far different. Except for a classmate's father running off with a married woman in our junior year of high school, I was unaware of much scandalous behavior by adults while growing up. There were plenty of things both sides of my family kept swept under the rug, and if such gossip was discussed, it simply wasn't done within earshot of me. Perhaps too I needed a sense of security sorely enough that I dismissed facts whose acknowledgment would have threatened destabilization of any sort.

Curious about Sue's situation, I queried Liz about how Sue made a living for her girls and paid for college too. Already concerned with my own debt to my uncle Dale for money he had loaned me to go to college, I wanted to know how this woman was managing such responsibility. When Liz explained that Sue was on welfare and was receiving money from different programs to go to college and childcare expenses, my mouth shot open again. More shocked than anything else, I felt neither judgment nor envy. Instead, as my head involuntarily shook from side to side, I thought to myself, *I never want to wind up like that.*

If I had ever known someone who was on welfare (except my family, the winter my dad was gravely injured), I never realized it. Welfare was a word that made people shudder. Accepting help of that kind was truly a last resort, and when I thought of public assistance, I primarily associated it with dirty, stupid, lazy people who were probably from Missouri or Oklahoma.

As often as not, whenever I would encounter Sue, she would loudly declare, "Roy has a brother that would like you." I always managed to avoid that statement turning into a conversation. I had never given any thought to dating someone outside my race, and my side steps to her contention wasn't about the man's color. Roy's brother could have been any color and my attitude would have been the same. Based on experience, I believed *no* man would ever be interested in me. After the encounter I had had with the boy who first kissed me and another couple of incidents with guys that were more or less the same kind of scenario, I knew the feeling of being used by a guy. Those trysts had left me dejected with an alarming feeling of being capable of behavior completely incongruent with who I really was. At any rate, I could handle *no* more rejection, no matter the circumstance, and whether from a family member molesting me, a guy whose favor I wanted, or a total stranger, I could *not* endure another man indifferently using me for his pleasure.

For several months Sue pestered me with her idea whenever I saw her. I was tired of hearing her opinion on the matter and wished she would just be quiet. Being assertive was a concept I knew nothing about, and what I understood to be standing up for myself was really aggression once I had reached the boiling point on an issue. That point was indeed approaching, and I knew I had to do something. In the end, the way I solved the problem with Sue was to accede to her.

I was sure Roy's brother would not be interested in me. With that expectation already in place, I reasoned my feelings were therefore safe from further injury. My acquiescence to Sue was simply the way to quiet her incessant chatter about the subject once and for all, and that is why, in retrospect, the racial element of this situation I must have unconsciously deemed a moot point. And so it was in that mindset one evening in late August 1970, Roy and Sue came to Liz's house and picked me up to go meet his brother.

Liz's house sat only a few blocks from downtown Hutchinson and a half dozen blocks or so south of the Highway 50 and Plum Street intersection. Roy drove north to that intersection and turned left to go west. We drove past the McDonald's, crossed Main Street, and kept going that direction for several minutes. We were approaching the edge of town when Roy began to slow down and put on his left blinker. When he turned left to enter, I did a double take! We were turning into Zinn's, where Dad had stayed when Mom and we kids visited him in the summer of 1966!

I felt the rush of adrenalin as my pancreas got my brain's reaction and sent help. I might not have had strong feelings about interracial dating or the possibility of it, but I dammed well knew how my father felt, and of all places in Hutchinson this guy could live, here we were at Zinn's, pulling up to that very same apartment I had observed black men go in and out of four years earlier! I felt the bitter taste of fear in my mouth and would not have been a bit surprised had my father actually walked out of the apartment he had once rented or jumped out from behind a bush and began trying to kill me for where I was.

Roy pulled his car into the exact spot I had observed the tall, thin black man parking his car when I was a fifteen-year-old teenager. Sue continued talking, but I was so stunned I heard nothing she was saying. In a daze I opened the car door, really not knowing if my feet and legs were going to support me or not. I did manage to stand up, and as Roy walked around the rear of the car, his brother appeared from the opposite direction.

I was wearing the long-sleeved lilac blouse my aunt Tibe had made me. With them I had paired white knit shorts that were close-fitting but not tight and a pair of white sandals. I was comfortable in my outfit but was nearly mute with shock as the two men approached me.

Joe Louis Ford extended his hand as his brother, Roy, introduced us to one another. My heart pounded in my chest as I continued thinking about my father and how uncanny this all was. I said hello and shook Joe's offered hand. As I looked at him, I could not help but think of the Maasai tribe in Kenya, who are tall and graceful with a thin build, long limbs, and dark, handsome faces. Such was this man. Named after the former world heavyweight-boxing champion of the same name, Joe smiled, and a gleaming set of straight white teeth grabbed my eye. I immediately noticed that instead of a matching pair of two larger incisors in the middle of his smile, a smaller tooth occupied the center space, and the two large teeth were offset on either side of it. I had never seen dentition like that, and his unusual teeth added to the surreal sense that I might have fallen down the rabbit hole.

As indiscernible as attention from the opposite sex had always been to me, this man's instant attraction was equally clear. As it turned out, not only was he nine years older than my nineteen years, he was as confident as I was unsure, even to the point of having a bit of a swagger. Sue and Joe exchanged greetings, and with me still in a kind of fog, we four proceeded to enter his cabin through the same doorway I had seen him walk years earlier.

With all the conflicting thoughts and sensations going on in my mind and body, I might as well have been on an LSD trip. Chances are it would have been no more exciting or distressing. I was in quite a state but apparently appeared all right to the others. The only association I had had with black people was at college as classmates and with Donna White at Mrs. Fountain's house as a roommate. I knew nothing about black culture except for parts that were common knowledge. I was unsure whether myths I had heard as a child about black people were true or not. Now I was in an unparalleled situation, in the home of a much older black man for the purpose of potential matchmaking.

My world was expanding quickly, and all the unprecedented implications, sights, sounds, and even smells dizzied me. One myth I had heard somewhere while growing up was that black people smelled differently than white people, and upon meeting Joe, I had immediately noticed a very distinct odor about him. While neither pleasant nor unpleasant, it was fairly strong and uncommon. I tried to take it in stride and not indicate I was well aware of his smell.

As if his strange dentition, odor, really dark skin, and definite masculinity weren't enough, I was having a terrible time trying to understand what he said! I could tell what he and his brother were speaking was English, of some sort, but beyond that, I was stumped. While talking together, their pitches went higher, they spoke quite rapidly, and with an accent that was completely foreign to me. Apparently understanding my dilemma, Sue told both Roy and Joe that they would have to slow down and talk plainer if they wanted me to be able to understand them, which they tried to do.

One of them produced a pint of whiskey and asked if Sue and I would like a drink. Sue assented, and Joe poured drinks for her, Roy, and himself. I declined his offer and drank a cola that was then offered. We four sat and talked for quite some time, probably an hour or two. Despite all the strange aspects of the situation, I found myself becoming comfortable and enjoying myself. Little by little I was able to understand more of what Joe and Roy would say, and Sue did a good job interpreting their conversation for me when needed.

Joe's cabin consisted of two good-sized rooms. In the living room where we sat were an old sofa, easy chair, and ancient-looking television set on a simple stand. At the opposite end of the room was his bed, and the small bathroom adjoined the room we occupied. Through a door in the wall that divided the two rooms were an apartment-sized stove and single sink as well as a small table with two chairs. In that room was a small built-in closet. It was clear the remaining floor space in that room was intended as the area where the bed would sit, but for whatever reason, Joe had positioned his bed in the living room area. Just as when Dad had rented a cabin at Zinn's while working on a pipeline job around Hutchinson, the cabin was clean and provided shelter from the elements. It's style and arrangement hearkened to days long past, and the whole court needed an extensive facelift, but the area was removed from the hustle and bustle of residential areas and apartment complexes and the noise of downtown. The court of cabins was generally quiet, and though very humble, a person could have done a lot worse. Undoubtedly, most of all, it was inexpensive.

I learned that Roy and Joe had been born and raised in Longstreet, Louisiana. Roy had come north to Hutchinson first, and eventually three younger brothers followed. They were from a large family, had been raised in church, and stayed in touch with their mother although they had never returned to Louisiana to visit her. In Hutchinson, Roy had a decent-paying job at the slaughterhouse. Joe was more or less a loner and preferred his job as the night watchman at the big bakery near the middle of town. I would also learn that Joe had had a new Pontiac a few years earlier, but subsequent to a DUI that involved wrecking his uninsured car, he now drove an Oldsmobile that was nearly twenty years old while he continued to pay on the car that was long demolished in the accident.

At some point I figured out what the strange smell was that always accompanied Joe, except when he donned his denim work jeans and simple work shirt. Besides his work clothes and underwear, all other pieces of his clothing he faithfully took to the dry cleaners, and it was the residual odor from that process that was permanently pressed into his slacks and knit shirts and jackets. In my world, the only thing I ever saw my mother take to the dry cleaners was an occasional coat or sweater and never frequently enough to produce a lingering odor. No doubt Joe Louis Ford had become desensitized to the telltale vapor, but for the rest of the world, his clothing, redolent of a dry cleaning shop, was his signature of sorts.

When I departed Joe's cabin that evening, it was with a second meeting already on the calendar. There was no way I could understand that I had just experienced a watershed moment in my life.

Had my life been depicted in a newspaper, this event would have been the biggest special edition possible. This man *saw* me! This man liked my appearance, my conduct, me. He wanted to see me again. He did not disregard me. He did not look past me or through me or find me unsightly or unattractive. He did what no man or boy in nearly twenty years had done; he considered me a possibility. Because of him, I now knew how it felt to be a desirable female. This man vindicated me!

Despite provocative differences in our races, backgrounds, life-styles, ambitions, and cultures that would eventually come into play, for a time I walked on air. I felt as though a thousand pounds had been lifted from my heart and floated as if I were walking on air. I felt blissful, as though I had been reborn and had not a care in the world.

Joe picked me up in his old, raggedy car a day or two later and took me for another interesting, curious time. We drove into the black part of Hutchinson, to a dinky building, tattered and worn, as are most structures in such a neighborhood. The place was a small restaurant, and Joe asked if I liked pork chop sandwiches. I told him I had never eaten a pork chop sandwich.

As I exited the car, he took my hand in his, an ordinary gesture but another first in my life. Like the rest of his body, his hands were long, slender, and much larger than mine. I was keenly aware of how my hand felt pocketed inside his. Joe stood six feet, five inches tall, and I found I really liked his height. I enjoyed the acute sense of femininity and womanness that being with an older, confident male was evoking within me. I was beginning to acclimate to the difference in our skin color. Like a scar or birthmark, it is remarkable how some things that stand out initially quickly fade into the background.

My date showed me into the small building, holding the door open for me as I entered. There were three or four stools affixed to the floor in front of the counter and two booths positioned against the front window of the place. The lighting was not bright; the painted walls were fairly clean but in need of a new coat, and the smell of grease from a hot fry cooker permeated the air. Rhythmic, loud soul music blared from a radio sitting on a ledge behind the counter, and even with the dingy lighting and contrasting darkness outside, the two front windows clearly needed a serious cleaning. We seated ourselves in one of the booths, and momentarily, a woman appeared from the kitchen area, greeted us, and took our order. I had had no trouble understanding black classmates at the college, but in this setting, I was making out perhaps half of the small talk in which Joe and the waitress were engaging. I felt strangely out of place.

The fried pork chop sandwich was tasty, made even more so with a sprinkling of hot sauce. Conversation between Joe and me came easily while we ate our meal. My date enjoyed feigning exaggerated pride and vanity and was entertaining when he did so; even so, his actual personality contained copious amounts of these qualities. Joe was nice-looking, and though raised in church with corresponding Christian values, humility was a work in progress for him.

After we left the tiny eatery, we drove around a while, eventually driving to Liz's house. By that time, I was sitting more or less beside him on the bench seat of his 1953 Oldsmobile. We pulled into Liz's driveway, stopping the car beneath the windows of my bedroom. Three guys had kissed me before, one a teenager and two who were older and more seasoned. I had never been kissed by a man nine years my senior, and a black man at that. Some things take little getting used to. After Joe turned off the ignition, he turned toward me, put his arm around my shoulder, and slid the several inches in my direction. As if it were a movie, a scandalous movie, he very deliberately lowered his face to mine and kissed me, easily and carefully at first, then with increasing feeling as the kiss continued. When it did end, we remained in one another's arms for quite some time, like lovers suspended in afterglow. Eventually he escorted me to the front door, and we said our good nights, shared another kiss, and reluctantly parted.

As with understood subjects in English grammar, there was an unspoken yet mutual agreement between Joe and me about continuing to see one another. I gave no thought to any ramifications of dating this man. A person who cannot breathe does not relinquish their oxygen. What did register with me was how good, even vital, it felt to have someone's attention and affection. The racial issue would not be the only difference Joe and I would have to confront along the way, although I was rapt with the present and enjoying every moment of a part of life to which I had never before been privy.

As a black man who had been born and raised in the Deep South, Joe's reality was a far cry from mine. From experience, he knew all too well about racial prejudice and the varied expressions it could take. What I knew about racism came from hearing my father and other adults whenever their conversation included topics about anyone who was not white and especially black people. I also knew what I had seen by way of newscasts and television presentations. None of what I knew before beginning college was from a firsthand account. I also knew what I had learned as a little girl about everyone being God's children, and as it turned out, that belief was a cornerstone for much of how I viewed the world then.

The education I was receiving in black culture was every bit as interesting and exhilarating as anything I was learning at Hutchinson Community Junior College. I began hearing phrases and expressions I had never heard before. When my new boyfriend did turn on his ancient-looking television set, it was to watch sports and little else. A half pint of whiskey was the regular accompaniment to Dallas Cowboy football games. Much more often than watching television, Joe cranked out tunes on his old turntable. Listening to record albums full of rhythm and blues and black gospel music took Joe to places I could tell were far from where we were physically. He would sit in his chair with both feet on the floor, and his long, thin legs parted, his torso curled forward with his head somewhat bowed, elbows resting on corresponding thighs, and his right palm covering the back side of his left hand and both planted across his forehead. In his version of the lotus position and with a nip or two of whiskey in his bloodstream, he easily surrendered to the music and welcomed the comfort, protest, reassurance, associations, and recollections it summoned, transcending the outer world and all its difficulties.

Indeed, his music spoke mostly to pain, burdens, suffering, loss, and perseverance. In short order, I learned to hear it differently. I had never listened to Aretha Franklin, B. B. King, and others of that genre but quickly grew to like it and, in a new way, feel the strong emotions it evoked.

In a relatively short amount of time, we were together all the time Joe was not at work or sleeping and I was not at school. The importance of my relationship with him was quickly overtaking the one I had with Liz and Vickie. He did not like Liz's loud mouth and other aspects of her strong personality. Not surprisingly, Liz liked Joe no better than he liked her. She urged me to reconsider my relationship with him, neither of us apparently realizing how tethered to this man I had already become. Increasingly Joe voiced displeasure about my living at Liz's house and one day made a strong request of me. He wanted me to get an apartment of my own. Despite Liz's exhortations for me to stay put, and though I was very happy where I was, I didn't resist Joe very long.

I loved and appreciated the opportunities Liz had given me and the all-around generosity she had shown me. I loved her house and being in it. Nevertheless, I began looking for an apartment to appease my boyfriend. Moving from Liz's meant I no longer had a job or income. To finance my relocation, I went to Mrs. Maybelle Fountain, from whose house I had moved to relocate to Liz's home. I asked Mrs. Fountain to cosign on a $500 loan I had applied for from a local bank, and to my pleasant surprise, she trusted me enough that she agreed.

A few days later, with the loan proceeds in hand, I moved into a basement apartment of a private home that sat only a few blocks from the college. The apartment was neat, clean, and comfortable, and I settled in quickly. As it turned out, I lived at that address only a little longer than a month. Earbuds were not a part of the musical landscape in 1970, and almost immediately, the volume of my stereo put me on the outs with the landlady who lived upstairs. In her sixties, she was no fan of Neil Diamond or Simon and Garfunkel or any other artists to whom I listened, and I was unwilling to squelch my music to the level she considered acceptable.

Even though I resided in these subterranean quarters but a short while, that was plenty of time for a lot to transpire. I had the healthy body of a nineteen-year-old that coexisted with a severely afflicted emotional makeup. I was convinced I would never marry. I pretty much subscribed to religious expectations of remaining a virgin till marriage, but since I believed I would never marry, the point of chastity was lessening in import. Like most people that age, I had an intense curiosity regarding sex, and the necking Joe and I engaged in was naturally heading in that direction.

I thought about my situation at length and in the end decided I was going to have sex. I wanted to experience the act, I had a partner with whom I felt safe, and my highly stimulated body and its longings were becoming more and more difficult to deny. I had plenty of book knowledge, so I consulted the calendar to make sure the danger of becoming pregnant would not be an issue.

Late afternoon on D (for deflowering) Day, I bathed, perfumed, and lotioned my body. I fixed my hair with utmost precision and applied makeup most carefully. I didn't own any sexy lingerie but had my best nightgown ready for use. In the meantime, I put on pantyhose, a pair of flats, and then a skirt and blouse, making sure the buttons on the blouse were not difficult to fasten (or unfasten).

As if on a movie screen, I then turned my attention from the glamorous actress to the set. Several candles placed around my tiny living room area and in my bedroom provided a romantic glow. I dished up crackers and cheese and made a couple of sandwiches in case we felt like eating a bite. The bed was made up with fresh, clean linens. My lilac chenille bedspread with a stitched bouquet of flowers in its center crowned my boudoir. I had no champagne or other alcohol to complete my props, so I did the best I could with bubbly 7-Up.

When my leading man arrived that evening, I was surprisingly calm despite the emotional stew that was simmering inside me. The seduction I had choreographed in my mind went pretty much according to plan. The pain was more than I had imagined it would be, but at least it didn't last long. I felt a kind of power, a woman in her own place, furnished with her own belongings, and carrying out her plan in her own bed. My lover was excited but patient with me, and never was I afraid, although the site of a naked man with a full erection was a bit intimidating. I had to remind myself that other women managed to accommodate men's members, and my body was normal, so surely I could too.

I quickly decided I liked having sex, so a short time later, I asked Liz if I could use her engagement ring from her wedding set, as I had made an appointment with a doctor to procure birth control pills. My friend allowed me to use her ring and commended me for my responsibility.

I soon found another tiny apartment in the same neighborhood and moved from the basement to a duplex that sat end to end rather than side to side. Even closer to the college, my podiatric commute took fifteen minutes tops. Generally, by the time I had finished with class for the day and returned to my apartment, Joe had finished sleeping after work and was there till he had to go to work at the bakery around ten o'clock at night. With no landlord on the premises, life at that small apartment was easy, and my routine was just that. Until my $500 was gone.

Joe had asked to borrow some of the loan proceeds for some debt he owed, and though I knew it was wrong of him to ask that of me, I gave him the $150. Even though he swore to a repayment schedule knowing that was the only money I had, he never repaid a dime of that money. Before the end of the semester, I was out of money. Because of Liz's kind heart and generosity as well as her serious disdain for Joe, I had a place where I could retreat. Shortly before Thanksgiving, I moved yet again, back to my wonderful bedroom in Liz's dear old home.

Displeasure really wasn't a strong enough word to describe Joe's opinion about my move, even though he was a significant reason my situation evolved as it did. Through the scores of hours I had spent with him by this time, I was well acquainted with Joe's jealousy, possessiveness, and underlying expectation that I behave as he expected me to.

A few weeks later, Joe and I were at his place when a hot-button topic led to another watershed moment. Early on I had been told that I had a strong resemblance to a former girlfriend of Joe's. Their relationship had been a serious one, and it seemed to me he was still in love with her. The idea that I was a stand-in, a substitute for the person he really wanted to be with, was a burr that continued to produce animosity within me and one my insecurity could not allay.

Combined with alcohol consumption, disagreements about my living back at Liz's, and other incidental subjects that became quarrelsome, my romantic bliss was waning, and discord was gaining.

That afternoon began normally, but when Joe called me Barbara, the name of his former girlfriend, things went to hell. Both our voices rose, I made accusations, and he became very offended. We were standing in front of his television set, the tenor of our argument getting more ugly and tense with each exchange. Then, seemingly from nowhere, the side of my face and head was violently cuffed. The blow knocked me backward a few steps, and I was grateful for the wall between the living room and bathroom, which stopped me. I was enraged and instinctively fought back, putting my hands to his chest and shoving as hard as I could. With nothing except the sofa behind him, his lower legs stayed put, but the rest of his body awkwardly plopped down onto the couch.

Splayed out on the couch, I saw Joe's expression turn from angry to scary. The whites of his eyes reddened. He glared at me as his eyes narrowed to slits, and his mouth curled menacingly. He got his balance, rose to his feet, and strengthened by his anger, lunged at me, this time with ferocity. With his hand in a fist, he punched me in my left eye. I suppose because of my stout build, this punch knocked me backward only a couple of steps because I was still within arms' length of my attacker, and he immediately grabbed me around my neck with both his hands.

I soon realized that without self-defense training, even an outraged 190-pound woman was no match for a man. Instead of trying to engage him any further, I began shrieking and trying to get away from him. He loosened his grip around my neck, and I pushed past him and into the tiny bathroom, where I began trying to soothe my swelling eye with cold water.

An appropriate reaction to such a row would have been to seek medical attention for the black eye and scratched up neck with which the assault had left me, to press charges through law enforcement, and to immediately end my relationship with Joe. I refrained from doing any of the above. In fact, none of those things even entered my mind. Instead, after a day or two apart and isolating myself because of the black eye, we made up and continued as a couple.

Without even questioning myself or trying to think through the suffering I was living, I automatically stayed with Joe. The problem was not that I enjoyed the mistreatment. Getting hit, choked, kicked, and otherwise beat by a man is dehumanizing and degrading beyond description. Lack of self-esteem is the beacon that signals to men of this ilk, self-loathing its offspring. Since I had met Joe, I had deferred to him whenever pressed. That element of our relationship was already in place on the occasion of our first physical altercation, except the stakes took a dramatic shot upward with the introduction of physical violence.

Nevertheless, the thought of divorcing myself from this abusive relationship simply wasn't an option. Despite whatever I had to endure, the paltry emotional payoff was far more important to me than no relationship at all. Predictably, episodes of physical violence continued as a part of our relationship.

By the time winter was nearly at an end, so was my stay at Liz's, and for the same reason as before. The place I moved to next would not have been acceptable to most men but was to Joe and illustrates how deeply he resented Liz and how confident he was about my fidelity.

Boyd Coy was a man in his late sixties who also worked for Liz and with whom I had easily gotten acquainted and of whom I had grown very fond. He drove the second mail route Liz contracted and lived in a mobile home with his son, Keith. Boyd was a grandfather figure, coworker, and pal all rolled into one. He was a widower and an honest, upright person. Along with Keith, who was in his midthirties, Boyd had a terrier which he adored, and whenever I was at his place, he always insisted I help myself to a cold bottle of Pepsi from the refrigerator and make myself a bologna sandwich. I felt welcome in his home and very at ease with Boyd.

While pouring my heart out to him one day about my plight, he said, "France"—he never pronounced the *s*—"just come and live with Keith and me in the trailer. You can have my bedroom and drive my truck to school." I had no money and no income, and here was a third adult in Hutchinson that was going out of their way to be extremely kind to me.

Within a day or two, I was living at Boyd's and had averted a showdown with the man who claimed to care about me. Boyd liked Joe no more than Liz did and basically for the same reasons. Joe could have been as white as I and the feelings would have been the same. Even I liked him less all the time, but the emotional derangement that debilitated me left me unwilling and unable to loose the shackles of this dangerous situation.

As if my life wasn't tumultuous enough, I was to suffer another bizarre trauma at the hands of my family.

My mother knew of my relationship with Joe but had told no one else. Whether out of fear or embarrassment, she had remained mum, but that was about to change. On a trip home that spring, Mom and I talked about what I planned to do after graduation in May. I informed her I was going to stay in Hutchinson so I could be with Joe. Not surprisingly, she was very dismayed and said if that was the case, I would have to tell my dad and siblings that I was dating Joe.

After dinner the next day, my mother called Dad, Bruce, Lonnie, and Stacy into the living room. The scene hearkened back to the circle we formed when I was in fifth grade when we kids had to vote on whether or not our parents should remain married. I sat across the circle from Dad, truly afraid for my life. I am sure everyone could tell that regardless of what was going on, it was serious, and they should brace themselves for whatever information was about to be shared. Lonnie sat to my left, and Stacy sat to my right. To Lonnie's left sat Bruce and then Dad. To Stacy's right was a chair for our mother. Gayla, the only absent member of my family, no longer lived with our parents, her husband having returned from Vietnam in 1969.

Mom was the last to take a seat, and after doing so, she turned to Dad and said, "Fran has something to tell you." Dad looked across at me, his face guarded.

"Dad," I said, "I have to tell you that I am dating a black man."

Dad was mute, Mom cringed, and Bruce showed little change in expression, as if he weren't surprised. Lonnie and Stacy's eyes widened to the point they looked too big for their faces and appeared to bulge out considerably. The tiniest pin dropping would have been deafening. But then so was the silence.

Had my dad tried to guess what I was about to say, I daresay my bombshell would have been his last guess. I am sure Dad's initial thoughts were about him and not me. The disgrace and embarrassment he felt showed on his face. I had sat down in the chair closest the front door and was ready to bolt if Dad had moved with the intention of doing me physical harm. However, I think he was in stunned paralysis for several moments, for he appeared not to move at all.

His lowered head shook back and forth in an involuntary mode and continued for what seemed an eternity. When he did speak, his words weren't what I expected.

"I should have seen the handwriting on the wall. I should have seen it."

This reaction alluded to the many discussions he and I had engaged in as I was growing up, about current events and politics. His views were nearly always very conservative, and like most young people, mine were generally the exact opposite. It was obvious that in his wildest dreams, Dad never guessed my views would manifest themselves in this particular way.

I had needed Dad's attention and his affection throughout my childhood and struggled as I tried to make do with the scraps I did receive. The situation was no different for my siblings, but different personalities experience situations from their own perspective and react to them in different manners. For the first time in my life, another man's attention had become more important to me than my father's.

I didn't get hit or cursed out. However, I was asked how long I had been dating the guy and if I intended to keep dating him. I felt nauseous and was sure I was going to be sick. Thankfully I was leaving for Hutchinson not much later that evening, and my ride mercifully arrived early. I left Ulysses that day further removed from it and all it represented to me than ever before. I would always call it home, but it was a place I felt I needed to run *from*, not *to*.

Though I loved my family, I didn't necessarily feel close to them. I had tenuous relationships with Bruce and Gayla. Lonnie and I were not as close as we had been as children, and because Stacy was getting older, she and I were forging more of a relationship. I had pleased my parents in many ways through the years, but I had also always been the perplexing child with the penchant for disturbing them and rocking the boat in strange ways. Now this latest upset threatened to sink the damn thing completely.

In Hutchinson, graduation was approaching quickly. Life at Boyd's was calm and relaxed. He and I spent many fine hours together, and my own blood could not have treated me any kinder or gentler than he did. He didn't even mind all the music I played or the volume I believed to be necessary to achieve maximum enjoyment! One time when my grandmother Bea was in Hutchinson, I took her to Boyd's and introduced them with the hope that perhaps Cupid would smile on these two individuals I held in the highest regard. That never happened, but I was proud of myself for the idea and the attempt.

My mother and Stacy were coming to my graduation. As with my high school graduation, Dad didn't attend because of his job. My grandmother Bea and aunt Karen were also traveling from Ulysses to attend the proud occasion, and Boyd was no less excited than any of my family about my achievement. Joe was so puffed up it was as if he were the one graduating.

A couple of days before my graduation from junior college, he and I scuffled, and as always, the effects of it showed on my face the next day. I was beside myself because my face and neck were scratched up for the day that I had lived for, for so long. I knew my family would not believe the lame story I had concocted and applied as much makeup as I could without completely overdoing it. Beneath my graduation robe, I wore the beautiful lemon-yellow knit dress my aunt Tibe had made me two summers earlier. Of course, Boyd had seen my face and nearly wept when he saw further evidence of what I was choosing to tolerate.

On graduation day, I mustered as much courage as I could and met my family when they arrived in Hutchinson. Boyd was handsome in his suit and grinned from ear to ear as everyone gathered at his home before proceeding to the college. I endured my family's reaction to my appearance and, with their help, had a wonderful day. Joe also looked very handsome in his suit and was nearly euphoric as I introduced him to my mother, grandmother, sister, and aunt. In order to not spoil my day, my family was civil to him without being actually friendly.

After graduation was over, our group enjoyed a celebratory meal at one of the local restaurants, and as we enjoyed dessert, I opened the gifts they had brought me. Not long afterward, Joe began badgering me to leave with him. This wasn't the first time he had behaved selfishly and pressured me to choose him over other things or people or occasions that were important to me. Again I participated in the sick exercise and gave him his victory. How I could have relegated my family to a lower priority saddens me even now. After saying goodbye to all of them, Joe and I left the restaurant. He had borrowed Roy's car for the day, so we drove to his house to return the vehicle and then, in Joe's old Oldsmobile, road across Hutchinson toward his place.

AFTER JUNIOR COLLEGE GRADUATION

I walked on air for several days after graduation. As an HCJC alumna with an associate of arts degree, my confidence was being invigorated by the pride in which it was being immersed. I had earned sixty-four college hours, and my transcript reflected a 3.25 grade point average. Thinking about my accomplishment and gazing at my impressive degree in its red binder caused me to smile involuntarily. With good reason, I was proud of myself. Inwardly, I jeered my hometown. *Take that, Ulysses. I succeeded without your help.* Accomplishment truly is self-doubt's antithesis. Had I been as well equipped emotionally as I was in the classroom and as an employee, my ongoing personal life and portentous future would have unfurled far differently.

Whether or not Joe Louis Ford had been in my life, returning to Ulysses was something I would not have done. By the time I graduated high school, I was chockfull of painful memories and associations regarding my hometown, and I had come to loathe most of what it represented. And because Joe Louis was in my life, staying in Hutchinson was a given.

Also, being unsure of what major I wanted to declare and what I really wanted to do for a living was stymying further plans of college at that time. Not incidentally, for the first time in my life, I was in debt. I owed my uncle Dale for financing my first year of college, and I owed the bank in Hutchinson for the $500 loan I had made to finance my third semester at school. Never having been in debt before, I was acutely anxious about being able to repay these loans as I had promised. No longer a student, the time was at hand to find a job, support myself, and meet my obligations.

Although I had earned my associate's degree, my area of study was liberal arts, and the courses I had completed were not ones that prepared me for work in a specific field. During the winter of 1968 and my junior year of high school, I had taken a nurse's aide course offered by the nuns at the hospital in Ulysses. I did so with the hopes of being able to get a part-time job at the hospital, like one of the girls in my class. I did well in the course but, unlike my classmate, was never able to get even an interview, let alone a job. I held no grudge toward my classmate for her good fortune; it wasn't her fault her mother also worked in the nursing department of the hospital. Such scenarios and the benefits that can trickle down from them are some of the unfair but real facts of life. As I realized what was happening that winter, my possible interest in the field of nursing waned while my loathing toward life in my hometown waxed. In the summer of 1971, however, that I had taken that training served me well in securing work in Hutchinson, and I got a nurse's aide job at the hospital in the downtown area.

As soon as I was finished with school, Joe's acceptance of my living with Boyd and Keith reversed itself. Right away, my handler began badgering me about getting my own place. Boyd did not like the idea and protested, without success, and soon after I began working at the hospital, I found an apartment in a duplex within walking distance from my job.

Hutchinson was a town of approximately forty thousand people and was fairly spread out. As much walking as I did on and off the job, it is surprising I weighed the two hundred pounds I now did. At a used appliance store, I bought a black-and-white television set and made payments on it till I had that $25 debt paid in full. The television and my stereo set kept me company and provided many hours of entertainment and distraction, a particularly important point considering I was living a completely isolated life. With no phone, I had difficulty keeping in touch with my friends, who lived more than walking distance from where I was renting. My entire life was my relationship with Joe. My job was simply a necessary routine in which I had to engage in order to be able to maintain my relationship.

Not once did Joe and I discuss living together. I was already violating social mores by being involved with a black man. Living together did not get the social pass that it does these days, nor did I think it was morally right. Besides, although he never expressed it aloud, I have no doubt living together was as far from Joe's mind as were a couple of other subjects that were becoming increasingly important to me.

Consciously or not, my boyfriend had me right where he wanted me. Our relationship might have been my life, but it was merely a part of Joe's. I was deferring to all his wants, was at his disposal as he saw fit, was rigorously rebuked with physical assault if I protested too loudly about anything. Other than the time we went for the pork chop sandwich and celebrated my college graduation, there were no dates. We simply spent time at his cabin or my apartment, engaged sexually or eating meals that I had prepared, watching television or listening to music, and increasingly arguing. The extremely high price I was paying trying to satisfy my emotional needs was bankrupting me in every other way.

The slop our relationship was feeding me was an imitation of love at best. Any and all the fruits of love were absent in my relationship. Each day I was a little worse off than the day before, but the worse off I became, the more my desperation grew to hold on to the craziness that was my life. Where there should have been a sense of calm and caring, I was anxious and filled with doubt. Where there should have been a sense of fulfillment, I felt drained. Instead of physical lovemaking leaving me content and assured, I was left always wanting more. In the end, actions really do speak louder than words. To my detriment, I ignored that fact as long as I was able.

Light years from understanding it then, letting go of Joe would have been a possibility only if there were something of strength in my life for me to grab onto. No such thing existed. Long before I met Joe, my emotional life had become a downward vortex. Absent the means to break free from that spiral, the question was not if I would continue the downward path, but only the speed at which my descent would claim me.

Sooner or later, partnering with a personality like Joe was the natural, inevitable outcome along the protracted course of my emotional handicap. Like predators and prey in the animal world, men with constitutions similar to Joe's are drawn to females they can dominate and otherwise prey upon. Likewise, countless women of all ages, races, religions, educational levels, and social strata whose ranks I had joined tolerate the intolerable and sacrifice who they are or might become, even unto death.

That fate, however, would not be the outcome of my distressing tale. I would soon be wrested from this labyrinth by a completely surprising turn of events, one that would shake me to my core in ways heretofore unquestioned yet provide the out from the perilous situation in which I was entwined.

Reflecting so many of the attitudes with which I had grown up, I generally took an either-or view of the world. In my personal life with Joe, that approach quickly came to the fore after I finished school. Joe had told me he loved me, and from what I understood love to be at that time, I certainly believed I loved him. The truth was, what I really felt was my emotional neediness and desperation compounded and complicated by the overpowering and intoxicating effects of a sexual relationship. I was bound up in a web so strong the more I struggled, the more vulnerable I became.

In my immature view of the world, my inexperience coupled with my idealism and emotional state to form a volatile mixture. I believed because I was finished with college, because Joe and I loved each other, because the natural course of events was to proceed to the next level in a relationship, we should get engaged.

My logic served not only as the catalyst for ugly confrontations between Joe and me, but ultimately as the elephant in the room whose presence I couldn't deny. I was always the one who brought up this charged subject, and Joe's reaction was always the same: complete resistance. I could not understand why he would not want to become engaged if he loved me. The more he resisted the idea, the more I insisted, and by the end of summer, I was in tears as often as I was not. The idea that a situation will eventually work itself out if those involved can't manage to do so is exactly what happened in my pseudo love life.

As a rule, Joe was very cautious about white people's attitudes and behavior toward our relationship. As a black man from the Deep South who preferred interracial relationships, he had a realistic view of our situation and the trouble it could attract in central Kansas in 1971. I accepted the precept intellectually but had no experience to serve as my internal sentry. Even if I had realized the likelihood of ugliness befalling us, my need for attention and affection would have overruled caution.

At my job, there was a young woman a few years older than I, another nurse's aide, whose husband was a black man. As this was no secret there and I was not aware of any repercussions she had experienced due to her marriage, I perceived her status as a signal of tolerance.

My shift at the hospital ended at 11:00 p.m., and except on Joe's nights off from his job at the bakery, I walked the few blocks to my apartment after I finished at work. On his nights off, Joe would park in front of the hospital and wait for me there. I had been working at the hospital nearly four months when one night, instead of waiting for me in his car, Joe disregarded his own rule and took the elevator to the floor where I worked. He appeared punctually as most of the dozen or so nursing staff was readying to leave. Instantly I felt a wave of nervousness wash through my stomach and walked as quickly as I could to where he stood near the elevator. We departed without incident, and I thought no more about that evening.

From my first day at the hospital, any feedback I had received from patients or staff was positive. Inside myself, I also knew I was doing a good job. I completed my tasks, enjoyed my patients, and they enjoyed the care I gave them and often told me so. Because I had had no complaint from patients or nurses, I had no reason to think anything was amiss. Two or three days after Joe came onto the floor where I worked, the nurse in charge called me into the office for a discussion. I entered thinking such action was probably routine, and I smiled as I anticipated whatever this was about would be positive.

I had always worked comfortably with the charge nurse and had never sensed she was irritated or dissatisfied with my work or me. Nurse Ammons was in her forties with brown skin and jet-black hair, and although I never asked her, I figured she was from Hawaii or somewhere in the Pacific Ocean. As I entered the office where she sat, I did so with the familiar confidence I possessed regarding school and work.

Immediately, though, I saw her face was sober, and her tone was serious. I sat in total surprise as she began assessing my performance. Not only did she not give me any praise or kudos of any sort, she didn't encourage me, thank me for my efforts, or one time relax her severe carriage. I had worked with this woman over three months and had never seen her with this kind of a demeanor. I was utterly devastated as she harshly impugned my work, telling me it was sub-standard and that my performance would have to improve quickly. I was mute. I couldn't squeak out the weakest whimper, let alone protest in any way or insist she cite examples and qualify her asser-tions. I felt as though I had walked into an ambush. I was about to become physically ill. When she finished, she instructed me to sign the document that recorded the session. In ways both like and unlike any situation I had ever encountered before, I did as I was told and signed the paper. As I had done times earlier in my life when I was altogether decimated, I simply silently rose from the chair where I sat, turned, and robotically shuffled toward the door, carrying within my chest my shattered heart.

I had worked at paying jobs since I was ten years old, begin-ning with the one where I cleaned my grandparents' laundromat and house. I had cleaned people's houses, done families' ironings, babysat children for several families, washed dishes and waitressed in cafés, maintained the swimming pool in Seattle, rogued in maize fields, clerked in a drugstore, and hauled US mail, all for people who were pleased with my work and were sorry when I left. As with good grades in school, I realized doing well at a job was a self-imposed standard and important to me; however, I had no idea just how important it was until the nurse's awful words and opinion eviscerated me.

I have no idea if I had any recourse in that situation. I was so distraught that had there been a grievance procedure, it wouldn't have mattered; I would not have had the wherewithal to protest. As it was, I was operating on emotional fumes, and this incident was my coup de grace. Stupefied, I was genuinely overwhelmed. Between the different aspects of my relationship with Joe that translated into extreme pressure and now this attack on one of the cornerstones of my psyche, I simply broke down. Sometimes all a person has is what they know about a situation, and in this one, I knew my work had been good. The remaining questions surrounding this nurse's criticism of me remained unanswerable. Years would pass before the possibilities involved in this assault on my character would finally allow me to make some sense from it.

I understood prejudice from a rational point of view. I had even experienced it as an overweight female throughout my life. I was still so very naive in ways, though, and to have someone express this scourge maliciously and cruelly in order to discredit my work was so egregious it was incomprehensible. In the end, that probability was the only explanation that ever made sense to my intellect or my gut.

In the hospital that evening, in a nearly continuous motion, I bent forward, signed the nurse's form, stood straight while I turned away from her, opened the door, and was literally gone. With a word to no one, I made a beeline to the elevator, rode it to the ground floor, where my purse and sweater were stored in my locker in the employees' lounge, grabbed them, and ran from the building. I never looked back. I didn't even return to resign officially or collect my paycheck.

The fragile world I had created and was trying to keep from toppling had just been disintegrated. Despite a reluctant realization that my life in Hutchinson was tenuous, I hadn't the slightest warning when I went to work that afternoon that it would be dead before the end of the day. I also realized as great as they were, neither my will nor my desperation was sufficient to resurrect it. I grabbed at the pieces as I felt myself falling apart inside. I marveled how I could be coming apart yet still be standing. As if they had their own memory, my feet took me to my apartment. Once inside, I fell upon my bed, sobbing as tremendous torrents of emotion spewed upward from the deepest parts of me.

At some point, exhaustion overtook me, and I fell asleep for a few hours. When I awakened, my eyes were swollen nearly shut, and

I looked hideous. With a wet washcloth to wipe them and sunglasses shielding them, I walked the several blocks from my apartment to the nearest payphone and called my mother.

My mother accepted my collect call and between my crying and sobs quickly got a grasp of the situation. She tried to soothe me and help me calm down. I could hear the love and compassion in her voice, and they were a balm to my spirit. My mother declared that she would be there by evening and that I needed to promise her I would quit crying and not do anything foolish in the meantime. I assured her I had no thoughts of another suicide attempt, which was the truth, and promised I would try to compose myself.

After hanging up the telephone receiver, I walked back to my apartment where, completely spent, I crumpled on to my bed again, where I still lay when Mom arrived several hours later. We sat on the sofa in my small living room area, and I related the whole story about my job situation to her and disclosed the physical abuse I had been suffering at Joe's hands, as well as the other facts pertinent to the relationship. I had no strength left with which to hide the truth, nor did I even want to. Even when my mother asked me if I had had sex with him, I leveled with her. She cringed a bit at my admission, I believe not because of the race issue but because she appreciated the difference between a relationship that involves sex and one that does not. Mom then asked if I needed to worry about being pregnant and was understandably relieved when I explained that I was on birth control pills.

I poured my heart out to my mother on that couch. I oscillated between moments of calm, weeping, and sobbing to the point of not being able to catch my breath. Mom listened patiently and reassured me about love and life the best she could. The look on her face was one of sadness for her daughter's pain alternating with a serious frown of anger toward the man over whom I wept. At some point she simply declared that in the morning, we would pack up my things, and I was coming home with her. I had no idea how my heart would ever heal or how or when life might seem beckoning instead of something to run from. I did know that there was no valid reason for me to stay in Hutchinson, and home was the sensible place to be.

Within twenty-four hours we had packed up everything in my apartment and loaded it into Mom's car and had notified my landlord of my plans.

I had also told Joe of these developments and that I was going home with Mom. He made little protest. I don't doubt there was a part of him that was sorry to see me go. Just because the relationship was sick didn't mean there weren't real feelings of endearment that coexisted with the dysfunction. Nor do I doubt he felt a considerable relief knowing the dissension I represented was being conveniently removed from his life. At any rate, Joe stopped by that afternoon and told me goodbye. We agreed we weren't breaking up, as if there were a future to be had together. I continued weeping as he drove away, knowing down deep that chapter in my life was ending.

Back in Ulysses

Being more than two hundred miles from ground zero, where I had had my meltdown, was helpful. The strength and support my dear mother provided supplemented what I was lacking. We talked a great deal about my past, my present, and then about my future. Staying in Ulysses indefinitely was not an option for me, and I knew that even before we arrived there. Still, being there long enough for healing to begin was smart, and I also realized that.

Dad was not home most of the time but away working on pipeline jobs. Bruce had gotten married that year. He worked for our grandparents on their farm south of Lakin, and he and Laura lived in a house there as well. Gayla and Jerry lived several miles east of Ulysses in a house provided by the farmer who employed him. Lonnie was attending college in Dodge City on a sports scholarship, which meant Mom, Stacy, and I were the only ones at home. Stacy was in her sophomore year of high school, and that time at home gave me the opportunity to get better acquainted with my little sister, who was growing up. I liked her a lot and enjoyed the time we did spend together.

Being at home a while was the right place to be, but it would come with a price tag. Admittedly an exaggeration, I recollect Mom establishing the amount I would pay her in rent as we rolled into Ulysses from Hutchinson! Paying my bills was another plank in my character about which I felt strongly. I took my responsibilities very seriously and abhorred those who didn't. The expectation for me to pay rent and the two debts I already had all helped me keep going instead of sitting around, giving in to sadness and depression.

Another requirement my mother insisted upon was that because I had been sexually active, I go see the doctor to make sure I wasn't pregnant or infected with some sort of venereal disease. Not only had I loathed Dr. Dodson since he belittled me as a ten-year-old for being overweight and rebuked me for attempting suicide, now I was going to have to reveal my most personal body parts and behavior to him.

Although I was no longer a virgin, I was still very innocent, and the thought of having to let Dodson touch my genitals was nearly more than I could bear. Mom accompanied me to his office the day of my appointment and went to the exam room with me when the nurse called my name. When the doctor entered the room, my mother told him what my situation was, including the fact that Joe was a black man. She explained she wanted to be sure I was not pregnant or diseased.

I suppose enduring that examination was no more difficult for me than for any woman except that I detested the doctor to my core. I was neither pregnant nor sick with any sexually transmitted disease. Utterly humiliated, I could not exit that clinic fast enough.

Several days after returning home, I found work at Western Prairie, the local old folks' home. I was fortunate to be able to work the evening shift. The LPN in charge was the mother of one of my schoolmates, who was easy to work for, cared deeply for all the residents in her charge, and was so good at her job she made it look easy. One of the aides was an older woman with whom I had worked years earlier at my aunt Tibe's Café. She was pleasant, dependable, and very professional yet gentle in her approach to the old folks. Another of the aides was a classmate's mother I had known for years. She smiled most of the time, was always lighthearted yet serious about her work. The third aide on our shift was Lupe Meza, younger sister to Clementine, who had taken care of me in the hospital when I broke my arm ten years earlier. Also neighbors of ours on Texas Avenue, I knew her and her family well and thoroughly enjoyed her as a friend and coworker. Lupe had a precocious nature and was always finding ways to make work fun and provide free entertainment. Like all the other staff, Lupe loved the folks we were hired to care for. Jane Mills rounded out our complement of aides. I had known Jane since second grade, and in high school after her brother and my sister began dating, we became good friends. Because they later married, we were nearly related, and when Gayla gave birth to Kelly, we were both aunts to that sweet infant. Jane had attended college her freshman year in Fort Scott, Kansas, and subsequently enrolled at the business college in Hutchinson, where she completed a one-year program while I was in my sophomore year at HCJC. She had come home afterward, and it was at Western Prairie where we were able to reconnect.

The workload at the nursing home was always formidable. The building was built with three wings extending from the nurse's station. Each wing had approximately eight rooms on either side of the hallway. Some were private rooms, and some were home to two people. Overwhelmingly, the population was geriatric-aged folks, but there were a couple of middle-aged people who were residents. Ironically, one of them was Clementine Meza's husband, who was completely disabled from a terminal illness.

Because I had the good fortune to work with coworkers who possessed sound work ethics, were proficient at their job, and who easily got along with one another, I thoroughly enjoyed my job. I also quickly came to love the folks whose personal needs I was hired to meet. Several decades later, the memories of the patients, the coworkers, and the fun I enjoyed in my job at Western Prairie are some of the fondest memories of my life.

When we weren't at work, I spent free time with Jane and/or Lupe, and the innocent mischief, laughter, and fellowship we shared helped as much as anything in my recovering from the heartbreak and the crisis of confidence I had suffered in Hutchinson. During that same period, Clementine told me, "Frances, what gets you over one man is the next one." I took that bit of philosophy to heart and was surprised by the number of black men my escapades managed to flush out in southwestern Kansas that fall.

By this time, I no longer looked at white men as romantic possibilities. Their complete rejection of me in that regard had left me feeling only anger and hatred toward them. After I became involved with Joe and was able to experience the wonderful sensation of a man liking my full-figured, ample build and being stirred by it (exactly what my leaner counterparts had experienced all along from white boys and men), my attitude toward men of my own color changed completely. I was like a eunuch toward concubines: there was absolutely no sexual attraction.

I was young, my physical health was excellent, and the accomplishment of each day built on that of the days already past. Emotionally, my pain was still excruciating, but my choice was to keep going one day at a time or give up. I wasn't ready to give up, and I had also gotten an idea that was a source of hope for me.

During my high school days, when I was busy trying to foster connection with my father, one of the thoughts I conceived was serving in the army, as he had done during World War II. Now that idea was occupying my thoughts again, and for several reasons, it seemed like a promising possibility. I talked to my mother about it, and she agreed to drive me to the nearest recruiting office, which was sixty miles away in Liberal, Kansas.

On my next day off, we made the trip to Liberal and were soon talking with MSG Marvin Loudermilk of the US Army. He was a dark-haired handsome man in his late thirties, but more than looking at him, my eyes were transfixed on his uniform. I had not a clue as to what all the ribbons, chevrons, hash tags, or colors meant. I didn't care. Immediately I knew I wanted to wear that same uniform. I would never come to doubt or regret that decision.

Had I not been forty pounds overweight, I could have committed to service that day. I learned that for my height and age, the maximum I could weigh was 158 pounds; I weighed 200 pounds even. I told the recruiter that I would go home and lose the necessary weight and then I would be back to see him, ready to enlist in the army. He was very polite and encouraged me to do just that. He gave me several pamphlets and other reading material and his business card and told me to call him with any questions I might have. He thanked my mother and me for coming in, saw us to the door, and we said our goodbyes.

It was mid-September when Mom and I visited the recruiting office. Back in Ulysses, I swallowed my pride and again visited the awful Dr. Dodson to find out the fastest way I could take off the necessary weight so I could enlist for military service. He advised me to eat lean beef and all the green vegetables I wanted, and to drink a lot of water. He further said to eat fresh fruit when I needed something sweet. There certainly was nothing mysterious or hard to remember about Dodson's advice, and I was eager to begin losing weight.

My mother was the epitome of support in my weight-loss venture. I am quite sure she grew very tired of frying hamburger steaks and making salad every day, but she never once faltered, which of course enabled me to stay on track more easily. Every evening at work, Mom would send Stacy up to the old folks' home with a big plate of food for me, aluminum foil acting as a guidon for the important contents it covered.

When I felt an acute hunger for a bit of chocolate candy or some canned fruit or other item disallowed by my diet plan, I would make the decision whether or not to cheat, always reminding myself what was at stake. Such choices had negligible effect on the rate at which I was losing weight. I was a youthful twenty and a half years old, my job was one where I was always moving and therefore getting a lot of exercise, and in four months, the forty pounds I needed to lose were gone.

In mid-January 1972, Mom again drove me to Liberal to see MSG Loudermilk. When I walked through the door of the recruiting office that day, he looked up from his desk and halted a minute, as if he were trying to place me. His expression was one that clearly conveyed he should recognize me but was unable to recall exactly how he knew me. Finally I spoke. I said hello and followed by, "Sergeant Loudermilk, I lost the forty pounds."

Instantly remembering me then, his faced beamed, and he took my hand and shook it vigorously. After a bit of small talk, he said how glad he was that I had returned. He further confessed that when I left his office that September day, he figured he would never see me again. How wrong he was! He congratulated me many times over, and I was never happier than I was that afternoon.

Most importantly that day, the sergeant established a date on which he would come to Ulysses and pick me up. From there he would drive me to Liberal and put me on a bus bound for Amarillo, Texas, where I would undergo a battery of aptitude tests, a physical examination, fill out the necessary paperwork, and absent any glitches, be sworn into the army. I was walking on air as I departed the recruiting office that day. An excitement distinctly different from any I had ever felt consumed me.

Even though I was twenty years old, had been self-supporting for two years, and had completed two years of college, I was required to have my parents' consenting signatures before I could enlist in the army. My father eventually signed the necessary paperwork but without enthusiasm. His attitude was rooted in the stereotype that women in the military were loose, homely, looking for a husband, or a combination thereof. No doubt his estimation of me was already jaded because I had broken the unspoken family rules designed to protect the adults before the children. A small range of emotions and his either-or view of the world kept life simple and unthreatening to Dad. My unhappiness and some of the behavior it spawned over the years were incongruent with Dad's reality, and I would guess instead of troubled, weird would have described his perception of me.

The weekend before I was scheduled to leave for the army, my sister Gayla held a family gathering at her house. She cooked dinner for us, and we all spent the afternoon together as a family. My parents, siblings, brother-in-law and sister-in-law, nieces and nephew were there. Lonnie brought his girlfriend along to enjoy this happy occasion, and my dear friend Liz drove from Hutchinson to see me off. It was a special day and the perfect prelude to my departure that would also be a brand-new, pivotal beginning in my life.

Around noon Monday, January 24, 1972, MSG Loudermilk's olive green government sedan rolled down Texas Avenue. The eye-catching sight of a government vehicle was no small deal. As the vehicle pulled up in front of our hybrid trailer home, I was filled with a pride I couldn't have imagined. As if the army sedan wasn't impressive enough, when MSG Loudermilk emerged from that car dressed in his imposing uniform and strode toward our front door with polished military bearing, I nearly swooned. I hoped the whole damned world was watching.

Mom was uncommonly emotional as I prepared to embark on this part of my life's journey. I knew she was proud of how I had pulled myself together and found a worthwhile goal to pursue. As she hugged me and kissed me goodbye, we held onto one another a good long while. Then it was time to go. The sergeant put my suitcase in the trunk of the sedan as I eased myself onto the passenger side of the car's seat. I pulled the door closed and looked at my mother standing on the step of our home. That powerful snapshot memory of my mother is forever etched in my mind.

I waved to her, and she to me. We continued waving as the car's transmission engaged and distance between my old life and new one began to accumulate as the sedan moved east down Texas Avenue. With some reluctance, I finally turned away from the direction of my childhood and my mother. The time had come to fix my sights forward.

Had I been a cancer patient, I would have been considered as being in remission. That which had already plagued me for nearly a score of years and threatened my well-being, even my life, and the authentic person whom my maker had intended me to become was undetectable at least for now. I was effecting a radical change in my life, hoping to be forever separated from those nightmares and forces that were real and capable of pulling me completely under. As the army recruiter's passenger inside the government sedan that day, I was trying to finally break free of mindsets and behavior that only harmed and enslaved me. That day, at least, was a day for broad smiles, a sense of tremendous relief, and well-fought-for anticipation of a bright future.

Bruce, Gayla and Frances (infant) outside trailer home. Early 1950's.

Frances in 4th of July little beauties pageant, representing
Miss Elliott Laundry. I won second place. (3 years old)

My younger brother Lonnie and I at Pearl Carter's. Behind
me is the fence from which I fell and broke my arm the first
time. I had just gotten the bandage/cast removed. Arm was
not yet able to hang completely straight. (4 years old)

Frances as a kindergarten student, the year I injured my head at recess
and was taken home to a place with no address. (5 years old)

Frances on porch of newer trailer home with porthole window. This is where my uncle Bud molested me the first time. (6 years old)

Frances on playground at Joyce School, a second grader. This is how I would have appeared when Dad's co-worker molested me. (7 years old)

Gayla, Frances and Stacy at Easter time while we lived at Grama's house, where Dad's co-worker molested me. (7 or 8 years old in this photo)

Stacy and Frances with kittens at the Fairgrounds. Behind us is the structure we called the garage. This is how I appeared during the timeframe my uncle Bud molested me a second time. (9 years old)

Bruce, Lonnie, Frances and friend Zana with goats Lily
and Daisy on parade in Ulysses. (10 years old)

ULYSSES GRADES
1961-62

Frances as a fifth grader. The cast on my broken arm can
barely be seen at bottom of photo. (10 years old)

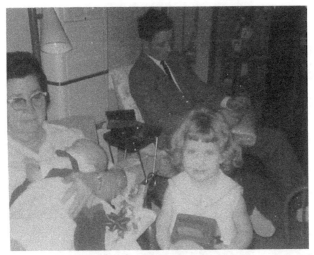

My grandmother Bea Elliott in early 1964. This is how she looked when I was in her employee at her Laundromat.

Gayla (age 13) and Frances (age 11) in band uniforms on porch in Florence, Colorado. Shortly before I started my periods and shortly before the Cuban Missie Crisis. (1962)

Frances as an eighth grade graduate, shortly before
my grandfather molested me. (13 years)

From the rear view, our addition to our trailer home Dad built
and in which I had much sweat equity. The addition more
than doubled our amount of living space. (196 7 or 1968)

Frances as a tenth grader in 1966, a year before
I was ever kissed by a boy. (15 years)

My grandmothers Valta Vanhoozer and Bea
Elliott. (Taken during the 1970's)

Joe Louis Ford and Frances on my graduation day
from junior college May 1971. My right eye is messed
up from him punching my face. (19 years)

My family and I. Stacy had not been born yet.
1954 or early 1955. (3 years old)

About the Author

Frances Smith was born and raised in a small town in Kansas nearly seven decades ago. Her time spent growing up became the impetus that would eventually lead her to write about those twenty years, including the many recollections of that part of her life that span the entire gamut of emotions and seemingly more at times as a number of these reminisces provoke intense and darkly disturbing reactions.

Ms. Smith's professional identity includes that of student, soldier, civil servant, postal employee, and besides author, most recently retiree in lively pursuit of varied interests while continuing to overcome some grave challenges. On a personal level, Frances is also a mother of a daughter and two sons and a grandmother of five grandchildren. She has a special affinity for animals, especially cats, and enjoys an esteemed reputation among friends and family of turning out delicious meals from her kitchen, her philosophy of there always being enough for another plate at the supper table well-known and frequently availed.

Ms. Smith has led a very interesting, eventful, and accomplished life made even more so due to the number of incredible circumstances through which she has navigated and her skill in relating her journey to those fortunate enough to read her story. Overcoming what some might deem more than a fair share of adversity, Frances shares her story with the hope that by so doing, anyone reading her book will benefit from it.

CPSIA information can be obtained
at www.ICGtesting.com
Printed in the USA
BVHW080837261120
593861BV00001B/47